'You can almost taste the sea air ... [Moderate Becoming]
Good Later. This incredibly mo... one family's story and shows the sense of hope and love that
can be found through adventure even when things don't go
according to plan. It's a privilege to be allowed a glimpse into
life offshore Britain through Toby and Katie's words.'
Elise Downing, adventurer and author of *Coasting*

'The perfect book for our times: from tragedy and stormy seas,
come hope, connection, and elemental awe. Exceptionally
beautiful and moving, a book that conjures connection to
people, places and the ocean with the immediacy, grace
and clarity of a kayak cutting through sea spray.'
**David Gange, historian and author
of *The Frayed Atlantic Edge***

'An incredible read of adventure and life that will draw you
in and inspire you to pursue your own journeys. Katie has
truly honoured her brother with this gripping recount.'
**Jenny Tough, adventurer and author of *Tough
Women Adventure Stories* and *Solo***

'*Moderate Becoming Good Later* is a wonderfully salty adventure, a
quixotic odyssey driven by equal parts grit and good humour around
the stormy shores of western Europe. But what really elevates this above
other travellers' tales is the astonishing and moving story of the book's
completion – a remarkable collaboration across the ultimate gulf.'
Tim Hannigan, travel, nature and history writer

'What a brave and tenderly written account of one man's
fortitude in coming to terms with a shortened life using
visits by kayak to the familiar Shipping Forecast sea
areas as "stepping stones" on his final journey.'
**Peter Jefferson, broadcaster and author of
*And Now The Shipping Forecast***

MODERATE BECOMING GOOD LATER

An Hachette UK Company
www.hachette.co.uk

Summersdale Publishers
Part of Octopus Publishing Group Limited
Carmelite House
50 Victoria Embankment
LONDON
EC4Y 0DZ
UK

www.summersdale.com

The authorized representative in the EEA is Hachette Ireland, 8 Castlecourt Centre, Dublin 15, D15 XTP3, Ireland (email: info@hbgi.ie)

Printed and bound by CPI Group (UK) Ltd, Croydon, CR0 4YY

ISBN: 978-1-80007-610-5

This FSC® label means that materials used for the product have been responsibly sourced

MIX
Paper | Supporting
responsible forestry
FSC® C013604

Substantial discounts on bulk quantities of Summersdale books are available to corporations, professional associations and other organisations. For details contact general enquiries: telephone: +44 (0) 1243 771107 or email: enquiries@summersdale.com.

TOBY CARR
& KATIE CARR

MODERATE BECOMING GOOD LATER

Sea Kayaking the Shipping Forecast

summersdale

*To those who didn't choose to have their
adventures curtailed, may you find solace and delight
in what you can do, in the time you have.*

CONTENTS

Foreword by Charlie Connelly   6

Part 1: Squally Showers   **13**
The Challenge   14
Limbering Up   31

Part 2: Northern Skies   **35**
Southeast Iceland: Land of the Midnight Sun   37
Faeroes: Sea of Flames   55
Utsire (North and South): Dangerous Waves and UFOs   73
Fisher: Sand, Surf and Cold Hawaii   91
German Bight: Salty Dreams and Starry Skies   105
Humber: Welcomed in the Gates of Hell   123

Part 3: The Seas Between   **133**
Thames: Venus, the BBC and Gourmands   135
Dover: The Ship and Viking Bay   151
Wight: Visiting Old Friends   165
Portland: Islands in the Middle   179

Part 4: Ends of the Earth   **195**
Biscay: Wild Seas and Green Spain   197
FitzRoy: Spanish Fjords and the *Beagle*   217
Trafalgar: The Last Hot Dog   237

Part 5: South-West Storms   **251**
Plymouth: Safe Harbours and Home   253
Sole (Lundy, Fastnet, Plymouth): Scilly Stories   273
Lundy: An Uncomfortable Landing   291

Part 6: Rough, Becoming Very Rough   **297**
The Unforecastable   298
Flotilla   315
The Challenge   324

Acknowledgements   329
About the Authors   333
About the Illustrator   334

FOREWORD

It's still dark as I write this early in the morning on a little peninsula in area Malin, looking across a sea loch to the opposite shore where a string of tiny lights bisects the blackness of water and sky.

Above the string of lights is the invisible magic of the heavens. Somewhere up there are patches of high and low pressure with currents of air moving between them at constantly changing velocities. Francis Beaufort devised a scale to grade those velocities, and while we can at least have a decent stab at predicting their speeds and directions in the short term, those movements in the skies will always remain way beyond our control.

The darkness below the string of lights is of a different order. The sea, beholden to the moon, is constantly on the move, from the infinite shifting shards on the surface to the relentless peaking and troughing of the tides. An unspoken cooperation with those invisible movements in the skies makes the sea tricky to predict; with storms and squalls come surges and swells, turning the sea into something John Ruskin described as 'bounding and crashing and coiling in an anarchy of enormous power'.

We will never tame the sea any more than we will tame the weather; knowledge you would think might foster a little humility in us humans, but no, we still swank around like we own the place, hemmed in by a sea that couldn't give a toss whether we're there or not because it's the sea that actually owns the place.

The best we can do if we can't tame the sea is at least try to predict what it might get up to in cahoots with the weather. The best we can do with those predictions is try to ensure that people out on the roiling, unpredictable sea are as safe as possible.

The best we can do to achieve that is the Shipping Forecast. Seamus Heaney called it a 'sibilant penumbra', while for Carol Ann Duffy it's 'the radio's prayer'. We can take poets' word for it because the litany of the Shipping Forecast is a form of poetry, a national epic even, recited four times every day, always different yet always the same, reassuring in its regularity, comforting in its progress around the map through familiar places – Dover, Hebrides, Wight – and locations that defy conventional mapping – Dogger, Sole, Bailey.

Yet for all its recondite meteorological phrasing and the reassuring rhythms of its recitation we must never lose sight of how the Shipping Forecast is there to save lives. Arguably it's the greatest piece of public altruism ever devised; for a century the Shipping Forecast has been broadcast for the benefit of whoever needs it, wherever they might be. There is no profit to be made from the Shipping Forecast, no bottom line to please the bean counters. There is no hierarchy of usage because everyone is equal under the Shipping Forecast, from the salty old seadog in his brine-encrusted fishing boat to the oligarch on his superyacht. The Shipping Forecast represents the best of us.

Estimating how many lives have been saved by the Shipping Forecast is an impossible task, but the reassurance provided by its rhythmic incantation goes much further than practical application for seafarers. Hearing the broadcast wakens something inside us, this poetry of protection an evocative reminder that not everything about being an island nation is insular or inward-looking. In fact, the Shipping Forecast is about as outward-looking as it gets, always facing the horizon, the shore at its back, watching over those at sea, binding us to our continent through relentless compassion and the invisible briny grid of a map that reaches from Iceland to Germany, Portugal to Norway.

The beauty of its composition and delivery is what elevates the forecast in our national consciousness to something way beyond a short-term prediction of the weather. Long-embedded in the culture of the nation, the Shipping Forecast has inspired poets, artists, photographers, musicians and writers. How is it that something composed to a strict template using a specific vocabulary with absolutely no scope for nuance can inspire such a rich range of artistic exploration?

The mystery retained in that composition must have something to do with it. From the names of the areas to phrases like 'low Trafalgar 1009 moving steadily south-east, losing its identity', the Shipping Forecast can, for landlubbers at least, be as enigmatic as it is addictive.

Longevity must count for a lot – broadcast in something approaching its present form for a century, a string of generations has grown up listening to the Shipping Forecast – while living on this rain-lashed archipelago probably contributes to the forecast's elevated significance. France and Spain also have long-established Shipping Forecasts, for example, which don't enjoy the same heightened cultural affection as ours.

Perhaps ultimately it comes down to its inherent goodness, the concern for fellow humans that thrums beneath the four daily broadcast incantations. The calm compassion inherent in the forecast unites people in a world growing ever angrier and more divided.

Either way, the Shipping Forecast supports a surprisingly large and varied community of enthusiasts. A few years ago I made a similar journey to the one on which Toby Carr sets out in this book, visiting – or at least passing through – each of the 31 Shipping Forecast areas. It's almost 20 years now since the book I wrote about my journey was published but to this day I still receive messages and tweets from people excited to know they are not the only ones captivated by the mystery of the broadcast's curious prosody, keen to share their stories about this quirky meteorological enigma.

One day, one of those messages came from Toby Carr.

'I'm writing regarding a slightly mad project I am about to embark on, which I think you could be interested in,' he wrote, leading to our first meeting on a stormy night in a dingy old seafarers' pub a pebble's toss from the English Channel. Overlooked by framed posters commemorating Victorian wreck sales and damp-crinkled old prints of sailing ships, I listened over a couple of pints to Toby's plans for the voyages contained in these pages, his eyes flashing with excitement in the candlelight for what lay ahead. I could sense even then his gentle kindness, not to mention a fierce intelligence worn lightly and a steely determination concealed behind immense personal warmth.

Toby's journey was much more ambitious than the one on which I had embarked, which essentially involved turning up in a place, squinting at a distant lighthouse, wandering through a museum with my hands behind my back trying to look clever, tripping over a mooring line and decamping to a pub because it was raining (it was always raining). Toby went further by actually taking to the water, some of which was, as you'll discover, pretty lively.

No vessel brings you closer to the water than a kayak, but nobody was more at home occupying that shimmering meniscus between water and air than Toby. Even the last time I heard from him, an email sent just a week before he died, he described his delight at being back in the kayak after a long absence for medical treatment.

'I was so pleased to get on the water yesterday,' he wrote, 'and even just floating around with the sun on my face has done me the world of good.'

Having only met Toby in the last years of his life I dearly wish there had been more time. Thank goodness for this remarkable record of a remarkable adventure, in which his personality shines through along with his zest for life, uncanny knack for unearthing stories and adventure and his delight in seeing new places, new horizons and meeting new people. For those of us fortunate enough to have known him, even a little, this book is a wonderful testament that will sustain his legacy. For those who didn't know Toby personally, well, you're the lucky ones, about to meet a unique human with an incredible story.

That Toby's voice remains with us in these pages is down to the extraordinary work of his sister Katie, who somehow managed to assemble his scattered notebooks, blog posts, video and sound recordings and the few chapters he had managed to complete, then turn them into the wonderful book you're holding in your hands. Writing a book is difficult enough at the best of times; to do so in the circumstances Katie endured is a truly remarkable achievement.

The orange smudge of dawn is now beginning to pick out the silhouette of the hills above that string of lights across the water. The early Shipping Forecast has already described the day ahead as 'south or south-east three to five, becoming variable three or less later. Fair. Good.'

Fair. Good. Two words to which we can all aspire.

Fair. Good. Ideal kayaking conditions.

Fair. Good. Safe travels, Toby.

Charlie Connelly
Argyll, Scotland
February 2023

Please note the maps included in this book are for information purposes and should not be used for navigation.

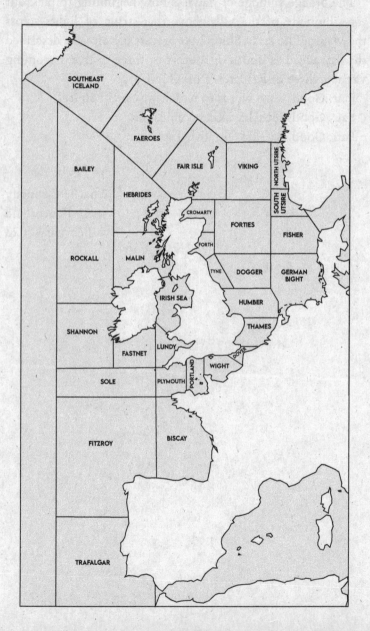

Part 1

SQUALLY SHOWERS

THE CHALLENGE

Rosemary oil infuses the air as the early summer light begins to flood through the slightly open window, as if there is hope for another day. My brother-in-law Andy and I have spent the night in St Joseph's Hospice in Hackney, where my brother Marcus is slowly and painfully dying of throat cancer, his body wasting away, until on this mid-May morning, he takes his last breath. It's not dramatic; it's a fading, a sun finally slipping below the horizon on a grey day. He was 38.

We sit in a thick silence for a long time. We've been talking to him all night, Andy sharing memories of the places they visited together: New Zealand, Denmark, Spain, South Korea – we travelled the world that night. If he had heard us, Marcus might have been glad of the peace. When we leave him for the last time, I feel nothing. Andy goes to Sainsbury's to get some breakfast things and I float around Victoria Park, where the lightness of the trees in bloom is meaningless, almost mocking the enormity of what has just happened. Everything and nothing has changed.

Marcus and I shared a little-known genetic illness, Fanconi anaemia which affects around one in two million people and has improving but relatively poor survival rates. At seven, I was told I would be lucky to reach 30. Since reaching this milestone five years ago, I sometimes get the feeling I'm living on borrowed time.

'And now the Shipping Forecast, issued by the Met Office at 00.15 hours on Thursday 11th May 2017…'

The night of the day Marcus dies I listen to the late Shipping Forecast at 00.48, one of the four-a-day broadcasts on BBC Radio 4 of the maritime weather forecast for the waters around the British Isles. The words I have heard my whole life comfort the emptiness I feel, giving gravity to the enormity of losing my brother. Like many others, I often listen to the Shipping Forecast to drift off to sleep at night, its repetitive rhythm a reassuring and reliable constant for me. Whatever is going on, the bigger forces of nature are still active, and while the names of distant places drift in and out of my comprehension, somewhere out there, someone will be on the water.

We weren't a particularly boat-oriented family, but for around seven years when I was a child we had a small boat called *Hullaballoo* which we sailed out of the river Orwell on the east coast and were definitely what someone described to me recently as 'a bit salty'. We spent most weekends and holidays there, come rain or shine. Marcus, my sister Katie and I often joked on particularly dismal, grey and windy days that it would be a good day to go on the boat. Typical jobs would involve scraping the barnacles off the bottom, reapplying the antifouling, pumping out the bilge tanks and writing down the Shipping Forecast for Humber, Thames and Dover. We explored the rivers Deben, Alde, Orwell, Stour and the Walton Backwaters. My dad Mike (who, like our mum Bron, we always called by his first name) was never happier than when on the water. Even when we were on land with no prospects of sailing in the next few weeks, he would turn up the radio when the Shipping Forecast came on. For Mike the forecast also became a way to soothe the pain of losing Bron, to a debilitating viral brain injury which she never recovered from.

One sunny July morning in Barrowden, where I grew up riding bikes around the village green and climbing trees, Bron woke up confused, unable to remember her name or recognise who any of us were. It was 1988 and I was six. She was rushed to hospital and we were thrown into a world of uncertainty: a life with a mother who was physically there but emotionally and mentally incapacitated. Long-term mental healthcare in Britain in the late eighties left a lot to be desired and Bron came home after five months in hospital. Home life for all of us was a challenge. Despite improved support and care over the years, Bron's rehabilitation never happened, and she would not recognise me in the street if she saw me today, even though I visit as regularly as I can.

Mike was insistent that we should keep sailing our 'floating caravan' of a boat. The time spent close to the water had a big impact on me, Marcus and Katie. It gave us a sense of the possibilities and freedom of the sea, a place to escape as well as a taste of adventure and discovery. I distinctly remember the feeling of driving from the coast in the back of the car after a weekend outdoors, sunburnt, with dried saltwater encrusted on my face and the smell of toxic paints and muddy wellies in the boot. Feeling tired and exhausted but content.

I never really got into sailing and after Mike sold the boat, aside from regular holidays to visit grandparents in Eastbourne, I didn't have much to do with the sea. This wasn't a choice but something imposed by my condition. Fanconi Hope, the excellent charity supporting those affected by Fanconi anaemia, defines the disease as 'a rare, life-limiting genetic disorder causing bone marrow failure in children and a predisposition to gynaecological, head and neck cancers, together with other complications both in childhood and in later life.' If there is such a thing as a typical Fanconi patient, I am one.

At the age of 12, I became seriously ill and my body stopped responding to the steroids that had been propping up my failing bone marrow. Dependent on blood transfusions for several years, I was part of an experimental gene therapy programme in the National Institute of Health in Bethesda, Maryland. While visiting New York, Washington, D.C. and New Orleans was exciting, the treatment didn't seem to help. The only option was a transplant. Back in the UK, my condition worsened into leukemia and the prospects were dire. Neither Katie nor Marcus were matches and several searches of the register drew a blank. Things were not looking good as I developed antibodies to most blood products and was living in isolation. A referral to the international register highlighted a partial match with a donor from Germany and although risky, we went for it. At fifteen, I had a successful bone marrow transplant with various complications which left me with a severely weakened immune system, but alive and eternally grateful for the kindness of a stranger who saved my life.

The treatment, transplant and recovery meant that for long periods of time I was kept in isolation and for several months couldn't go outdoors at all. I read books about long journeys and followed them in my imagination. At night, with one of the other inpatients – Tom, a wise-eyed 15-year-old with a penchant for breaking the rules – we used to explore the hospital stairways, silent corridors and hidden departments. There was a covered tunnel where staff took a cigarette break; we used to call it 'Smokey Mountain' as there were always grey clouds hanging in the air. It was cold and uninsulated but had a view of the sky in contrast to the heat and bright lights of the wards. Further on, an underground subway painted with a beach scene linked the two sides of the building. The flooring changed as you walked down the ramp; it went from a hollow-sounding timber to solid concrete, from yellow to blue, which was the line of the seawater in the mural. We were gradually immersed into an underwater world, coming up on the other side for the canteen and X-ray department. It was a simple artwork but it took me to another place every time I went through it.

For years afterwards as I went through my GCSEs, A-levels, degree and professional architect training, I was advised that I shouldn't spend time outdoors. I felt disconnected – this cotton-wool self-care expected of me was limiting my enjoyment of the life that so many had helped me to hold on to. I got into cycling, both around my home city of London and on longer trips in Europe, but it wasn't until after Mike's unexpected death from a heart attack in autumn of 2010 that I reconnected with the sea.

For as long as I can remember, my aunt and uncle Nicky and Kevin have been adventuring by land and sea. It wasn't unusual for us to spend an evening after a family meal lying on the green carpeted floor in my grandparent's lounge looking at the latest pictures from their journey to Spitsbergen or Greenland. After Mike died, they invited Katie and I for Christmas at their home in Jersey. Straight off the plane and we were in wetsuits jumping off the pier into the bay. A few days of surfing, kayaking and swimming around this beautiful island was all I needed to reignite a connection to the ocean, the refreshing sense of freedom and possibility of the water.

That same Christmas, I found a worrying lump in my throat and soon after I was diagnosed with cancer. I underwent several operations to remove tumours in my mouth and throat, which didn't stop me from joining Tower Hamlets Canoe Club and starting what would become a life-changing connection with these small one-person boats. Kevin has described kayaking as 'aqua rambling', and one of the great things about the sport is that it's easy to start and get better at, even if you're recovering from cancer.

From the moment I got in a boat, I loved the simplicity of it: the kayak, the paddle and the water. I loved the connection I felt to the wide variety of people at the club who showed me kindness and patience as I built confidence and strength in things I thought I wouldn't be able to do. I loved the way it sucked me out of London and on to wild coasts around the UK at the weekends and on holidays. Joining Tower Hamlets Canoe Club took me from often feeling alone in the grey of the city to being connected to nature and others.

In the years leading up to Marcus's death in 2017, I spent most of my spare time in a kayak. I balanced British Canoeing training and assessments with as much experience as I could get. At first, me and other newbies were taken out by more experienced kayakers – I remember feeling my heart race as the wind picked up and the sea got choppier. Later I found myself with kayakers of a similar level where we struggled to apply our navigation and meteorology knowledge to the state of the sea, and later still I led groups as an Advanced Water Sea Kayak Leader and Coach. Kayaking is a much more cerebral activity than you might expect, so while you need to know all the rescue moves should you get into trouble, most of the training and practice is about understanding what's going on in the atmosphere, water and land: a change in one of them can change everything.

In the five years between the Christmas in Jersey and Marcus's death, I led groups on much of the south-east and south-west coasts of England as well as in parts of Wales, and organised expeditions in the Scilly Isles and Outer Hebrides. My personal paddling took me even further afield to Arctic Greenland, the French Alps and Sardinia as well as training in the Channel Islands, Cornwall, Anglesey and Pembrokeshire. I'd already kayaked in 13 of the Shipping Forecast areas. Despite the physical part of kayaking often being considered akin to a hearty walk, you need a lot of training and experience to kayak alone in the wilderness where the sea meets the land.

The numbness that engulfs me in the wake of Marcus's death in 2017 subsides as the summer sets in and gives way to an overwhelming desire to change my life in as many ways possible. I've been angling for a solo adventure since cycling the Trollstigen mountain path in Norway the year before, camping in the lush undergrowth along the way, but something was holding me back. I'm far from the best kayaker in club, yet people with less skill have been on big adventures. Over the course of a few years, and many trips, I've developed the kind of reliance on the deep friendships only attainable when you spend a lot of time problem-solving together: it is easier and more fun to do things with others, even if it's less of a challenge. Marcus's death changed that and as I drift through the rest of that year, I realise now is the time for a proper solo adventure. But what?

The devastating outcome of the Brexit referendum has placed the division of the UK from the rest of Europe on the horizon, and it is starting to feel like sauntering around Europe in a kayak might not be as easy in the future as it is today. In this time of disconnection, it feels more important to connect. It dawns on me that the Shipping Forecast is one of the ways our island is connected to our neighbours, its 31 sea areas bridging the water between the British Isles and mainland Europe: from Southeast Iceland in the north-west, down the entire coast of Western Europe to Trafalgar including the tip of Portugal and a tiny point off Morocco in the south: shared seas, shared stories. In each of the four daily broadcasts, the Shipping Forecast is recited in the same format and order, giving mariners information on gale warnings in force, a general synopsis, and forecasts for each of the 31 sea areas, containing wind direction and force, weather, and visibility. Broadcasters achieve this in three minutes, the lyrical place names, repetition and rhythm making it sound more like a poem than an informational broadcast. Few people use the broadcast as a way to understand the weather, but any attempts to curtail its airtime have been met with uproar by the British public. The names of the sea areas are so familiar to me, I often wonder what places like Faroes, South Utsire, Biscay and FitzRoy are like, and by the time the Shipping Forecast hits the headlines in August 2017 for celebrating its 150th birthday, I've decided it's time to find out.

I had heard about the Winston Churchill Memorial Trust (or the Churchill Fellowship as it later became), who fund international trips of all types under the slogan, 'Travel to Learn, Return to Inspire'. It's a wonderful institution which has been on my radar for a while. In fact, I've had their list of Fellowship application questions open in my phone notes for three years. It's these questions, no doubt honed to perfection over the 50-plus years the Fellowship has been in operation, that now force me to define what would otherwise be a vague excuse to go kayaking.

It's mid-September, the leaves outside my tiny London flat are crispy, just about to turn, and the sky threatens to add more wetness to my afternoon where I'll be kayaking with my friend Owen at the Lee Valley White Water Centre. For now though, I have coffee and I'm determined to fill in the form. I start with the easy bit: name, address, employment history, additional information... then project details. Right, now we're getting to it. I'm momentarily distracted by the movement in the trees, a police siren, and the thought that I should warm up my coffee. 'No,' I say to myself, with the restraint gained from years of detailed desk work as an architect, 'stick with it'.

'Project description.' It doesn't look like there's much space so I put, 'Moderate Becoming Good Later: sea kayaking the Shipping Forecast.' The name has taken a few iterations but

I'm happy with it. A phrase from the Shipping Forecast, it refers to visibility on the sea, but I like the sense of hope it conveys. A kind of learned optimism that has got me to where I am despite my setbacks. It could also refer to my level of kayaking.

I say none of this on the form and move to the next part: 'Countries?' The Shipping Forecast covers nine European countries as well as the four in the British Isles, but the form is looking for specifics and because Churchill's 'living legacy' is all about learning from abroad and bringing that knowledge back, the destinations have to be outside of the UK. I look at the Shipping Forecast map and pick Iceland at the very top, Portugal at the very bottom, Spain and the Faroe Islands because they sound interesting. I feel a well of excitement as I write these down. I have no idea what a trip including these places would look like but I can figure that out later. Next, 'Number of weeks.' My guess is I'd need at least two for each so I write eight. That's probably the maximum time I can get off work as well.

Outside, the grey sky is excreting a fine drizzle that my houseplants would enjoy. 'State the background to your proposed project,' says the form. 'Oof', I think, time to make another coffee while I deal with that. I've never liked talking about my illness, or Marcus's or Bron's, I find the glimmer of pity in listeners' eyes paralyzing, as if it were a confirmation that I shouldn't be out doing what I'm doing. But I know I need to include some context. So after a pot of coffee, my fifth draft is as short and to the point as an explanation of my backstory can be. I start: *Diagnosed with a rare genetic disorder as a child…*

I think of the reaction most people would have to it: 'Oh that's terrible!' 'It must have been so hard!', 'I'm really sorry!'

– and there it is, the pity. I don't want pity, I want to look forward, because to look back is to submerge myself in the boggy ground of grief and hopelessness. On the water you have to read the signs in the moment and look forward, predicting what might happen, so that you're ready to react when something else does. I like this as an approach to life as well. I copy the draft from the Word document into the form and move on.

'Describe the aim(s) of your project and what additional knowledge or understanding your Fellowship project will contribute to what is already happening in this field in the UK.' I've been thinking a lot about this and I know it's something I will refine as I go on. For now, the project is about how active engagement with outdoor environments and physical challenges can help to overcome personal adversity and how a curious approach to these can deepen the experience. 'Is that enough?' I wonder. The Churchill Fellowship has a huge scope and while it supports adventures and discovery, many Fellows focus on the challenges facing society today. I am inspired by UK explorers like Sarah Outen and Justine Curgenven, whose expeditions, documentaries, books and talks help others, including me, to broaden horizons.

I can't believe how useful these questions are in shaping my thoughts, and I seem to be on a roll, so as the drizzle turns to proper London rain, I text Owen, a good friend of mine even before he was a kayaker, to let him know I might be a bit late getting to Lee Valley. Back to the application form. Only three questions to go.

'Describe how you will carry out your project.' I wonder how much detail they want. Planning a trip generally requires a big investment of time, good navigational skills, local knowledge and a large helping of logistical problem-solving. I get momentarily sidetracked thinking about how one might get a kayak to Iceland, before realising that's not what I'm being asked.

Sometimes with a challenge it's easier to ask, 'how will you know when you've completed it?' I realise that my eventual ambition with the project is to have kayaked in part of all 31 areas of the Shipping Forecast. The sheer size of the land masses involved means that the aim is not to kayak the entire length of the coasts but to select the most interesting parts and link them together by land or sea. This will be a solo project but I hope to contact local paddlers and communities to build my trip and have some company on the water. The foreign part of the expedition would take me to the outer reaches of the map to explore the northern extremities of the forecast (Southeast Iceland and Faroes) and the southernmost points (Trafalgar, FitzRoy, Biscay). By visiting and engaging with the extremes in a sea kayak, I hope to learn both how the environmental conditions change and lead to different human responses.

Penultimate question. The rain has stopped and a grey orb looms in the sky, looking like it might break through the clouds. 'Please tell us your thoughts and plans for sharing or implementing your findings.' I'm ready for this one: I've already reserved a domain for my blog, thought about school visits and planned to use social media to provide live updates and reflections on the places visited. I imagine compiling videos, interviews, sound recordings and photographic footage of the trip into a series of contrasting perspectives of people and places. I put all this down, thinking about how much I would enjoy this part as well.

Final question – I'm going to have to skip lunch but we'll have time for a good session. 'Please describe the benefits, or impacts, of your project for others as well as yourself.' I haven't really thought about this before, but my morning's work pays off and I quickly compile a list. I save the document, grab my stuff, and text Owen as I walk out of the building. After a morning inside, I'm keen to get on the water. A few days and revisions later, on the first birthday on which I don't receive a card from Marcus, I send the application.

By the end of October I receive an email telling me I've been shortlisted out of 1,096 candidates and am one of the final 266 being interviewed for the 150 grants on offer this year. The interview will be in early January but before that I'm asked to fill in a more detailed form about my trip. This time they are expecting me to plan it day by day and come up with a detailed budget for the journey: things I know I need to do anyway but have been avoiding. I spend a few weeks of winter's evenings in front of my laptop taking notes on scraps of paper in red fine liner – it's a pleasant way to hibernate. The first thing I realise is that I need to redefine which countries I will visit, as if I'm going to complete all the Shipping Forecast areas outside of the UK, there will be more than I put on the form. I like the idea of starting in Southeast Iceland, which is always the last area to be mentioned on the Shipping Forecast, so I work my way down from there.

I've often been asked how I plan my trips and I don't think there's much mystery to it. I start by finding out what might be interesting in the area I'm focusing on. This could be national parks, remote islands, caves, recommended places to kayak, even museums or cities. The information comes from Google, guidebooks and, most effectively, from people who know the area. Then I look at the logistics. How can my kayak and I get to these places and onwards? Airports and ferry terminals often dictate what is and isn't possible. As I structure the trip, I note down the routes and costs of travel, the number of kilometres to be kayaked and the best times of the year to visit. Everything is weather-dependent so there needs to be some flexibility.

Later of course, I will plot navigation routes on nautical charts, carefully looking at the weather, tides, landing spots and places to camp, but for now, it's the basic structure I'm asked for. I start a list of contacts in each place, determined that this trip will be about connection and learning from others, not isolating myself in a small boat. As I think through Southeast Iceland, Faroes, North Utsire, South Utsire, Fisher, German Bight, Biscay, FitzRoy, and Trafalgar, I feel butterflies in my stomach, excited about what might be possible. By the time I send the form, the sea areas are already more than their lyrical names, I now know how to get to them, the names of places in them, and everything seems more real. The end of the terrible year where I lost my brother is suddenly twinkling with the possibility of opportunity in the next.

No matter how positive you feel, illness can still step in and quash those dreams. On New Year's Day I wake up in the Wye Valley where I've been kayaking with some friends, but halfway home, at Leigh Delamere Services on the M4, I am scraped up by an ambulance crew, completely incapacitated, vomiting, sensitive to light, unable to move my head and in severe amounts of pain, despite having been off the booze for the last week. Quick-thinking paramedics administer IV antibiotics and antiviral treatment on the way to the closest A&E, in Swindon, for suspected meningitis – an action which on reflection probably saved my life and ensured there was no lasting damage.

The next day is hazy as I'm given high-strength painkillers, hallucinogenic anti-sickness treatment and a lumbar puncture. I begin to feel brighter as the antibiotics start their fight. Katie arrives having jumped on a flight from Spain, where she has lived for the last sixteen years, about as excited as the rest of us to spend time in Swindon. By the afternoon I can finally look at my phone again. Although I'm hardly able to sit up in bed, I draft a careful email to cancel my interview with the Churchill Fellowship, scheduled for two days later in London. A reply comes quickly, 'Unfortunately, as you cannot attend the interview we will have to allocate your designated time slot to an applicant on the reserve list.' My heart drops. Most of the time I manage to stay out of the destructive spiral of how my illness limits my opportunities, but today I dive into it. Of all the times I could have become ill, it had to be now, just before my interview for an opportunity I have spent every free moment thinking about and have pinned more hopes on than I'd care to admit.

I feel devastated, but within twenty minutes I manage to pull myself together enough to draft one last-shot email. 'At the core of my application is encouraging others to overcome the barrier created by poor health,' I state, 'so I'm very keen to find a way that this could work…' I go on to suggest that I could attempt to get a doctor to sign off on a day release, but this seems unlikely within the timeframe, as Katie is still having to wear full PPE when visiting and I'm not allowed to leave my room due to infection control (meningitis is sometimes infectious and always treated as such). The reply comes in less than five minutes: 'We'd rather you rest and recover fully and we will do all we can on our end to find a suitable slot to fit you in.' A better outcome, but by no means a certainty.

That evening my diagnosis is confirmed as the non-contagious pneumococcal strain of bacterial meningitis meaning that at least I haven't put the lives of friends and family at risk. Two days later, I'm offered a new slot for my interview in London later in the month, and I feel lucky to still have the possibility. My aunt Nicky arrives, bringing with her a copy of Charlie Connelly's book, *Attention All Shipping* – a witty account of his experiences in the areas of the Shipping Forecast. I spend every moment I can lapping up his tales about each area, keen to get to each by sea and find my own stories.

Eventually, discharged and back in London, I am placed in the care of The Homerton, a local community hospital, who carefully monitor my blood counts and manage my release back into the wild. I'm just well enough to attend the interview in person, the canula in my hand giving me more credibility than my smart jacket and new haircut. I didn't expect it to be emotional, but as the interviewers delve into the details behind my application, I find myself, uncharacteristically, holding back the tears. This isn't the intention behind their questioning, but is the result of a hard start to the year and a feeling that I'd escaped death yet again. As I leave, I'm even more determined to start my journey around the Shipping Forecast.

A few days past Valentine's Day, a large envelope slumps through my letterbox, marked with the logo of the Winston

Churchill Memorial Trust. I'm excited as I rip it open to find an acceptance letter and welcome pack. At first, I can't believe it and read the letter through several times to check that they have actually offered it to me. Once I'm sure of this, my eyes mist up. I'm delighted and daunted that such a prestigious institution believes in my project. I realise that this hasn't just been about the grant I've been awarded (although this of course helps) but more the confirmation that what I've set out to do isn't a crazy idea. I almost skip my way through the park to the wine shop to see if I can find a bottle of Pol Roger, Churchill's favourite champagne. Raising a glass with friends later, I feel a mixture of trepidation and excitement: there's no going back now!

LIMBERING UP

By the end of February, it's good to be back on the water, even if I'm a bit tentative. It is easy to forget that just a few weeks before, I'd been unable to make the smallest of movements in my neck without shooting pains from head to toe. Carrying my kayak on my shoulder to the River Conwy in Wales, the advice I've received from many to 'take it easy' echoes in my head and I'm not sure if this is what they had in mind. Over the next few months, I continue to plan my trip, guided by the Churchill Fellowship.

There's a lot to do: besides building strength, planning and figuring out logistics, I've committed to creating a website and blog to record my trip, opening social media accounts and reaching out to anyone who can help. I get better at explaining what I'm doing and why and send out various emails a day to people I don't know. As I press publish on the 'my story' part of my website, I'm worried about what people will think about the detailed information I share on my past struggles.

At the beginning of March, through a blanket of snow that remains surprisingly white in Central London, Andy, Katie, her partner Josep, their son Llorenç and I take Marcus's ashes up to Hampstead Heath and put them in the ground under a tree. We raise a glass of champagne from Marcus and Andy's wedding three and a half years ago and leave him to his views of the city. The next day we celebrate his life with a party in the pub with friends and family. This wasn't something anyone felt like doing after his funeral, but it feels good to give him a send-off now. To acknowledge that life does go on. I feel more grateful than ever that my trip is keeping me looking forward, dreaming of what's to come.

Working through more logistics, the huge scope of the trip I've proposed begins to weigh me down, and I consider breaking it down into several legs. After a seminar with other Churchill Fellows at the end of March, my head is full of advice from those who've completed their trips. 'You have to establish a balance between research and taking advantage of the places you are visiting,' says one. 'Beware of overplanning,' says another. 'Keep days free and allow time for reflection.' It's not said but I leave with the idea that less is more. After a lot of thought, I remove the southern part (France, Spain and Portugal) from my plan. I will continue in these areas next year within my Shipping Forecast project but outside of the Churchill Fellowship, for which I must hand in a report by the end of the year.

Just before Easter, I receive my business cards from the Churchill Fellowship: 'Toby Carr, Adventurer, Educator, Architect.' I feel pleased with myself. It's often hard to use a new label to describe yourself and I've dared to put it before the two I feel more comfortable with. Sometimes, I think adventure and exploration are states of mind as much as physical experiences. There are people who agree with this, and people who don't. Among those who don't are my Czech friends Natalie and Michal, expert kayakers who can be relied upon for most things, especially a bit of fun and cutting the bullshit. One evening at their house, I'm talking about my trip again and proudly show them a card. Natalie grabs it, has a good look and rips it into four pieces. 'I'll put this back together when you've actually done any adventuring,' she says in her lightly accented English, with a stern caring smile perfected as a Special Needs teacher.

'Oi!' I say, but I don't dare to argue.

I make a pilgrimage to Stanfords in Covent Garden. This treasure trove of maps and travel books rose to prominence in 1862, one year after the broadcast of first telegraphic weather warning (the precursor to the Shipping Forecast). It was this year that Edward Stanford published his *Stanford's Library Map of London*, which made him famous and is still on sale today. The shop now forms the starting point of many a journey. Once you've bought the charts for a journey, you have to do it!

The harsh weather over Easter as I visit the Farne Islands on the north-east coast of England helps to dissolve any doubts I had about saving the southern part of the Shipping Forecast for next year as me and other kayakers spend more time on windy beaches looking at the sea than on it. I manage to negotiate a sabbatical from the architects' firm I've been working with for nearly nine years: I can leave at the end of May and come back in September. Everything is falling into place.

I book my flight to Iceland and two weeks before I'm due to leave, I make my first appearance on BBC Radio 4, on their *Saturday Live* programme. I'm excited to be on the radio and the atmosphere in the studio with other guests is light and playful. I talk about my trip and the Shipping Forecast, but when presenter Aasmah Mir says, 'You and your brother were born with the same condition: Fanconi anaemia. What does that mean?' I find myself flailing. I still haven't told many people about my illness and I ramble on about it. Listening to the recording later, I notice a change in my breathing and hope it wasn't too obvious. Katie says it made for better radio, but I'm not so sure. I'm keen to give people more to talk about than my medical history.

Before long, I'm taking my kayak up to Immingham on the Humber Estuary for it to be shipped to Iceland for the start of the trip. I drive into the port, past silos, what looks like a blast furnace, a chemical works and an oil refinery. Dave from the shipping company helps me wrap up the kayak. He's a small guy whose arms show signs of constant heavy lifting. 'No rush,' he says, 'I'm enjoying the sun'. It's frenetically busy as they offload pallets from trucks, forklifts whizz around and a crane swings above us stacking filled containers. My little car is out of place amongst all this and suddenly the kayak seems very small and vulnerable. Dave questions me excitedly, and his reaction to my answers veers from 'I'd like to give it a go' to 'you wouldn't catch me doing that.' We carry the kayak into the warehouse and leave it among small motorbikes, toilet tissue and nappies that with any luck will arrive the following week in Iceland. It's exciting to think that the kayak is already starting its journey and a sudden rush of the reality of the trip ahead hits me.

Part 2

NORTHERN SKIES

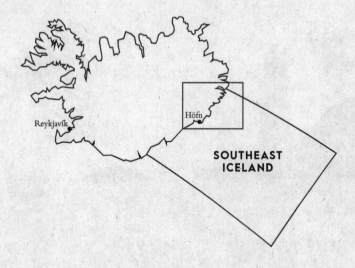

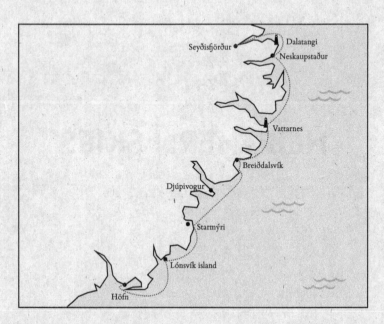

SOUTHEAST ICELAND: LAND OF THE MIDNIGHT SUN

I spend a busy few weeks finishing work projects and packing up my flat. The night before I leave, Björk is headlining at the All Points Festival in my local park, and it seems rude to eschew the Icelandic connection, so I go with a uni friend, Dave, and my kayaking buddy Lindsey. We adjourn to the pub for a farewell drink and some laughs. In the morning, I have a quick interview with BBC Radio Wiltshire about my trip, meningitis and recovery, and I'm off to Gatwick. Katie and family have been visiting and are flying back to Barcelona so we go to the airport together. I eat a hearty Full English brunch, hoping it will tide me over until I'm on the water, and we say our goodbyes in matching Moderate Becoming Good Later t-shirts. I hug my one-year-old nephew Llorenç extra tight. Despite all the planning and precautions, kayaking alone in unknown seas and wild camping along the way has its risks. I'm nervous as I check in. My bag gets a tag saying 'heavy' in case there was any doubt I've overpacked.

The plane begins its descent into Keflavík airport in Reykjavík and I get a clearer view of the strange landscape below. Volcanic rocks form mounds sticking out of the light green flatlands of a lava field, like piles of sand heaped up for shipping. Straight lines are scored across the ground with a trace of previous structures embossed in the rough terrain. The sea makes a white border around the black coastline and a gentle swell is washing in. I can't wait to get on it. I've never been to Iceland before and the forecast looks good.

The Southeast Iceland Shipping Forecast area covers about 300 kilometres of Icelandic coast from just beyond Vík in the south to just above Eskifjöður in the north. If we consider the finger-like ins and outs of the East Fjords the distance is much longer. I'm hoping to kayak the length of it over the next week and a half, flying into Vík, kayaking up to Seyðisfjörður and getting the ferry to Tórshavn in the Faroe Islands. As the plane lands in Reykjavík, I'm desperate to stop talking and start doing.

I feel like a VIP as Guðni picks me up at the airport and it might be the first time ever I've been waved off and welcomed in. Determined to make connections in all the sea areas I'm visiting, I'd reached out to friends of friends in places along the way. A fellow kayaker in Cornwall put me in contact with Guðni in Reykjavík, who circumnavigated the island in 2013 and who, over the past few weeks of helping me with logistics, has become a friend. As I breathe in the cool fresh air, I'm suddenly awake, excited, ready to absorb everything this country has to offer. Conversation flows more freely than the traffic on the drive to the hostel I've booked. Having recovered from the Financial Crisis in 2008 where all three of the country's major banks failed, the capital is now growing fast and traffic problems are testament to this. It's on the edge of the wilderness and is affected by substantial geothermal activity. So much so that the meaning of 'Reykjavík' is Smokey Cove.

'Paddling in Iceland will all come down to the weather,' Guðni says in the car. 'Icelandic weather is known for changing really fast.' I've experienced this in Cornwall especially and naïvely think I know what he means, but the next day the weather is nothing like the forecast I looked at in London. Strong winds whip up the sea and standing in the shelter of the bright yellow Ingólfsgarður Lighthouse in Reykjavík harbour, I know I won't be leaving for a couple of days. In the meantime, Guðni arranges the logistics of getting the kayak to the south-east coast: it will travel by lorry whereas I will fly or take a bus. The only problem is, I still don't have my kayak.

'It's here but I can't release it,' I'm told in no uncertain terms by a man in a grey beanie at the dock warehouse. Apparently, it has to clear Icelandic customs. As the wind dies down over the next day, my frustration builds. Now would be a perfect time to leave but I can't. I try to calm my itchy feet by moving from the hostel to a camping ground. Guðni and his partner Eva look after me, including me in their plans and inviting me round for delicious dinners.

'You need to get on the water,' says Guðni one evening. 'Tell me something I don't know.' I think, before he continues, 'Tomorrow you can come with us for an evening paddle with the club.'

'That sounds brilliant, thanks!' I reply as Guðni sends some messages to get me a boat, equipment and clothing. The next day I go out with twelve other kayakers, who share their experience of Icelandic waters and some traditional stock fish (a natural high-protein snack). It feels great to be on the water, and I'm overwhelmed by the warmth shown by the people of this cold island.

The next day, I walk around Reykjavík listening to a track by Icelandic singer Bubbi Morthens about a shipwreck off the island of Skrúður. It's on my route, but for now the song is as close as I can get to Southeast Iceland, which is 200 kilometres away. Large houses in eclectic styles line the street. The road falls away to one side and the buildings are cut into the hillside, planted with pines and brighter green trees just coming into leaf; it's June now. In the background, the city disperses and gives way to impressive black mountains with snow-streaked sides, their tops shrouded in the early morning cloud. A yellow glow like melting butter on warm toast lines the horizon as the sun breaks through and warms the chilled air. I enjoy the moment, but I feel like the weather is taunting me.

It turns out that Icelandic customs are notorious for delays. 'Yeah, it's going to take long but, that's what you've got this time!' Guðni consoles me. I'm not as ready as he is to accept the situation and I convince him to call customs while I try the British Consulate and, not wishing to underestimate their reach, the Churchill Fellowship. All three are helpful, but my kayak is still not released, giving me no choice but to put back my departure to the Faroe Islands and give myself time to complete my first leg of kayaking.

One afternoon, I chat with Guðni in the campsite, sitting in the open boot of his car as he tries to stop his two-year-old daughter picking up various things, including spare batteries. 'What's your experience of the Shipping Forecast?' I ask him.

'Well, Iceland also has one which is broadcast on national radio twice a day: people love it.' he says. 'I used to listen to it with my grandfather who was a fisherman in the West Fjords. We'd listen to the midnight forecast and he'd decide whether to go out the next day. If he tapped his hat that was it.' He smiles wistfully and I wonder how many similar stories there are around the seas. Guðni finds the Icelandic forecast and I listen to it a couple of times, the deep rhythmic voice of the presenter and repeated words making it similar to our own.

After five days in Reykjavík, the weekend arrives and still no news on the kayak. The woman at the shipping company promises she will 'get aggressive' with customs on Monday morning; I wonder why this hasn't happened already. Even if I get my boat on Monday, I won't have time to do the whole of the Southeast Iceland coast. My best option now is to fly to Höfn in the middle of it, although planes only go on Mondays and Thursdays, so it's going to be tight. I try to accept that 'this is what I've got this time,' and decide to have as good a weekend as possible.

By mid-morning next day, I'm facing misty snow-capped mountains, standing on the edge of a rough lava plateau, next to a vast wooden structure where thousands of cod heads are drying. I'm with Arian, a friendly Swiss woman with short dark hair and a wry smile, who I'd met at the kayak club. She's taking some visiting friends on a nature tour and asked me if I'd like to join. After the fish, our next stop is a lava cave, and she leads us into a dark sideways gash in the landscape. I try to take in the colours, smells and shapes. I feel so lucky to be here.

The same day, Guðni gets me a ticket to a friendly football game between Iceland and Norway. While I can't say I'm a football fan, the chance to see a national game on home turf is too good to turn down. We've got seats in the same stand as the band that travels with the team and I form part of the renowned 'huh' Viking war chant and, as the cold wind blows through the drizzle I feel a link to eons past shiver down my spine. Norway scores the winning goal and a silence descends. I walk back with the sound of 'Ég Er Kominn Heim' (the unofficial song of the Icelandic national teams) in my ears and the colours of the Icelandic flag smeared across my face, wondering why people are staring at me.

The next day, it's the Day of the Seafarer in Iceland, a yearly celebration of the fishing fleets and memorial to those who have lost their lives. Down at the harbour, we see women pillow-fighting on a pole over the water, a display of fish, a rescue demo by a helicopter crew. I try sour whale meat and pickled herrings as well as Iceland's best ice cream then I'm invited back for homemade pizza at Arian's house. It's been a fantastic weekend and in many ways I'm pleased that customs have dragged their feet.

On Monday at quarter to ten I get the mail I've been waiting for: my kayak will be released today, but only if I pay 102,111 Icelandic króna (about 700 pounds) which I will get back when I leave in ten days' time. Since I've hardly started my trip, I have the money but quickly find out that there's no way to pay it from a UK account. This is deftly resolved by my Icelandic support team and they swing into action to help me get myself and my kayak to Höfn that day. We pay the money, get the boat, pack it and take it to be transported overnight. It's frantic but exciting, I feel the thrill of the chase.

At the airport as I leave, Arian pushes a small package into my hand: 'traditional sheep's head pâté, to keep you going,' she says with a smile. As I say goodbye to Guðni in his blue polarised glasses and red hat, I can tell he wants to come too. In the void between one adventure and another, I'm sad. I don't want to leave Guðni and Arian but I have to start my trip. After a week waiting, I am thrilled to be nearer to launching for the first leg of the trip; I just wish I could take them all with me.

The conditions are perfect, and I have a clear view of the coastline, glaciers and mountains for the whole of the fifty minutes of the flight. A hitched ride from the airport, a celebratory 2.5% beer, an overnight camp and before I know it, I'm following a forklift with my kayak wobbling along a bumpy road in a desolate industrial area of the port to a small slipway. I'm happy to see my boat; taking it out of the plastic wrap is like opening a present. Truck drivers stop by inquisitively as I get my new drysuit on and faff with my stuff, trying desperately to ram it all into the small boat.

I stand on my own and watch as the water level drops in the muddy harbour at the back of the Skinney-Þinganes fish factory, the largest employer in Höfn. It's not the romantic image I had of my Southeast Icelandic launch, but I don't care. I know that soon I'll be in the wild. I stop to breathe in the moment, and my heart races as I think about what lies ahead. I mark the moment with a few photos, and push the kayak into the water, lowering myself in. I'm on my own in unknown waters.

The tidal harbour is drying out quickly and I need to get going on this tide to make the most of the day. I push off and slip through the weeds towards the orange lighthouses marking the entrance to Höfn harbour. A calmness comes over me despite the underlying menacing feeling of the steep slopes of black sand. As I paddle out of the harbour the bulky Ikea bag I've strapped to my back deck catches the wind and spins the bow of my boat around, making it hard to stay in a straight line. I've got a long paddle of about 50 kilometres up to Starmýri today, so it's not ideal.

Considering how far you can realistically get in a sea kayak in a day is an important part of trip planning and is more dependent on the weather and the tides than on your strength and skill as a kayaker. A sensible, sustainable distance for someone with my skill level, paddling with the wind and tide as much as possible would be 20–30 kilometres a day. But this is my first day. I'm behind schedule, still fuelled by delicious Icelandic food and ready to push myself a bit. The furthest distance ever covered by a kayak on flat water in 24 hours is around 250 kilometres, so my 50 kilometres in eight or nine hours isn't that impressive.

The scale of the landscape is immense, jagged grey rocks rising up in an uneven zigzag from the sea, the teeth of a saw. Limited landing places on the first stretch heading north-east up the coast mean that I can't take a break until I reach Lónsvík island about four hours in. Seals bathe in the sun and surprised birds squawk and fire their streaky poo at me, while I stretch my legs and eat some lunch.

Back on the water I spend hours staring at the same headland, seemingly making little progress. I wonder what Marcus would make of my trip. It's over a year since he died, but I still can't believe that he's not on the other side of a text or call. I'm pretty sure he'd be worried about me out here alone, but also a bit proud. When Mike died, as the 'sensible' one, Marcus stepped into a paternal role, often checking that Katie and I were okay. He and I would go for a monthly drink at the Pub On The Park, where his Cocker Spaniel Eric would scramble under the table on the bare wooden floor to snaffle fallen food. Invariably, before we had finished our pints, Marcus would switch to serious mode and say something like, 'I'm a bit worried about all this time you're spending outside, I hope you've got good sunscreen.' He'd be pleased to know that I have. My skin is so fair that even on grey days I have to reapply it to my face and hands every few hours.

On a long paddle like today, I stop on the water every hour or so to drink water, apply sunscreen and eat some sweets or an energy bar. Landing is always a bit of a hassle and I keep thinking, 'if I can just get past that next bit…' After another four hours, I'm ready to land; all I need now is a good spot. I often use Google Earth before I launch to scope out possibilities further up the coast. Generally, I'm looking for a small cove that's sheltered from the wind, has a flat area at the back where I can pitch my tent and enough space above the tide line to leave my kayak safely. It takes me another hour to find somewhere suitable but I am rewarded by a perfect camp spot for my first night in the wild and a stunning fish-skin purple sky, reflected on the water and the white of my kayak.

The simple dinner of pasta and cheese cooked on my camping stove tastes delicious. I'm feeling pleased with myself. I've been sleeping in my small tent for a week now and am used to the colder weather. Tonight the temperature will drop to about 6 degrees centigrade – it's like March in the UK.

Still, I'm glad of my thick sleeping bag and extra layers. It's amazing to sleep to the sound of the sea lapping on the shore and I crash out quickly. At 3 a.m. I wake up to bright sunshine. I find the endless day comforting: I don't have to worry about what happens in the dark, it feels safe and relaxing. I cover my eyes and wake up again when the tent starts to get too hot around 6 a.m. It's a glorious morning and the sea caresses the beach like massage oil, smooth and reflective. I dip my feet in quickly, have a wash and make myself a cup of coffee and some porridge.

I need to get rid of the bag on the back of my boat so I take everything out. Firstly, I divide the food into piles: snacks, breakfast, lunch and dinner. I've got a week's worth in 3 small dry bags. I carry 15 litres of fresh water as well. I move on to clothes – I'm ruthless and set aside an entire dry bag that I don't need. It feels good, I don't know why I brought a shirt to this wild place! From the technology bag I extract a small projector and many cables. Finally, 3 books and some maps go on the pile. The pile goes in the Ikea bag, which I will try to post back as soon as I can. It's sunny so I take my time, enjoying the view, the impressive scenery, giving me lessons in my own insignificance.

I launch in the early afternoon. It's such a beautiful place and I feel at ease, happy to be there on the rise and fall of the sea. A thin wisp of cloud crosses the blue-green sky as if someone has rubbed out a line across a drawing, and puffins join me to bob along next to boat. Fuelled by Haribo and chocolate bars, with the help of a tail wind, I cover about 45 kilometres. I've been aiming for the town of Breiðdalsvík and it's a glorious evening paddle into the sun as I approach. I find a landing spot on the other side of the fjord where I won't be disturbed and make myself a sausage and mash dinner, sitting in sunshine until it dips below mountains. It's windy, cold and foggy overnight and the tent moves constantly. I berate myself for choosing such an exposed place to camp.

In contrast, the next morning, there is an intermittent stillness on the water as the sun beats down in the deep blue sky. I'm quicker at packing my boat and make the 3-kilometre crossing to Breiðdalsvík, a small town whose website claims has a population of 139, and a post office. I'm way too early so I hang around in 'The Old General Stores,' a shop and cafe, waiting for the post office to open and charging my phone. A steady stream of American and German tourists arrive. 'Oh, it's from a machine. Are those freshly ground beans?' demands one woman in shiny new outdoor clothes. I wonder if she realises how remote this place is.

At the post office, when I hand over the unwanted package, now wrapped in an orange survival bag (the Ikea bag itself is too useful to get rid of), the Australian/Icelandic woman at the counter happily tells me it will make me 8 kilograms lighter. It is a big weight off my mind. There's a large part of a trip like this that is just about lugging stuff, packing and repacking everyday, so I am pleased to ditch it. When I do the currency conversion later, I think it might be the best 60 pounds I've ever spent.

Leaving in the afternoon, a low mist sweeps in, first like a cloud sitting on the sea, later becoming a London-esque fog. On the next stretch up the coast, after Route 1 (the national road that circles the entire country) moves inland, the wilderness begins. The bird life is fantastic. It's been active up to now but in this untouched corner, it goes into overdrive. Fulmars and gulls fly low, right over the bow of the boat, and flocks of puffins, guillemots and kittiwakes flap and bob on the water. Later, the constantly surprised 'Oooohhh' call of eider ducks makes me chuckle as they sit and gossip around my boat on the beach, ducklings waddling and bobbing behind.

The water is teeming with life and the bright green mossy ledges contrast with the black, charred rock faces. They are bulbous and strange, like whipped cream splurging out of a layered cake. The mountain faces are formed in steps, laid down as the lava set. At around 13 million years old, Iceland is a relatively young landscape. The East and West Fjords are the oldest parts. I pass between Skrúður and the mainland, pleased to see the island I'd listened to the song about in Reykjavík, and spend the night next to Vattarnes lighthouse. Embraced by a gentle mist, the bright orange lighthouse is like an enormous chess piece and the place feels surreal as the wilderness disappears into a thick fog.

My two compasses give different readings for the hour-long crossing of the Reyðarfjörður fjord ahead of me: it's totally disorientating. The wrong bearing could easily send me way out into the Icelandic Sea. Tentatively I push on, keeping the just-visible sun behind me and checking the GPS I'm carrying. My route track looks like that of a drunken spider until I settle into it and gain confidence. Visibility improves and I'm joined by a raft of puffins. Further up, around the next headland, waterfalls cascade over the rusty rocks into the sea and I discover dark caves behind them that I paddle through. 'This is what exploration is like,' I say to myself, pleased that every day I dare to do more.

When I stop in Neskaupstaður, one of the largest fishing ports in Iceland, I've paddled out of the top side of the Southeast Iceland Shipping Forecast area. I've been in contact with a man called Ari who has built and runs a kayak club here. When I arrive, he is away for work in Reykjavík but tells me to camp next to the new clubhouse in a beautiful spot by the side of the fjord until he can open it for me. I have a very civilised dinner at a picnic table and pitch my tent around the back. I've averaged about 40 kilometres a day over the last four days and decide to stay in Neskaupstaður for a few days – I deserve a break.

I spend a day looking around the town including its open-air pool and hot tubs, and I'm glad of the wash. The Museum House is home to three museums one of which, Safnahús, is about the fishing industry, rocks and wildlife. Later I become intensely interested in Icelandic knitting as I stretch out a coffee long enough to charge my things in a wool shop and cafe. Knitting is a big thing here and jumpers are on sale for upwards of £150 handcrafted by a 67-year-old man in the town. I almost buy one.

After breakfast, coffee and wifi at the town garage, I'm back in my tent looking at maps of the Faroes in the green tinted light, when I hear voices. Ari is later coming back than expected, so has sent his dad Benedikt to come and meet me. He greets me like a good friend and points up the road, 'Here's my house, come if you need anything. I can do your washing. Come for coffee.' He opens the timber-framed clubhouse, which smells of beeswax. 'You'll need a mattress.'

'No, no, it's fine,' I say as he runs off to get one anyway.

'Here you are,' he says less than five minutes later as he places the mattress on the floor. 'Would you like to go to the valley to see the horses?'

'Yeah, that would be great,' I reply without thinking. I don't have any plans, and this sounds like the sort of thing I wouldn't do on my own.

Later that evening, I'm sitting with Ari's parents enjoying delicious cod, fried simply in lemon, pepper and butter accompanied with rice and potatoes, the yellowy flakes of fish almost melting in my mouth. The drive into the valley was a journey across generations. Amid laughter and back-patting, I met all the family. Ari arrives after dinner, and I'm pleased to finally meet him after the hospitality he's indirectly offered me. I do a double-take when he tells me he's 45 and a grandfather; his boyish looks and relaxed attitude made me think he was much younger.

It's past midnight and despite the late hour, he shows me round the club. It's a brilliant project driven by a few people's vision, which involved moving an old frame building from further down the coast on to land donated by the community and funded by the local fish factory. He tells me stories of the first modern kayaks in Iceland that were brought here from the UK strapped to the bridge of a fishing trawler. 'Sea kayaking is a new sport in Iceland', he tells me. 'Traditionally, small boats were for getting kids used to the sea before they went to work as fishermen. Have you heard of Neil Shave?'

I admit I haven't.

'He was a British man who ran activity trips for people with learning difficulties. He learnt Icelandic and taught us all to paddle.'

'Wow!' I say.

'Shave introduced the British Canoe Union coaching scheme to Iceland and changed the perception of kayaking from an unnecessary danger to a sport to be enjoyed safely. But he took his only life.' It's a sad ending and something about Ari's expression gets under my skin, the emphasis on 'only' making life seem even more precious. Before I set off the next day, filled with fish and clued up with local knowledge, I visit Neil Shave's grave in a small churchyard looking out over the sea. I pay my respects and think about how our adventures can be curtailed for lots of reasons.

I'm glad I've had time to look around Neskaupstaður. I have a few days before my ship leaves to the Faroe Islands from the next town of Seyðisfjörður. Hopefully I'll have time to explore the coast and hills after I've made sure the kayak is there on time by paddling the 45 kilometres around the headland and into the fjord. It's fairly wild as I pass Dalatangi, the oldest lighthouse in Iceland. I carry on through the now very lumpy but mesmerising sea to the southern side of the entrance to Seyðisfjörður, where the hillside is covered in a carpet of blue alpine lupins. It's a controversial non-native species in Iceland that has been introduced to rebalance nitrates, reduce erosion and help other species grow. I camp on the grass near the flowers and dare to try the sheep's head pâté. It is like a pork pie without the pastry, and with some thick slabs of bread it's a good hearty meal.

Checking my messages in my tent, a few people have asked if I'm okay and I realise that my GPS tracker has stopped working and it looks like I've dropped off the map. 'I'm fine, it's just a technical issue,' I assure them, a little bit happy that my moves are no longer being followed from afar. Although designed for use on the sea, the tracker is waterlogged and I'm not sure if it's salvageable. This is not good news since it is an important piece of emergency equipment. I still carry a Personal Locator Beacon (to transmit my location in an emergency), a handheld waterproof GPS (to know where I am and my speed), and a VHF radio (so I can contact the coastguard or other boats). I also use an analogue compass strapped to the front of my boat, and printed charts in a plastic holder. I carry flares I can set off if I'm in trouble and I have a phone. So even without the tracker, I don't think you could say I am taking a laissez-faire attitude to safety.

Over the next day, I make it my mission to get back to the Dalatangi lighthouse. Ari suggested leaving my kayak and hiking back over the hills, but after spending a few hours scrambling up a vertical scree face, I realise the Icelandic meaning of 'hike' is rather different to ours and return to the kayak. In the evening, I take to the water for the quicker route back. Most Icelandic lighthouses are bright orange or yellow and stand out clearly in a landscape that is green and black, like small castles.

As I wander ashore near the lighthouse in the evening light, I'm met by three sheep dogs running towards me barking; they skid past at high speed, rolling over each other before returning to jump up at me. Playful and friendly, they are followed by a woman in blue overalls riding a quad bike. 'Hello,' I say. 'Are you the lighthouse keeper?'

'That's me.' She offers me a friendly smile.

'Great to meet you!' I say with more enthusiasm than is necessary.

'I saw your boat yesterday, why are you here?'

I explain a bit about my trip and she asks if I'd like to look around the lighthouse. 'The foghorn isn't used any more,' she tells me, 'but sometimes I fire it up just for fun!'

'So how did you become a lighthouse keeper?'

'I took it over from my parents,' she replies, before adding, 'It's just a job'. After we complete the tour, I wave goodbye and pat the dogs before paddling back to my camp spot next to the blue flowers.

Seyðisfjörður is a pretty place and knows it. Quaint could be a way to describe it, tourist trap could be another. It is rammed with motorhomes, motorbikes, Americans and Germans. Makeshift craft shops and galleries give it an arty edge, with a rainbow pavement leading to the church and a street-art-covered Nordic house on the high street. A classic car buzzes past as I try to readjust to this strange film-set-like place and find a less expensive beer. I've had a great final day paddling down the fjord, with snow-topped mountains ahead of me and the mist chasing me in. A passing cruise ship is miniature against the mountains, a final reminder of the scale of this place.

Maybe I'm emotionally on edge, maybe I haven't had enough sleep in the land of the midnight sun, maybe it's because it's my first leg of this journey, but there's something about this volcanic island in the North Atlantic that makes me smile and cry at the same time. I've been welcomed so open-heartedly by its brilliant and warm people, I've been treated by the weather to a spectacular show of scenery and bird life as well as interesting and challenging conditions on the sea. I stand on deck of the boat that will take me to the Faroe Islands watching Iceland drift away, sorry to leave this beautiful, friendly and varied island.

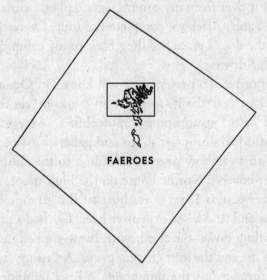

FAEROES

FAROE ISLANDS

NORTHERN ISLANDS

Tjørnuvík
Saksun
EYSTUROY
Oyrarbakki
Vestmanna
STREYMOY
MYKINES
Tindhólmur
VÁGAR
Tórshavn
KOLTUR
HESTUR
SANDOY

FAEROES: SEA OF FLAMES

It was always going to be difficult, I knew this before I started. I've had a bit of a fascination with the Faroe Islands for a while after seeing photographs of its waterfalls in a gallery in London. I'd read a post online from someone asking about kayaking in the Faroes and the reply from an irate tourist saying, 'it's far too dangerous, don't even consider it!' Now, you know what happens when someone says not to do something... There was a strand of common sense in her reply and a wise warning about these turbulent seas. I put the idea to bed until it cropped up again as one of the Forecast areas: now I had to do it.

The Faroe Islands are an archipelago located between Iceland and Norway, the closest being 330 kilometres off the north coast of Scotland. They are the only land in the Faeroes Shipping Forecast area (which uses the Faroese spelling).

I bought the second of Justine Curgenven's *This is the Sea* films in which she documents a trip to the islands where they are battered by strong winds, hampered by quickly changing conditions and fighting wild tidal currents.

Nigel Foster wrote about it in the 1980s in the book *Raging Rivers, Stormy Seas*, which I'm able to get online for 2p. I assume the huge areas of red tails flowing from the islands shown in the beautifully hand-drawn maps mean 'bad'. I later find this was the inspiration for a trip by two Norwegian kayakers that they called 'Sea of Flames'. The red tails on the charts show dangerous currents flowing around the islands caused by the movement of the tide. None of this helps to make this area seem more approachable.

Nevertheless, I stand in the queue alongside the motorbikes with a small piece of blue paper saying 'FAROE ISLANDS' fixed loosely to my kayak, which I have on a small trolley that I keep inside the boat. The ferry, operated by Smyril (Eagle) Line who brand themselves as 'Explorers of the North Atlantic', is called the Nøronna. The constant thrum of the engine reminds me of trips as a child where we crossed the channel in *Hullaballoo*, returning low in the water, laden with booze stored at the bottom of the bunks in the hull with the idea that customs officials wouldn't want to wake small children in the middle of the night. Invariably they'd come aboard for a drop of whiskey with Mike and be on their way. The gently swaying motion of the ship helps me drift off to sleep.

In the blurry light of an overcast dawn, the islands emerge out of the sea like the silhouettes of sleeping reptiles. The journey takes around eighteen hours and we arrive in Tórshavn at 3.30 a.m. to strong gusting winds and lashing rain. Just the welcome I'd expected. I stand on the freight deck in front of a pack of lorry trailers being readied for the half-hour turn-around before the ship continues to Denmark. The squeal of an industrial alarm pierces the air until the ramp clangs into place, revealing a cluster of soaked passengers waiting on the quay. I find a quiet sheltered corner by the side of the ferry terminal, gather my thoughts, and try to get my bearings. After wheeling the kayak around the harbour for a while, I tie it to some railings outside a grass-roofed government building, hoping they'd be understanding. I don't want it to blow away and it would be hard to steal. I crash out at a campsite along the road, up a small hill.

I've brought a slightly broken iPhone with me, which was a bad move for lots of reasons, mostly that a working phone gives me access to the latest forecasts, different charts and is a way of getting help if I need it. I left a new one at home and a friend has sent it poste restante to the Faroes; after some searching, it's found in a drawer in the main post office. I've just enough time to restock on food and check my plans before meeting Jan-Egil, a local kayaker who I'd reached out to on Facebook, who meets me in the harbour. Despite describing himself as a 'timid kayaker' he's a wily short-haired man who has an excited, wild look in his eyes. He leads me with a quick movement in his step, up the small hill behind the grass-roofed parliament buildings and around past the cluster of fishing and sailing boats. We weave our way through the shipyards, where huge trawlers are hauled up on slipways for repairs. 'This is our boat shed,' he says, showing me a single-storey timber building sitting in a row of similar structures facing out towards the sea. 'We keep the key here, in case you want to stay'.

'Thanks, so is there much of a kayaking community here?' I ask him, thinking about my friends back in Tower Hamlets Canoe Club.

'There are a few of us, but it's a lone-wolf culture.'

'What forecast do you use?'

He chuckles. 'Your best bet is to look out of the window and see what's happening. Only trust the forecast for eight hours, check the weather stations and webcams around the coast, don't plan, you can't plan!' This makes things more complicated than usual, I think to myself, before asking him if there are any places I should avoid. He points out a few in the Northern Islands. Jan-Egil thinks I'm mad and as we say goodbye, he waves cheerily and says, 'I hope you survive.' It feels like a test.

I have good phone reception but no data connection – this is a change from Iceland where even the remotest corner was covered. I'd come here to get away, in part at least, to experience wild nature, to challenge myself, not to update my Instagram and Twitter feeds. But without data, I won't be able to check the sea state unless I'm in a harbour, which isn't ideal. Still as I prepare to leave Tórshavn it doesn't seem important. Connected to wifi, I study the long-range wind forecast and the swell. It looks okay and I think, 'this is my chance'. I'm never going to have perfect conditions here and I'm impatient to leave the tourist traps and fancy bars.

Still, the decision to go is never easy. To leave a place of relative safety and comfort and head out into the unknown. There's a gap in the weather over the next few days, and the wind forecast is dropping. Residual swell from a storm that hit Ireland is making its way up the Atlantic and I can track the approaching big red and orange blob heading our way (red means bad again). Guðni in Iceland recommended an app developed by fishermen to show the notorious tidal movement around the islands. This is a game-changer as it makes tidal planning easier. I'd like to do a circumnavigation of Streymoy, the largest island in the Faroes, and get out to Mykines, the smallest inhabited island, where Jan-Egil works as a bird warden and guide. I decide to kayak as far as I can north away from Tórshavn to position myself to take on the exposed west coast in the weather window.

It's early evening by the time I bite the bullet. Pulling the loaded kayak over the smoothed, worn granite slabs takes determination and the silencing of all the 'what ifs' chattering around in the back of my head. I plunge my hands into the icy cold water and give myself a final push. The heavy, loaded kayak floats out into the harbour as I stretch the spraydeck over the cockpit rim. This piece of neoprene around my waist will seal the gap between me and the cockpit of my kayak, keeping the inside dry, with a quick release on the front in case I need to get out fast. A sense of relief and nervous excitement pulses through me. I'm here and I'm off! 'I can always turn back,' I think, knowing that I probably won't.

I leave the harbour and round the corner to the east of the island of Streymoy, heading north, flanked by its neighbour Eysturoy. The sharp salty air enters my nostrils and immediately refocuses my mind on the sea, blowing away any trivial land-based worries. The cumbersome kayak transforms into a sleek and buoyant vessel as it regains life in the dark waters. The strips of land are like ancient sea monsters waiting in the waters just showing their backs, the green and black colour palette like scales. Sharp shafts of light piercing through the moody grey skies highlight spots of vivid green on the hillsides. The effect is a dramatic contrast like a fresco in an Italian cathedral. I half expect to see an arm reaching out of the sky ready to save me from eternal damnation.

Instead, the wind gets up and it starts to rain. I'm uneasy, worried about what might come at me next. Then after ten minutes, the water gently smooths, the wind stops and the sun comes out. I relax a bit, going back to my aqua-rambling, my mind so focused on what's going on around me that I can't think of anything else. Later, a cold side-wind blows down the fjords, forcing me to change gear to something like a jog then a sprint; still progress is slow and despite my determination, I wonder how long I can keep this up. I sustain it for as long as possible battling against the sea, but with the power of a building tide against me as well as the wind, it all gets too much. I'm weak and tired when I find a place to land and decide to pitch the tent under a road bridge next to the water on a raised bank and wait until the flow starts going the other way.

I've been paddling for nearly seven hours and the hot drink and food I've fantasised about for the last few of them don't materialise as my stove seems to have run out of gas, another thing I didn't think about in Tórshavn. Great. I eat some sweaty cheese and salami I've been carrying for a few days. Flies chase around as I take off my sodden paddling clothes and pull out some dry ones. I can hear the water rushing under the bridge as I lie down in the tent, stretching out my back and loosening my neck. Red lights on the bridge flash and fade away as I drift off into an exhausted state. Waking at around 5 a.m., I see the water is starting to flow the other way. I pack up quickly. The flat-topped mountains in the distance look like a collection of jaunty hats.

As I approach the northern end of Streymoy island, the

swell gets big and a bit chaotic. I tell myself it's because of the headland and the water being pushed into a thinner channel from the open sea. I thought my get-out could be the surf beach at Tjørnuvík, but a glance over to it, as the swell builds and crashes, confirms that's not an option. Landing a fully loaded kayak on a beach with big swell and surf can be a dangerous operation leading to broken boats and equipment or perhaps worse: broken bones. It is often safer to stay on the sea. I push on and round the corner which reveals a sculptural wedge of a cliff rising at an angle out of the sea with its black face looking a bit like a slice of rich chocolate cake. Puffins are bobbing up and down on the water and seem very tame considering they've been hunted on these islands for centuries.

The looming cliffs of this exposed coast reveal themselves as I make the turn into a building sea. Pushing hard into the current with waves crashing over the kayak, I realise that I'm not making any progress, bad timing having put me right where I didn't want to be, in the tidal current at its strongest flow. I keep telling myself that I'm prepared and I've been in conditions like this before – but perhaps not all combined and perhaps not on my own with a loaded boat in a hard-to-reach corner of the world. I head into the cliffs in search of weaker flow but am wary of breaking waves. Gradually I start to make progress, and taking breaks just to sit and feel the movement of the water makes me feel more at ease in this challenging sea.

I'm willing a gap in the cliffs to emerge and signal my first landing opportunity. It comes after about five hours on the water, and couldn't be soon enough. I'm exhausted and need some food. I've managed to eat the three energy bars I had in the pocket of my buoyancy aid, but the rough sea has made it hard for me to open the day hatch, normally accessible from my seat, where I keep better food, snacks and safety equipment. I'm shaky as I get out of the kayak below the sheer black cliff faces surrounding the flat beach.

It's imposing and empty and as I look around I am reminded of the smallness of my craft. I feel the tiredness in my body, aches in my shoulders, back and legs. It's a common misconception that kayaking is all about using your arms; in fact, the whole body is involved, and a lot of the power comes from your legs and feet, pushing against the foot pegs. When I first started, my back would ache from sitting down for so long, but our bodies are quick to adjust and I know my kayaking muscles are strong, they've just been through an endurance test today.

The tiny town of Saksun is nestled behind a channel cutting through rocks, but isn't visible from the beach. I know it must be there as tourists mill around in the distance, giving a scale to this vast landscape. I watch as the sea level drops and the dumping surf builds. I know I can't stay on the beach as if the conditions change there's a high chance I won't be able to leave. The town would be a long walk especially with heavy bags and a kayak, up steep and narrow footpaths. So, I refuel on cheese and refocus, launching into the surf for the next few hours' stretch under the towering cliffs. I begin to realise how isolated I am here and how quickly the conditions can change. It's an interesting feeling – in one sense liberating and exhilarating, in another humbling and daunting.

Scouting for places to land, I become a scavenger. In desperation, I head towards the town of Vestmanna which has a camping symbol marked on the map. It turns out to be a dodgy trailer park with nowhere to pitch a tent. The town is grim; kids play with broken fences and car parts as I will them to go to bed so I can put the tent up in peace. Having fought the tide all the way in, I'm exhausted and crash out in the tent, hidden between some fishing huts on the edge of town. It's not a peaceful night, but my body switches off and I get some rest. The next morning, a heaviness descends on me, like when I was diagnosed with mouth cancer. Fitful sleep has allowed me a break from the reality that the morning sun is now illuminating in full. I decide to try to get to Mykines, the tiny island on the west of the archipelago where Jan-Egil has promised to welcome me, 'if I make it'. After a tough few days, I'm craving some connection and the feeling that not everything is against me.

Rounding the headland at the corner of Vágar, the tidal flow is chaotic with eddies and streams colliding and the occasional flat section that always makes me suspicious, because you never really know what it is doing. The swell has dropped significantly overnight; this bit of the coast is sheltered from the south-west, the flatter seas allowing me to explore some caves and arches, and get closer to the cackling and cawing of the cliffs. Every ledge is crammed with precariously balanced gannets and fulmars which launch, dive and swoop, joining the cacophonous crowds filling the sky.

I'm aiming for a headland in the shape of a witch's hat which I need to get to soon, before the tide changes and the crossing to Mykines becomes impossible. As I round the bumpy point, I am suddenly hit by a strong headwind. Fog starts to descend, and I check my bearings in case I lose sight of the island. I'm using my GPS to guide me, but since I can't always read the tiny screen as I paddle and never fully trust it not to fail, I also use the compass strapped to the front of my boat. Pointing it towards where I want to go and memorising the number representing the degree from north, I just keep going in that direction, checking from time to time that I'm on course.

As I near the eastern tip of the island, I can see a large, wide tide race – an area of fast-moving current – building across the channel. It's picking up quickly and I push harder towards the point. It looks like the kind of thing that in other situations could be fun to play in and makes me think of good times kayaking in similar waters with Natalie and Michal. It's big and fast, so right now I'd prefer to avoid it. I skirt round the headland and into two further races mixed with building swell from the south-west. It is not a relaxing paddle. I push so hard against the foot pegs that they come lose, making it harder to paddle. I continue along the layered green cliffs of the south coast of Mykines, now covered in a blanket of fog. The wind pushes my boat in the direction of surf waves breaking on the jagged rocks.

Fulmars and guillemots come to check up on me as I desperately will the harbour to appear. At the last minute it does, a small wall tucked in behind a narrow rocky cove with some sheds and huts on the clifftop about 50 metres above me. The harbour looks like an Inca temple with over a hundred stone steps leading up to the top. A sense of relief descends. I can feel the conditions building and know the weather is closing in. There's no clear place to leave the kayak. I'm dragging the heavy boat up a narrow ledge when I slip over, getting a nasty gash in my leg. I sit down to inspect it and to warm some tomato soup on my stove set up on the rocks, and to text Jan-Egil. True to his word he soon pops up and I clamber up the steep steps. 'You're late!' he smiles. 'I thought you got into trouble.'

'Well kind of,' I say, neither wishing to play down the challenges of the past few days, nor look stupid.

At the top of the cliff Jan-Egil negotiates in Faroese with harbour master and other islanders. From what I can tell, an old man with a Collie dog suggests we haul the kayak up on the trolley winch (a flat piece of sloping concrete not unlike a slide in the middle of the steps), and the bearded harbour master agrees. 'Tomorrow there'll be waves of six metres.' He points down to my boat, making me glad that it will be well out of the way of the battering that anything in the sea's way will get.

As predicted, the wind and rain set in and there are just a couple of others camping on the hill outside the village. Gusting blasts of Force 9 classed as a 'strong gale' on the Beaufort Scale give my tent a good slamming. The neat scale classifying wind from Force 0 ('calm') to Force 12 ('hurricane') was developed by Admiral Sir Francis Beaufort, hydrographer to the Royal Navy between 1829 and 1855. Before this, uncategorised wind strengths like 'a bit blowy' or 'windy woos' would have been rife. The Beaufort Scale is used in the Shipping Forecast, and today the Faroes gets a mention in the gale warnings at the beginning – a relatively common occurrence as far as I can see.

I spend the next day almost entirely in my sleeping bag, trying to keep warm and stay dry. I'm worried about getting stuck here and feel weak and unwell. The village comes to a standstill, the other campers have taken shelter in a public toilet and the angry sea makes the small harbour look like the top of a frothy coffee. Huge swell has developed, and the crashing waves pound their energy into the small inlet. There won't be any boats for at least a few days. There's a *Mary Celeste* feeling about the village, as life stops until the next day when the sun comes out and the wind starts to drop. Slowly people emerge from their houses and various jobs start again, building sheep pens, cleaning up and preparing for the return of the tourist ferry. I take a walk to the lighthouse at the westernmost tip of the island. The wind is still strong and it's hard to stand up in places.

In the early evening sun, I'm standing looking down at the harbour when a man comes up to me. 'Hi, welcome, I'm Heini,' he says and smiles.

'Thanks! I'm Toby,' I reply. There haven't been many people to talk to, so I'm happy to have the chance to do so now. He's friendly, and I tell him about my project and ask him if he has any Faroese stories of the sea. It turns out he's a former fisherman and now a tourist guide, and his dad was the last lighthouse keeper on the island.

'Not here, come with me,' he says, beckoning me to one of the few houses on the island.

The warmth and comfort of his home is a welcome refuge after a couple of days being battered in the tent. The 2018 football World Cup is on the TV in the background and an elderly beagle lies next to me on the sofa, snoring. A large picture window looks out over the coast and on the opposite wall hangs a puffin-catching net, or *hafwar*. 'Do you catch puffins?' I ask, looking at the net.

Heini makes a backwards circular movement with his hand. 'We use it for fulmars, not puffins. You can't catch puffins any more. From 2002 they had a tough time, they couldn't feed their chicks for twelve years in a row.'

'Because they were overhunted?' I ask.

'No, because they couldn't find food. Puffins eat small fish and reduced stocks close to the shore meant that adult birds had to fly farther away from the nests, leaving pufflings hungry and defenceless.'

'What's it like now?'

'The puffin population is slowly recovering, but they are still considered a vulnerable species,' Heini says as he leaves the room, coming back moments later with a cup of hot coffee and some pressed meat and cheese, which he pushes towards me. 'Eat, this is really good!' He's right, it's much nicer than anything I would have cooked for myself on a camping stove in the rain. Such kindness from a stranger makes me feel a sense of belonging on this remote island with a population of eight.

'Do you think the human community will die out?'

'I don't know, but I hope so. Why should you stay here in wintertime, why?' I wonder what it's like in winter; if almost-midsummer is anything to go by, conditions must be terribly harsh. 'In the world we live in now, why should you stay here and not live somewhere else?' Heini continues. 'The island won't die out. It will be more alive if no one lives here all year round. It will always be an attraction, it will always exist, how can it die just because people don't live here? It would be more alive!' he finishes, raising his voice with conviction. It's a perspective I haven't heard often, a clarity that as humans we are not the most important thing. There's nothing like being on a tiny boat in the ocean to remind you of that. There's a slight pause as we sit looking at the television.

'Who do you support?' I idly ask. The Faroe Islands are self-governing but remain a part of the Kingdom of Denmark.

'The Icelandic,' Heini says. 'I could support Denmark, but if Denmark played Iceland, I would support Iceland,' he said, hinting at a slight animosity I have detected from others over the relationship with the Danes. 'We have a Faroese team,' he says proudly, 'in the Island Games.' I'm familiar with this competition, which is like a mini-Olympics for small island communities, because my cousin Lisa recently competed in mountain biking for Jersey. It strikes me as a wonderful way to connect through sport across the seas.

'Do you have a broadcast weather forecast here?' I ask, changing the subject.

'Yes, it's on the radio every day from seven o'clock. On weekdays you can hear it almost every hour.' He smiles. 'At twelve o'clock they read the list of people that have died that day, and at six o'clock, it's the forecast and who's died.' Having kayaked in the lively waters here, it seems fitting that deaths are connected to the forecast.

I get the sense it's time to leave as my host disappears outside to clean the windows, but I'm quickly ushered back in and given some cured lamb to try. 'The weather's too nice to stay inside, we have to go out on the edge and see the sunset,' Heini suggests. I amble up to the ridge above the village and Heini arrives on a quad bike. As we watch the setting sun, I ask him about the solid stone monument nearby. 'The side facing the sea is for those lost at sea. The other one is for those who have fallen from the land catching birds,' he tells me seriously. 'You see the part lying down?' I look but can't make it out. 'We update it every week, for all those who have lost their lives kayaking...' He laughs heartily and, once I realise he's joking, so do I. As I wander back down to the tent, I feel lucky to have had this chance encounter and go to sleep with stories swirling around my head.

It's been suggested by a few people that I take the ferry back with my kayak, but looking at the tides and the calming seas the next day makes me think otherwise. I watch the ferry leave before we haul the kayak on the trolley winch back down to the harbour. To get back to Tórshavn, I need to get to various places along the way at the right times to avoid getting caught in unhelpful tidal currents, so I plan carefully. At around 60 kilometres, it will be the furthest I've kayaked in one day so I'm glad for the favourable conditions and a westerly wind which will push me back.

The wind growls in my ears as the sun pushes through the cloud and highlights in vivid velvety green the grassy backs of dark cragged rocks jutting out of the sea. To begin with my mind is so focused on what's going on in the moment that although I'm not relaxed, I feel a sense of peace. I settle into my journey as I pass the islet of Tindhólmur, a near perfect right-angle triangle whose base is the same width as its height. Its hard lines are a dramatic contrast to the flow of the seas below. In one faster stroke, my wobbly foot pegs break and I find it hard to get comfortable. I realise that so far in the Faroes, I've only kayaked in survival mode in seas bordering on dangerous. Today though, despite the lack of foot pegs, I feel like I'm back in touring mode, able to enjoy moments in this Yorkshire Dales by the sea.

Later, I follow the tide along the coast off the island of Vágar, and paddle between it and the islands of Koltur and Hestur, the first like a long run up and jump, reminding me of the bike ramps we would build in the garden as kids, Katie and Marcus always making me try them out first. It's hard being the youngest. I think how I would selectively tell Marcus about this part of the trip: calmer reflective seas but a marathon nonetheless. We'd sit in the kitchen that I designed in Marcus and Andy's house (or Mandy's, as we called it), around the family table we'd sat around at as kids, and tuck into a delicious meal they'd prepared. 'So, what were the Faroes like?' Marcus might ask. 'Beautiful and wild,' I'd say, 'and a bit scary.' I still find it hard to believe that Marcus isn't at home in his tastefully decorated town house surrounded by scatter cushions and carefully chosen furniture.

Sandoy island reveals itself as the wind changes direction slightly and the tide against me starts to build. A hilly part of the marathon, I think, and increase my effort level accordingly. I keep on going. In the late evening, I round the headland of Streymoy on the home straight to Tórshavn, in jubilant or delirious excitement, and am treated to a beautiful sunset through the whipped-up clouds. I find some interesting caves, their large mouths open to the ocean, worn and smoothed by the waves undercutting the land above. The reverberating crash and crackle of the water wards off any interlopers.

I've been in the kayak for over twelve hours by the time I reach Tórshavn, and stumble wearily out of it, cook a quick dinner and fall asleep on the floor of the Canoe Club. I spend the next day fixing kit and repacking my boat ready for the ferry ride to Norway. I'm exhausted but happy to have made it back. As expected, it's been challenging, not just physically but mentally too. I've had to push harder and draw on my stubborn determination, adjust to changing situations and have faith in my ability and judgement. The exposed coastline that was brooding in my mind has rewarded me with spectacular, unique scenery, dramatic skies, interesting seas and fast-changing weather. I board the ferry in the early morning rain, pulling the kayak behind me, pleased to have made it and thankful not to have my name added to the fictitious monument in Mykines to fallen kayakers.

NORTH UTSIRE

SOUTH UTSIRE

UTSIRE (NORTH AND SOUTH): DANGEROUS WAVES AND UFOs

The sweet smell of fairground hot dogs fills the air as we glide about 10 meters above the sea, on what from this angle is a floating cafe, whose large windows boast impressive views across the fjords. I'm on the ferry from Sandvikvåg to Halhjem, just south of Bergen in Norway, my fourth ferry in three days. It's been a logistical challenge to get here from the Faroe Islands but it feels good to finally be inside the North Utsire Shipping Forecast area. Named after the island of Utsira, the North Utsire area runs down the side of Norway's fjords from about 70 kilometres north of Bergen to 3 kilometres north of Stavanger, while South Utsire continues around the coast to the entrance to the Skagerrak, the strait between Norway and Denmark.

I'm with Alina and Ivar Kim, Norway-based kayakers who were sufficiently excited about the trip to pick me up from the ferry port in Stavanger at 5.30 this morning, greeting me with smiling faces, a personal sign and a flask of strong coffee. I'd met Alina in Cornwall at a kayak symposium four years ago, then gone on to do some of my kayak leader training with her, where we'd shared our struggles and laughter. When I knew the Shipping Forecast would bring me to Norway, I got back in contact, and she was keen to join me.

We'd decided to paddle north from Stavanger to Bergen (stopping at the island of Utsira on the way), but the northerly wind blowing when I arrive and the forecast for the next few days makes this difficult because we'd be kayaking against the wind. Our first planning decision is made in the ferry car park when Alina's boyfriend, Ivar Kim, offers to drive us the five hours up to Bergen (including two ferry rides) so that we can do the trip in reverse to make the most of the conditions. I'm taken aback by his kindness – it will be a ten-hour round trip for him – but I'm not about to refuse the help, especially since my stomach is starting to hurt and I regret gorging on the seafood buffet on the last overnight ferry.

On my route to Norway, I've passed through several Shipping Forecast areas. I'll visit Fair Isle, South Utsire and Fisher again later with my kayak, but Viking, is one of the four areas - alongside Forties, Dogger and Bailey – which does not include any land. Located in the middle of the sea, the only ways to reach these with a kayak involve boats, helicopters and oil rigs. I haven't written off the possibility yet, but I'm not hung up on visiting them. The Utsires, or Utsiras as they should be spelled (according to everyone except the Shipping Forecast), are some of the newest areas of the forecast, having been added in 1984 following new common area boundaries throughout the North Sea region. The same areas appear in the maritime weather forecasts of Norway, Denmark and

Germany, although those countries use the modern spelling of the name which has been in use since 1924. Utsira itself is a 6-kilometre-square island about 17 kilometres off the coast of Norway and the key place I'd like to visit here.

We've spent most of the car journey chatting about how we might get to Utsira, but it's not until the forty-five-minute crossing to Halhjem that we spread our collection of charts out over the thin Formica table in the ferry restaurant and get a clear view of what we are considering taking on. Above Utsira the words 'DANGEROUS WAVES' in capital letters printed in shocking pink jump out at us from the charts. I've never seen this on any charts before, so it is worrying to say the least.

'Ah that's the Sletta,' Ivar Kim says knowledgably, as if talking about the big bad wolf. He has kayaked most of these waters and is keen to help us with anything that might keep us safe. Between the islands of Espevær and Røvær, this open stretch of sea littered with rocky outcrops is infamous among ferry passengers and mariners for its heavy seas. 'It's very deep but also has lots of shallows that make the sea very messy in windy conditions,' Ivar Kim warns. 'Usually it's not that bad, but people here have always been told, "the Sletta is dangerous, you should keep away from it and definitely not cross it in a kayak unless you have a boat following you, or a death wish!"' Alina and I look at each other, wide eyed but smiling, realising how difficult this might be but excited by the challenge.

It's no surprise that many ships have sunk here. 'A boat my dad used to work on went down there,' adds Alina, not making any of us feel more confident. 'The Finnøyglimt was a sand cargo ship. Two members of the crew survived, but the captain was never found. He and another crew member were people we knew.' Neither of us are particularly keen to end up the same way, so we plan to go but be ready to cancel if the sea doesn't look good. A tactic I like to think the Faroe Islands have taught me.

'It's okay because "dangerous waves" will be written on the sea when we get there,' I joke.

'Yeah, it will be flashing in neon lights,' Ivar Kim replies. We all laugh, knowing this crossing will be something to take seriously, but can be made light of for the moment. Fleetingly, I think about my illness: it can be easy to let big looming challenges stop you before you start, but sometimes it's better to prepare as best you can and not think about them. We continue with the planning, deciding where to stop and stay each night if the conditions are as forecast. We know these plans will change, but by the time we are folding up the maps and going back to the car, we have a clear idea of which islands we'll be hopping to down the coast of Norway for the next six days.

My stomach is rumbling as we drive through the low cloud and drizzle that apparently signals that we must be nearing Bergen. We set off from Hjellestad, a harbour just south of the city where people are going about their Sunday afternoon business of tinkering with boats. 'I'm going to need a bit of time to repack my boat,' I warn Alina and Ivar Kim, whose time I'm worried I'm wasting as I stuff things into smaller bags and try to distribute the weight around my kayak. They don't seem to mind. I'd forgotten my broken foot pegs and am stuck with the not-very-high-tech solution of wedging a couple of sandwich boxes down the boat in the hope they will provide the resistance my feet need to put some power in my paddling strokes. I eventually manage to stuff everything in and look over at Alina's kayak. She seems to have lots of space and a whole hatch full of bananas. 'Healthy energy,' she says with an excited smile.

We both get into our drysuits, zipping up and tightening the seals around our wrists and necks. They are an overall-like piece of kit designed to keep the water out even if you fall in, essential for cold-weather kayaking. Good ones are not cheap. 'I bought this drysuit and it cost so much money,' Alina says. 'I thought, now I have to paddle all year.'

I laugh. 'Me too, with every piece of kit you're a bit more committed,' I say, slipping on my spraydeck like a skirt. If I capsize and can't roll I can pull the release on the front. Like all serious kayakers, I've practiced this move so many times that I'm no longer worried I might get stuck in the boat. On top of my drysuit goes my buoyancy aid which will keep me afloat if I do fall in. Before getting our kit on, Alina and I looked nothing like each other; now both in orange and grey, we look like we're playing for the same team.

We say our goodbyes to Ivar Kim. 'I hope you survive the "Sletta",' he says half-seriously before reminding us that he'll be with us in spirit, on hand to help with forecasts, logistics and anything else we might need. We push off the slipway and paddle in between the large yachts to the middle of the water.

It's 2 p.m. on a late June day but the cloud is still low and visibility poor as we negotiate shipping lanes between the islands. Thanks to my fishy feast on the overnight ferry, I have to make an emergency landing toilet stop and quickly get out of my drysuit, narrowly avoiding what could have been a horrible mess. I'm reminded of a Raymond Briggs book we had as kids where Father Christmas goes on holiday and overdoes it on rich creamy food and shellfish, something that his Laplandic stomach promptly rejects.

Partly because of this, we've planned to start with a shorter trip to Havstrill Paddle Club on an island about 15 kilometres away. We've got a list of places where we can land and camp, including several kayak clubs who are happy for us to pitch our tents next to their boat sheds. The unquestioning support of like-minded people is becoming a theme of the trip. As we head south from Bergen, the land flattens and trees disappear giving way to large slabs of glacier-smoothed rock with wooden summer houses clustered like barnacles. There is a subtle pinkiness in the stone where deep wrinkles, creases and folds make it look like the life-worn skin of an elderly relative. We kayak for four hours on a flat reflective sea that has nothing like dangerous waves and if anything is a bit boring to paddle. I'm glad of the break, my stomach ache is slowing my progress and Alina is getting used to having to wait while I paddle in to the land for another toilet stop. I feel like I must be a bit of a disappointing kayak partner and hardly manage any of the fishcakes and mash that she prepares for dinner.

My stomach is slightly better the next day as we pick our way through small inlets and islands. I still feel tired and am noticeably slower than Alina, who is mostly in front. I stress about this for a while before relaxing into the rhythm of paddling and keeping pace as best I can. Nothing like the greens I associate with Norway, the land is craggy, seemingly sun-bleached, and from a distance looks like ice, with a faint backdrop of mountains behind. Around the islands, large fish farms are useful navigational aids, with their circular nets and yellow markers.

Fishing has long been a big deal in Norway, and although the top spot in exports was scrumped by energy when Norway found oil, fishing, fisheries and fish-processing are still the second most important industry. According to the Norwegian Seafood Council, exports amount to '42 million seafood meals every single day of the year.' Famously, Norwegians claim responsibility for getting the Japanese to eat salmon sushi. In the mid 1980s Japan was importing fish while Norway had too much of the stuff. The Norwegian Fisheries Minister of the time came up with 'Project Japan', where Atlantic salmon was distinguished from its Asian counterpart (not considered fit for sushi) and demonstrated to be an option in the more lucrative raw fish consumption market. It took fifteen years, but Norway increased salmon exports to Japan and convinced the world to eat salmon sushi.

Further on, the rolling sea and clear sky are deep blue with the occasional white of an eider family bobbing along. We have biggish swell and a Force 4 to 5 wind, both of which are assisting our progress as we push south. Force 5 on the Beaufort scale is often seen as the cut-off point for safe kayaking, although how safe it is depends on a lot more, including the wind direction, the kayaker's experience and where you are. This would not be good weather to cross the Sletta in, but the forecast for a few days' time predicts a drop in the wind, so Alina and I are keen to position ourselves further down the coast to take advantage of it for the crossing to Utsira.

It's a fast ride and we often lose sight of each other in the waves. We are both fully alert; there is no option but to be present and no space for niggling thoughts in our heads. I suppose it could be classed as a kind of extreme meditation. The coast is peppered with lighthouses and Alina and I do our best to try to spot them and pick out the names while both focused on our own challenge with the sea. About four hours in, Slåtterøy Lighthouse stands on an island that could be made of Stilton cheese and we decide to make a stop. Goats nibble our shoes and inspect our kayaks as a family from Oslo unload kids, bags, food and toys from a small boat for a stay in their summer cabin.

We find somewhere to sit and eat some lunch on the rocks. Perhaps it's seeing the family from Oslo or the feeling of being on the edge of humanity that makes us talk about our families. 'It was my dad who first took me kayaking on a lake in Poland,' Alina shares. 'I was 16 and I just loved it.'

'My aunt and uncle got me into kayaking, but it was sailing with my family as a kid that made me love the sea and the Shipping Forecast,' I say, letting my mind drift back to long days gazing at the horizon on the foredeck of *Hullaballoo*. We talk about our parents and siblings. 'I've got a brother and a sister,' I start before correcting myself. 'Well, my brother Marcus died last year.' By now, we know each other well enough for Alina to ask what happened and not just say she's sorry. Once I've explained she asks me something British people rarely dare to air: 'Doesn't that make you worry about yourself?'

'Yes, but I try not to think about it,' I smile. 'There's so much I can do now, that I'm just happy to be able to do it.'

'It's a good attitude, we should all have it.'

A goat about to stand on Alina's kayak brings an end to the conversation and we get ready to launch, aiming for Hiskjo, another 20 kilometres – or three to four hours – down the coast.

The wind has dropped a little and the islands all look very similar. To navigate we rely heavily on compasses and recognising manmade insertions in the rocky landscape. On the last section we're aiming for a road bridge, but I get it wrong and position us further down the map than we are. 'I've messed it up,' I admit to Alina, who, despite the frustration she must feel, is kind. At around 8 p.m. we see the bridge we are looking for and by the time we land on a small beach, the moon is nearly full and clearly visible. I cook cheesy pasta as the sky burns orangey pink and the air starts to cool.

We have a shorter hop the following day to the pretty island of Espevær. It's famed for an unexplained oval impression in the grass which appeared overnight in 1975 and has been attributed to a UFO landing. Several theories abound including that it's the work of rabbits, fungus or soil conditions, but none are confirmed. Alina navigates us skilfully to the hidden landing spot close to the imprint and we walk up to a flat grassy patch, next to the UFO site, watched over by alien faces painted on the rocks. Below them is a barbecue, picnic table, bag of charcoal and some lighter fluid which we decide is a sign from the extra-terrestrials about today's dinner. With a population of 100, the island has four times fewer inhabitants than the small village in Rutland where I grew up, but we are assured that one of its amenities is a shop, so go off in search of it.

The shop is one of a chain called 'Joker', which I find hard to trust, as if they'll leave banana skins on the floor just for comic-book laughs. The woman in the Joker thinks we're crazy kayaking to Utsira. 'If you miss it your next stop is England,' she laughs. I think she's exaggerating but Google Maps later informs me that a couple of compass degrees wrong and 600 kilometres later we would end up just below Newcastle. 'You can see Utsira from the hill,' she tells us, which fills me with excitement as the name of a place so familiar is suddenly within reach.

After our alien-assisted barbecue and our last beers before attempting to cross the Sletta, we take a walk into the woods where things are not quite what they seem. Small eyes painted on the trees follow us through the makeshift path, wooden fishes swing from ropes, and shoes are nailed to trees. 'People here get really into the story,' Alina says, 'they create these paths full of mysterious eyes to make you feel crazy as you walk around: am I being watched or am I alone?' The wind has picked up and whips away Alina's cap as we stand looking at the small wooden fingerpost sign pointing out the nearby islands including, right in the distance, a small speck of land: Utsira. To get there we will have to cross the dreaded Sletta.

'It looks far, but we will make it,' Alina says defiantly. I like her positivity and commitment to the challenge. 'We have no other option!' she adds. We laugh, both hoping the 'dangerous waves' decide to take a day off tomorrow. The forecast is good, and the wind should be lower than previous days where we've had waves of one to two meters, but you never know. 'When I see you near the rocks taking pictures, I think okay, he feels comfortable, and that makes me think it's fine too,' Alina says.

'Yeah, the problem with that is that when I see you paddling ahead, it makes me feel more confident,' I admit.

'Well maybe we're better together,' she says. 'Either that or we're both mad!'

As I get into my tent next to the UFO site, I think about my kayaking friends back home: Michal, Natalie, Lindsey and Esther. Alina is right on both counts; when kayaking with others you dare to do more and the sense of shared madness makes it all less scary.

I'm still not feeling right in the morning, but if we're to get to Utsira it has to be today. Back in Bergan Ivar Kim, presumably hoping to see his girlfriend again, strongly suggested that we first cross the Sletta to the island of Røvær and then go on to Utsira. The first leg of about 15 kilometres will take us right through where 'dangerous waves' is written on the chart. We paddle out through small channels, getting closer to the spectre of the notorious Sletta, expecting things to get difficult at any moment, and foreseeing a kind of Hollywood-esque battle with the sea to certain glory. But, it's sunny and the sea is flatter than we've seen it for days. Neither of us want to tempt fate until we get to Røvær, so save our 'we crossed the Sletta' celebration until we reach the island. Behind the walled-up harbour, fields of wild garlic and buttercups sway in the wind, while the seaweed around us is like ribbons or fluffy lettuces. My lack of foot pegs is making me a bit uncomfortable in the boat, so I reload it to distribute the weight differently, hoping it will perform better on the next leg to Utsira: an open sea crossing of around 18 kilometres.

Utsira is low so we can't see it to begin with and have to trust the charts and a compass bearing to take us in the right direction. We spend a long time staring at a speck in the distance that doesn't seem to grow any bigger. As well as GPS and charts, we have a comedic map of the island that is a large sheet of paper with blue all around and a small blob in the middle that is our target. When we are in the middle of the sea unable to see any land, it feels like the most accurate chart. We stop every hour for a break and food, bobbing along on the waves like the birds. There is a north and south harbour on the island which can be used alternately depending on conditions. We are heading for the north harbour with light swell and good visibility.

Two hours go by, the swell increases and we get a fun surf over to the island. Nearing what we think must be the harbour, we see the wind turbines on the coast. Utsira is famous for being very windy. In 2004 Norsk Hydro took advantage of this and installed the island's two wind turbines as part of the 'Utsira Project' – a full-scale initiative for energy self-efficiency, where the power of the wind was combined with hydrogen electrolysis to supply full energy for 10 households. Despite being largely successful, the project came to an end in 2008 due to issues with the hydrogen part of the system. The turbines continue to generate energy for the island and in the open sea further south, Norway has opened tenders for the creation of a floating windfarm.

As luck would have it, after unnecessarily negotiating some massive waves, we arrive into the small fishing harbour and land on a slipway next to the pub on one of the two nights of the week it is open. As we pull the boats up the slipway, I can't believe I'm finally here on Utsira. The north harbour is a relaxed place with wharf buildings lining the quay and some small fishing boats in the harbour. The bar is in an old timber building that looks like a fishing warehouse, its long tree-trunk beams creating a clear span across the main room. It has a worn, friendly feeling to it.

'You here to visit? Wonderful!' the softly spoken, tanned barmaid says, not expecting an answer.

'Yes, we're visiting, could we have two beers please?' I venture.

'Wonderful, two beers coming up.' She grabs some glasses. 'You looking for somewhere to stay? There's a wonderful place to camp up the hill.' I'm not sure I've heard anyone say 'wonderful' so much, but it's a nice welcome and good to know where we can stay. 'Just sorry about the loud music later,' she says, 'it's a big party tonight, but you can come. Wonderful!'

After a quick beer, we pitch our tents on the hillside overlooking the harbour and go back to the pub. We sit outside in down jackets in the last remaining sun of the day, pleased with our achievement and serendipitous planning. A group of locals inside are watching the World Cup on a projector. The loud music we've been warned against turns out to be speakers plugged into a phone through which the barmaid plays the song 'Utsira', which she says gets locals going but doesn't seem to impress the three other women in the bar.

'An exorcist friend of mine was flown here by helicopter to rid the school of ghosts,' says Alina in what I first assume is the beer and physical exhaustion talking but turns out to be a true story. 'Strange things were happening in the school, they tried everything, then the council paid for Ayna to come from the mainland to get rid of the ghost.' After another beer, we amble up the hill, stopping to look at the full moon bright against the pinky blue sky. It feels like anything could be possible here, but for now we crawl into out tents on the mystical island of Utisra.

We wake to thick fog. Visibility is definitely poor. The smooth flat water of the harbour reflects the eerie calm of the most immediate surroundings, but the rest is erased by this white blanket. We decide to take a walk to South Utsira, which seems quite intrepid from our new home in the north. One road leads there and it's not easy to get lost. We pass the red wooden town hall, outside which stands a monument to Aasa Helgesen, a midwife and Norway's first female mayor, who served in Utsira from 1926 to 1928, only ten years after women got the vote.

The fog starts to clear and we immediately pick out what must be the haunted school; its dominant presence on a rock and long, narrow windows make it look like a scene from *Scooby-Doo*. There is a macabre street-art exhibition in the basement gallery with fake blood and handprints on the windows, not helping the spooky feeling. Utsira is known for its street art, which has been promoted through the Utsirart Project, launched in 2014 to bring street art to 'the island without streets'. Street artists from around the world have contributed and I later notice the stick figures painted on the wind turbines are similar to many close to where I live in East London, created by the artist Stik. It's strange to find a little connection with home so far away.

We carry on to the south harbour which is more open than the north, the buildings scattered. Deckchairs give it a holiday feeling and we buy ice cream and postcards from the Joker on the harbour front. There is a small beach and a fleet of timber rowing boats. 'Which do you prefer?' Alina asks, referring to north or south Utsira.

'Definitely north,' I say, quickly aware I'm making a snap judgement. 'What about you?'

'Me too, and not just because it's got the pub,' she laughs.

The fog lifts and we amble back. As we're packing our boats a tall, bearded man comes over for a chat, telling us he's a volunteer bird guide. Alina and I had wondered if we'd bump into many birders, as Utsira is one of the best birding sites in Norway, with 317 different species. 'Thirty years on the island and I've seen two-hundred-and-ninety-nine,' says the birder, and we make impressed noises. 'I will have a party when I see them all,' he smiles. He wishes us well and it's time for us to round the island and make the 30-kilometre crossing to Skudeneshavn.

Leaving from the north harbour in an anti-clockwise direction around the island, we get a good view of the lighthouse. It takes longer to get to the south harbour than we expected but once there, we check our positions and point our boats into the endless sea, kayaking for hours to where we think the land must be. There is very little to look at along the way and we start singing songs almost immediately. I am annoyed that I can't think of any more ways to treat the Drunken Sailor than 'put him in a bathtub with a hosepipe on him,' so it's Alina's turn.

'This is a song about the sea where we're sitting and rowing. It says there are big waves and small waves coming at us,' Alina explains, 'the sea is moving in waves.' It seems very appropriate, so she sings it a few times, then asks me to teach her the areas of the Shipping Forecast. We start with the names, 'Viking, North Utisre, South Ustire, Forties, Cromarty, Forth, Tyne...' then move on to an invented version of the full forecast: 'There are warnings of gales in Shannon, Rockall, Hebrides and Faeroes...' After a few hours she could almost get a job at the BBC. In return for my services, she offers to teach me 'Row Row Row Your Boat' in Norwegian, which I struggle with as we realise it could be easy for madness to set in. We make slow progress but gradually shapes emerge in front of us. 'Land?' Alina says with a half-questioning tone.

'Yes, I see it too,' I reply. It's easy for your eyes to play tricks on you on the water, but we're on course. We round the corner towards Skudeneshavn and fall off the edge of my chart. Alina is armed with the detailed version. She also has instructions from Dirk the dentist – a kayaking acquaintance of hers – on how to get to the kayak club we can stay at tonight. It's all a bit complicated so she gives him a call. 'Call back in seven minutes while he's doing his op,' says the friendly hygienist. We do this.

'It's fine for you to stay at the club,' he says, as we imagine him drilling someone's teeth at the same time. 'I'll come and meet you.'

We land in Skudeneshavn as the wind picks up. Dirk arrives in shorts and a t-shirt, on a bike. It's cold enough that he has goose bumps as he kindly opens the club toilets and lets us camp in the harbour. He asks us about our plans for what will be our last day on the water, and when we mention the crossing we have planned to Finnøy he says, 'Watch out for the shipping lanes!' I have to admit that having crossed the Sletta, then to Utsira and on down to Skudeneshavn, I thought we'd overcome all our major obstacles, but as is often the case we still have a challenge ahead.

Alina cooks reindeer meatballs for our dinner which, with some powdered mash, is good solid camping food. Before going to bed, we stroll around the pretty town in the evening light. It reminds me of the east coast of England, places like Woodbridge where we used to sail. Red pantile roofs and white-painted timber cover the higgledy-piggledy houses with overhangs and roofs at jaunty angles. Large, shiny motor cruisers jostle for space in the harbour with traditional fishing boats, trawlers and drilling vessels. It's very quiet.

The next day we cross Boknafjorden, the widest fjord in Norway. It feels like it too. The shipping lanes we've been warned about turn out not to be as busy as expected, and we run the gauntlet across a group of sailing boats whose crews wave cheerily at us, so we can't have messed it up too much! We dodge the ferries crossing the fjord but have a crosswind most of the day, which makes it hard work to stay on course. Towards the end of the day, we near our destination in Finnøy, where Alina and Ivar Kim live. The sea picks up and pushy waves make the final stretch a bit of a slog.

This is soon washed away when we land and are met by Ivar Kim on the pier, who has cold prosecco in the fridge and homemade pizza in the oven. 'You made it!' he laughs, as we feign victory with our paddles held in the air. It's a relief to get out of the boat and to have completed it, and there are hugs all around. After a much-needed shower and washing and organising our kit, we spend the evening on their sunny terrace, excitedly telling Ivar Kim about our adventure before I convince him to read the Norwegian shipping forecast. He laughs as he finds it online, saying, 'It's in new Norwegian – that will be funny! Oh no, it's also in Bokmål.' Norway has three languages: Sámi, 'new Norwegian' (Nynorsk) and Bokmål, the latter two being official variations of Norwegian. He admits that the first time he'd heard the forecast on the radio was when they came to collect me at the ferry six days ago. It feels like we're old friends as we laugh about UFOs, crossing the Sletta and singing madly on the sea. I drift off to sleep on an inflatable mattress in their spare room, full of food, wine and conversation.

We spend the next day fishing from their small motorboat in the heat of the day and Ivar Kim dives for scallops. I'm pleased to catch some mackerel, although less excited about the fish blood I leave trailing down the side of the boat. My stomach is finally back to normal, and we eat our bounty later, cooked simply in butter. The scallops are tender and fresh. 'To the Sletta,' toasts Ivar Kim, raising his glass of beer.

'To the Shipping Forecast,' says Alina.

'To you guys, thank you,' I add, feeling like I should say more but knowing I'll get emotional if I do. 'It's been brilliant!' I feel that space between adventures opening up to swallow me again. As I say goodbye to them, a big part of me wishes I could stay.

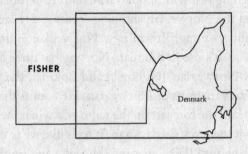

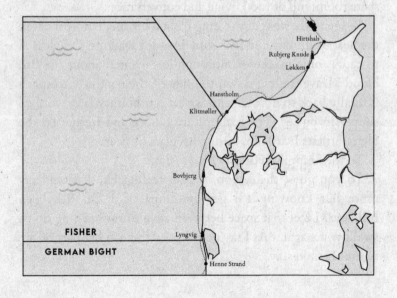

FISHER: SAND, SURF AND COLD HAWAII

There's a loose parallel with a life journey to that of a long stint on a ferry: high and low points, the celebratory feeling of the entertainment, the lows and boredom of mid-morning, the isolation and vastness of the surroundings and an inevitability that we're chugging away along a course to a definite end. It's a microcosm of life and it reminds me of times in hospital wards where beeping, whirring, humming machines drift on through the night. I emerge from my subterranean quarters to bright sunshine and the smell of fish wafting off the land. Gone are the rocky islands and in place is a long expanse of flat, sandy beaches.

I'm in Hirtshals, a seaport town on the top of the Jutland peninsula in Denmark. At about 125 kilometres from the Fisher Shipping Forecast area, it's as close as I can get to it by ferry. In fact, I've failed to find a way of transporting my kayak there other than paddling down the coast. I wouldn't normally mind this, but it turns out that this part of Denmark and all the way down the west coast to Germany isn't exactly a kayaker's dream, and most of the paddling in the country takes place on the other side where beaches are protected from the Atlantic surf, and islands and inlets make everything more interesting.

I've been in touch with Anders, a Danish kayaker from Copenhagen who has attempted circumnavigations of Denmark twice and is one of the few sea kayakers with experience on this exposed coast. His reply to my email asking for advice was less than encouraging. 'It is mostly the same sand with sand, sand and sand,' he told me. 'Further down it is mostly sand on one side and water on the other... Not the most interesting of sceneries after a few days.' Despite knowing this since April, as I pull the kayak off the ferry on a hot July morning with clear blue skies, I'm concerned about the next week of my trip and mostly how I might manage the boredom of it.

This strange dune landscape is a big contrast to the mountainous scenery of Iceland and the Faroe Islands, and the rocky ins and outs of Norway. The houses are noticeably different, made of bricks, with tiles on the roof; modest buildings, hunkered down to shelter from the wind. Walking around, it is so quiet that I can hear the rustle of leaves as they circle around on the pavement and the chattering of birds in the foliage. I'm keen to launch as soon as I can and get this over with, but a scattering of people clustered around a fish restaurant advertising a 'Shooting Star' as its special gets my attention.

The 'Shooting Star' turns out to be a kind of 'everything' open sandwich, which sounds like what The Very Hungry Caterpillar ate on Saturday: 3 herrings, 2 fried fish fillets, 1 piece of thick-cut smoked salmon, a spoonful of caviar, 5 prawns and 3 sprigs of asparagus, all balanced on a piece of rye bread with plentiful Thousand Island dressing. Apparently, it was invented by a famous Danish Smørrebrød chef in 1960 who named it 'Shooting Star' after Yuri Gagarin visited Copenhagen. It is delicious if a little challenging to eat. I do my best to extract the fragments of it from my increasingly impressive beard and walk with lethargic determination back to my kayak. 'Let's be 'aving you, Fisher,' I think to myself.

The Fisher Shipping Forecast area is named after the Great Fisher Bank, a sandbank about 275 kilometres off the coast of Denmark in the middle of the North Sea. Once a lucrative place to fish, trawlers and unsustainable fishing practices reduced the biodiversity of the area and subsequently the number of fish. Fisher Bank is now a protected area with carefully controlled European quotas. The sheer distance from the land makes a visit in a kayak out of the question. The only stop that anyone has recommended along this coast is 'Cold Hawaii', the nickname given to the area around the town of Klitmøller, so as I prepare to launch it's there I'm aiming for.

'Are you sure you know what you're doing?' says a stand-up-paddle boarder who's just emerged from the small amount of surf in Hirtshals, with the vague concern of a stranger who doesn't want to read the news of a lost kayaker tomorrow.

'Yes, don't worry,' I assure him, though his question makes me second-guess my preparation and worry about the surf. I've checked the forecast from the Danish Meteorological Institute and the paddle boarder confirms my understanding that the wind will be picking up further south – more reason to get going now.

I spend three long days covering the 120 kilometres to Hanstholm just up the coast from Klitmøller.

Occasionally something breaks the continuous line of dunes and sand, but mostly it is all the same. Concrete bunkers are intermittently slumped and sunken in the sand, shrouded in a veil of greenery, slowly claimed back by nature. These are the remains of the Atlantic Wall, an extensive system of coastal defences and fortifications built by Nazi Germany to protect Western Europe from Allied invasion. Constructed between 1942 and 1945, the defence system ran down the entire western seaboard of Europe from the top of Norway to the border with Spain. The northern tip of Denmark was one of the most heavily fortified, given its strategic position at the entrance to the Skagerrak (the strait between Denmark and Norway) which joins the North Sea to the Kattegat (the Danish Straits) which, in turn, joins the Baltic Sea.

On my long days, I think about this history and how lucky we are to live in a time of peace, friendship and connection across these seas. I hope that Brexit doesn't change this. It turns out I have lots of time to reflect as I let my perseverance kick in and just keep going. At times I focus on the beauty of it: the sharp shadows of paragliders projected on to the sculptured surfaces of the sand. Their colourful kites swooping and soaring like graceful birds. The turquoise blue of the sea as the light reflects off the sandy seabed, and the leaning tower of Rubjerg Knude Lighthouse, a spike in the sandpit.

At other times I find myself thinking of Marcus, scenes with him flicking through my mind: me proudly handing over a bottle of elderflower Champagne I'd made and decanted into an Ikea bottle (I would find out later that it had exploded, narrowly missing Marcus and Andy); Marcus's calm professional approach to dealing with Bron, whose mental illness leads her to make up all sorts of untrue stories about us, which Katie and I find difficult to manage; Marcus and Andy looking after me, feeding me soup and supplying me with newspapers in their cottage in Suffolk after my mouth cancer operation six years ago.

Most of all, I think about his resilience in the end. He'd been plagued by cancer for thirteen years on and off, and each time it came back it took a little bit more of him away. Generally, he just got on with things like being a doctor, seeing the world and living as much as he could. I remember only one time when his determination broke in front of me. In March last year, as the scarf round his neck stopped us all from seeing the cancer eating away at him, Katie came over with her three-week-old son, Llorenç, so that they could meet. He was a tiny piece of hope in an otherwise bleak world. Sitting on the sofa in the comfort of Mandy's, the house we had come to consider the new family home, Marcus burst into tears. 'It's just so hard,' he wrote, because by then he could no longer speak. We fought back our tears and the sense of utter impotence, only being able to hug his skeletal frame and say, 'I know.'

Tears roll down my cheeks off the desolate coast of Denmark and I try to focus on something else. I stop for a moment to shout at the sea. It is beginning to be a bit more challenging and deserves a telling off anyway. The different kind of exertion feels good. I think back to last week singing on the sea with Alina and spend some time doing renditions of all the songs I know. Maybe even the difficult sea doesn't deserve that! I head south, keeping the sea on the right, sand on the left. The Danes seem to love the beach and it's not uncommon to see the glinting reflection of cars and vans driven right to the water's edge. On more than one occasion, sleeping in the dunes, I'm surprised by the sudden flash of naked bodies darting out and plunging into the warm sea.

On the third day, the wind changes direction and increases speed, meaning I have to battle against it; crossing swells throwing the boat around. My route is no longer boring but I'm not sure I prefer this new alternative. The relentless noise of the wind rushing past my ears is like sitting in a room with a loud, untuned radio. Occasionally, I stop and turn my head away for a break but the wind pushes the kayak backwards and I lose ground. It's a slow slog to the wind turbines I can see across the bay in the far distance. By the end of the day I realise I'm quite far out and losing energy fast. Paddling closer in takes ages and I need to push hard to make progress.

The repeating rhythm of deep troughs and peaks sets in making the boat jump and slam on to the water, giving me a periodic soaking. Sun cream dribbles down my face, stinging my eyes to the point of crying; my bum is sore from hours in the boat and I struggle to shift myself out of a whimpering stupor. Despite the conditions, I feel a self-imposed pressure to round the corner that I've spent the whole day staring at, even if a small kinder voice in my head says, 'stop, relax, you don't have to do this'. Marcus had it worse, I think, keep going.

I land briefly to refuel and refocus, launching back into the surf and staying close in to the beach. I run the gauntlet through a flock of windsurfers and kites zooming around and jumping off the sharp, clean surf wave that's formed at an angle to the harbour wall at Hanstholm. I change my course to head south. A view down the coast ahead slowly reveals itself as endless dumping waves: big surf that crashes with all its force onto the beach, which is not good news. It is difficult and dangerous to land in sea like this, but it's what I'm going to have to do. I think I can see Klitmøller or at least something poking out along the coast but don't have the energy to get there. The weather is closing in and I know that wherever I stop, I'll be there for a few days. I decide to take my chances and head in while I can. The waves are steepening and are close together, the wind is howling and pushy, the kayak is heavy – together this is possibly the worst combination for landing. I need to choose my timing carefully. I watch as one after another the waves rear up, break, drop and pick up again before smashing down violently on to the steep shingle. The booming sound is followed by the sucking of tiny pebbles being dragged from the shore by the retreating water, churned, pummelled and spun before being thrown back on to the beach.

Watching closely, I choose my moment, turn the kayak to face the beach and start to paddle in. The white water of the collapsing peaks surges as I paddle backwards to gain control and get on to the back of one of the smaller waves. In a split second, the one behind jumps on my tail. It lifts the back of the boat up and pushes forwards fast, the boat rises and I lean back hard, pushing on the sandwich boxes I have as foot pegs to lever myself upwards and counterbalance the force. I'm practically standing upright, propelled towards the gravelly sand, when the nose of the boat digs into the beach and I'm sure I'm about to be catapulted over it. I dig harder with my paddle and brace as the wave breaks and violently sheds its anger on to me, the kayak and the beach. I rip my spraydeck off and quickly get out as the next wave fills the boat with water. I grab it and pull hard up the beach away from the roaring monster. The force of the sea hitting my head has ripped the lining out of my helmet and I'm lucky not to have broken anything else.

I'm shaking as I pull the boat further up the shingle beach, out of reach of the tide. If this is a sign of things to come on this coast, I'm not sure I want to continue. So far, it's been sandy, lonely and now dangerous – not a great mix. Beyond the shingle, the beach is backed by a margin of grassy dunes with spiky gorse bushes that are interrupted by a road running along the coast, and behind this, the dunes continue. I find out later they are the start of Denmark's last wilderness, Thy National Park. I use the last of my energy to pitch my tent in the grass and eat whatever I have that doesn't involve cooking. It rains overnight and the pegs come loose on the tent. I emerge, soggy and tired into the rising sun; it's only 5 a.m. The wind has picked up as forecast and the sea has become more violent overnight.

There's no way I'm kayaking, and after a bit of scouting, I decide to move everything across the dunes to the road and drag the kayak on its trolley the 12 kilometres to Klitmøller: 'Cold Hawaii'. 'The first bit of the name is for obvious reasons,' Anders had told me, 'but the last part is because the surf here is like that in Hawaii'. After yesterday, I'm not looking for the surf, but Anders' promise of a 'cool culture with fishermen, surfers and other water-users all getting along' seemed like as good a reason as any to go. I'm much closer to Hanstholm, but when I'd contacted Charlie Connelly, the only other person mad enough to visit all areas of the Shipping Forecast, his advice for Fisher was, 'Don't hang around Hanstholm unless your kayak is buoyant enough to resist the weight of a crushing sense of ennui.' Decision made, I struggle for three hours with the kayak on its trolley, testing my body in a completely different way, and finally wheel the kayak into a busy campsite, pitch my tent and collapse on the ground next to it exhausted but happy to be there. It's 11 in the morning and once I've recovered enough, I manage a trip to the Spar shop for some olives and beer. Back at the tent I celebrate my arrival with a bottle of Cold Hawaii, the zigzag blue and white waves on the label reminding me of the sea I've just left.

The next day, I see a car drive past with a kayak the same as mine on top. Sea kayaks are few and far between in these parts so I post on the Tiderace website, hoping that followers of the manufacturers of my kayak might know who he is. A bit later, Thomas, a smiley man with excited eyes, turns up. 'Nice kayak!' he says, kick-starting a conversation about what we love about the Tiderace Xcite boats, followed by a who-do-you-know-that-I-know interaction. After a while, Thomas goes back to his family, who are here on holiday, promising to come by later on.

As I start packing up my stuff, a man cycles past my tent, slowing when he sees my kayak. 'There's another kayaker camping over the other side of the fence, you should say hi,' he calls out. I do so and meet Morten, a tanned guy with a surf vibe who smells of coffee. He tells me he's on a tour of Denmark between two sea kayaking events and hasn't yet paddled on the west coast. As we wait for the swell to die down, I introduce Thomas and Morton and a plan is hatched to paddle together down the coast.

We launch from the surf spot 'Bunkers', hauling my heavily laden boat to the beach. The pockmarked, graffiti-covered surface of the bulbous concrete bunkers gives them an animal-like character. Like oversized dinosaur eggs hatched on the beach. The wind has shifted to the north and died down. It's great to be on the water again and to have company. As we paddle, Morten tells me how he listened to the Danish

Shipping Forecast late at night with his grandparents. 'My grandfather was a fisherman and my sister and I would be in their living room as the forecast was on... we had to be very quiet,' he remembers. 'Whenever I hear it, it takes me back.'

'I grew up listening to our Shipping Forecast too,' I say, before explaining more about Mike and the boat. 'Can you remember yours enough to do a pretend reading of it?' I ask.

'I can try,' he says before reeling off what sounds like a very convincing version of the Danish forecast. Despite my hours watching Danish crime series, I can't understand it, but the cadence and rhythm are similar and the familiar place names are beautiful to hear in this gentle language.

Neither of them can believe I walked the kayak from outside of Hanstholm, although both agree that it was a good choice. 'The only thing worth visiting is the restaurant whose Shooting Star has been voted the best in Denmark,' says Thomas.

'Still not worth it, you wouldn't have met us,' Morton chips in.

'That was worth the walk,' I tell them, 'and I had a great Shooting Star in Hirtshals.'

We have a glorious evening to surf our kayaks on the dropping swell down the coast to Vorupør, a small fishing harbour. Landing a catch here would be a tricky job as there are no real harbours, just beaches that boats are hauled up on to or unloaded at sea by smaller boats. Nevertheless, fishing has been the main industry in these towns and Vorupør is the home of Denmark's first fisherman's export cooperative, Fiskercompagniet – founded in 1887 and still in operation today. It was also a religious community, and the last thing fishermen did each day before putting out to sea was pray together. Having seen a bit of this sea in action, I can see how that would be a good idea.

'I'm happy to be part of your beautiful voyage about the forecasts for the sailors,' Morton says as the evening descends, and he and Thomas get a lift back to Klitmøller. It sounds so much more romantic that way, and as I'm left alone on the beach, I feel reconnected with the significance of my journey. It's been a great day with such nice people, and I realise I'm content for the first time since reaching Denmark six days ago.

That night, as if a reflection of my mood, the sky turns pastel pink and blue and the warm, light wind brushes my face. To the north, a cloud of sand dances along the beach and creates a light haze in the glowing evening light. I put up the mesh inner of the tent to stop the flies but leave the fly sheet off so I can see out. I'm slowly drawn into the spectacle of the setting sun which through the fine gauze is blending into the most amazing painting, subtly changing and moving. It's a delicious sensation: a renewed gratitude that I'm alive and able to be here, combined with the space and presence to enjoy it. As I'm enveloped by the sky, I drift off to sleep listening to the smooth melody of 'Sailing By', the Ronald Binge piece that always plays ahead of the late evening Shipping Forecast on the radio, originally to give sailors and fishermen the chance to tune their radios in properly. Its melody lulls me to a deep sleep.

The next day is Wednesday and I'm behind schedule. I've still got another 130 kilometres to go to reach Henne Strand Hostel, the only other recommendation from Anders down this coast. I'm on the clock because I've planned to paddle with some German friends over the weekend but that relies on me getting to Germany, or somewhere close.

A few days pass and I think I'm getting used to the surfy beaches and outlying sandbanks that kick up the salty soup without a moment's notice. There are usually two or three lines of breaking waves, the first two near the beach and the third much further out. The visibility is good and I can generally plan a route through and avoid the bigger breakers. Most of the time, the sea is rolling and doesn't have much energy, but occasionally the waves peak and slap the ends of the kayak, pushing it around or breaking on to the deck. I know what's coming when I see this starting to happen but it's quick and the only defence is to brace into the wave, but I'm tired and easily caught unaware. There's nothing quite like having what feels like a bucket of water thrown in your face a few times to wake you up in the morning. This is what I get on repeat as I average more than 40 kilometres per day.

One morning it gets a bit relentless, and I'm about to head into the beach to better secure the kit I've got strapped to my deck when the sea crashes over me. It's a surprise. Several rolls and some bouncy bracing later and I find myself smashed into the water with some of my kit; I quickly grab the paddle and the boat, then clamber on and surf in on the back deck. I've practiced this move in similar seas in Cornwall, but it's very different when there's nobody else around; my heart races and I think, 'I can't fuck this up'. Luckily I don't, but it's certainly not pretty. I was close to the shore, so most things end up on the beach and I run around collecting them. Years of dealing with difficult situations have developed my skills in crisis situations and sometimes I think I perform better in them than out. Once I've calmed down I realise I am without my pump, map case or frame for my small trolley, the sea having claimed them. I feel stupid and careless to have lost kit and littered the ocean.

It's a short paddle from here to Henne Strand and after a much less dramatic landing I'm happy to drag my kayak out of Danish waters for the last time, having kayaked the whole of the coast in the Fisher Shipping Forecast area and the entire west coast of Denmark. I feel accomplished and happy to be off the sea. I've booked a bed in Denmark's oldest purpose-built hostel, constructed in 1937, and I'm pleased to have a place to relax and pull myself together.

The building is simple, yellow rendered, with a large timber-lined hall in the middle and framed drawings of Danish ships hanging above the doors to the rooms along the sides. After the glorious feeling of my first hot shower in days, I sit drinking coffee and eating biscuits on the timber deck next to the sandy road in front of the hostel.

'Where have you come from?' asks a man in a smart jumper and a kind face, as he takes a seat at the table.

'Hirtshals.'

'What? Really? Hey Lizzy, this guy's kayaked from Hirtshals!' he calls over to the hostel owner.

'Hi,' Lizzy says, 'we get a few kayakers here, welcome!'

'Yes, five years ago, two people came from Germany and sailed north, up the Danish coast, and a year or two later two others came down,' the kind-faced man says, before telling me about the red-and-white-ribbon challenge to kayak around Denmark. 'Now you've done the west coast, the rest is easy,' he says, as I make a note to come and 'finish' Denmark one day.

After a while Lizzy comes by. 'Leave him alone,' she jokes to the man, 'can't you see he's tired. Stop talking to him. Let him have a sleep.'

'It's okay,' I say, because it is and I'm enjoying the atmosphere. The hot afternoon sun beats down on clusters of thatched cottages and crowds of holiday makers, and I'm pleased to have arrived in one piece and selected this as the place to end my surfy time in Fisher.

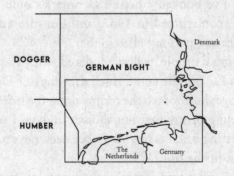

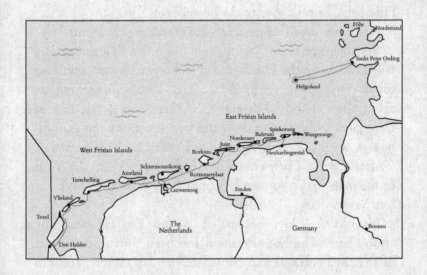

GERMAN BIGHT: SALTY DREAMS AND STARRY SKIES

I've always had a soft spot for Germany and Germans, something I could probably attribute to my German teacher in school, Frau Roberts, or 'Frau' to us. Despite Frau's efforts to home-school me after my (German) bone marrow transplant, the language didn't stick beyond GCSEs, but the love of her country did. So, I've been looking forward to getting my teeth into German Bight especially since I'll have company for part of it.

It's a hot dusty day when Doris and Felix arrive at Henne Strand to pick me up and drive me to Germany. We met at a sea kayaking symposium in Jersey a few years ago and since then have been on several adventures together. I'd contacted them almost as soon as I got the Churchill Fellowship grant. 'If you'd like to come to Heligoland with me, you'd be most welcome,' I'd written, understating my hope that they would join me on the paddle out to Germany's only offshore island.

Doris was quick to reply, 'Everybody we know who crossed to Helgoland told us it was dull, dull, boring, dull, and they wouldn't do that once more, but we'd like to join you!!! We can't wait!' Long sea crossings are often a bit dull and at 50 kilometres, this will be the longest I've done so far.

Heligoland is of special interest to me because in 1949, when the Met Office extended the reach of the Shipping Forecast to touch the shores of mainland Europe, the southern part of what is now German Bight was named Heligoland. In what was the shortest amount of time a Shipping Forecast area name has lasted, it was changed to German Bight in 1956, following a meeting of North Sea meteorologists who recommended it be extended and renamed to coincide with what to Germans called *Deutsche Bucht*, German Bight.

We've driven from the small, thatched villages of Denmark to North Germany, where fields and fields of maize sway around in the gentle breeze. The sun is so low, as we approach Nordstrand that it's impossible to see the road. Nevertheless, we find the campsite where we are sworn to complete silence until 8 a.m. This seems unrealistic, so we escape through a small gate labelled 'Costa del Sol' to the beach. The sunset is reflected in small rivulets running from the shore like the glittering skin of a mackerel heading out to sea. We absorb its beauty.

The next morning is calm, warm and windless, and we lie on the grass eating fresh bread with Danish ham, consulting charts, weather information and tides. We have four days before Felix and Doris have to go back to Paderborn in Central Germany. We look, then look again, and the three of us at once come to the same conclusion:

'If we want to go to Helgoland—' Felix starts.

'—we have to go today', Doris and I finish.

We can see a gap in the weather with almost no wind for a few days, and what wind there is should be largely behind us. We pack up quickly and drive through the Bourbon-biscuit brick villages to Sankt Peter-Ording, 40 kilometres down the coast.

It's a hot, languid morning and the whole of Germany seems to have crammed on to what little bits of beach they have here. We negotiate the parking and start the long drag of kayaks through the crowds of brightly coloured swimwear. Hot, sweaty and agitated, after loading our boats, we lather ourselves in sun cream and feel an immediate sense of relief as we float away from the busy shore. Visibility is crystal clear, almost strangely so, and the surface of the water is like a sheet of smooth silk gently billowing. It will take us around eight hours to reach the island, so we settle into a focused saunter, stopping every few hours to snack and regroup before pushing on. In the middle, where we can see no land, I feel an uplifting sense of freedom from the clear view out to the horizon in any direction. When we pass the yellow marker of a weather station and scour the horizon for the next point, Felix says enigmatically, 'The next big thing is right in front of us.' I'm not sure what he means, but it sounds optimistic and that's important in journeys like this, and in life. Eventually, we see tiny humps of land emerging in the distance.

There are two islands in the archipelago of Heligoland, a main red sandstone triangular rock which juts out of the water and the low-lying Düne which, as the name suggests, is flat and sandy. These lands have been inhabited since prehistoric times and over the years have been passed around between Denmark, Britain, and Germany. Before the 19th century they were mostly Danish, but having surrendered to the

British in 1807, they became an important centre of resistance against Napoleon, ending in their official annexation to Britain in 1814 as part of the Treaty of Kiel. Britain kept hold of them until 1890, when, in a typical colonial move, they were swapped for Zanzibar and became German. Germany used the islands as a strategic military base in both World Wars, before they were occupied by the British as one of the Allied Occupied areas in Germany, and eventually in March 1952 they were returned to Germany, whose coastline they are closest to. Part of this history is reflected in the different spelling of the name: for Germans and Danes it is Helgoland, while for Brits it is Heligoland.

Doris has spoken to a few people about the trip, and has been advised that we should not land on the main island but should try Düne, where the campsite is located. We're not sure if this has to do with the islands' duty-free status or the fortifications surrounding it. There's a military feel as we near the coastline and we can see the dominant, square lighthouse tower on Heligoland and a smaller red-and-white-striped tower on Düne. Nazi plans for expansion of the archipelago under Project Hummerschere (Lobster Claw) would have dwarfed the islands and are straight out of an evil villain textbook. The project was not completed but remnants of the fortifications, gun emplacements and harbour walls are still very much present.

Approaching the harbour in Düne, tall concrete walls with no landing stages loom above us and form a huge rectangular enclosure. There is a small steel ramp in the corner and we paddle towards it, very much ready to land. A cluster of people wait on the jetty and as we get closer we notice a man shouting and gesticulating wildly at us. 'He's drunk, ignore him,' say Doris, who I assume has a better handle on what's being screamed aggressively at us in German. As we near the end of the ramp, next to a banner saying, 'Welcome to Düne', more people come to shout at us. A small ferry arrives and a stern, orange-faced man steps off followed by his overweight colleague. A complicated conversation ensues in German. I can't make out what's being said, but every second word seems to be '*nicht*' accompanied by an angry facial expression. Felix later tells me it went something like this:

'What are you doing here. You can't be here.'

'Sorry, we didn't know.'

'It's written on the wall outside and on your charts. You must leave.'

'We can't leave, it took us eight hours to get here.'

'I'll call the Düne Inspector.'

'We'll stay at the campsite.'

'You can't stay at the campsite unless you registered on the main island.'

'But we're here now.'

'And you should come here on the campsite ferry.'

It's eventually agreed that we can sort it out in the morning, which is a relief as it's getting dark, we're tired and hungry and have no intention of going back today. With that, the lobster-coloured tourists waddle on to the ferry, glaring at us, and the little boat disappears, leaving us in the sinister harbour with a group of youths swigging a bottle of wine and throwing rocks into the sea, beneath a sign that points to a nude surfing beach. We pitch our tents in the dunes of the campsite, knowing we'll be told off again in the morning. It takes us all a while to relax, but Doris's garlic, red wine, pine nut and raisin pasta helps.

Oystercatchers busying themselves around the tents wake us up in the morning with their 'peep peep' sound like that of a dog's squeaky toy. They're massive and very tame, strutting their bright orange legs along the timber decking that runs through the dunes. We're up early as we plan to take the big ferry back to the mainland and want the explore the island of Heligoland before we do. We have the choice of getting there by the ferry whose captain hates us or sneakily paddling over. We all agree to the latter option. The workers painting the slipway are much more understanding. 'Just land on the North Beach,' they say when we carefully suggest we might be going to Heligoland. We're still worried about bumping into the ferry so make an undercover launch into the forbidden harbour and swiftly round the entrance. I half expect the James Bond theme tune to play in the background.

There's a noticeable tidal push against us as we cross between Düne and Heligoland. Some other kayakers are launching on the beach and, keen to find out where they stayed, we go and say hello. They were not warmly welcomed here either and have camped near the beach with the begrudging agreement of the nearby hostel.

'When do you paddle back?' they ask us.

'We'll get the ferry back,' Doris relays to them, and we feel a bit like we're cheating.

'That'll be hard,' they say, before explaining that the mainland ferries anchor off the islands and passengers get to them in smaller boats with no space for kayaks. Apparently, you can't just kayak up to the ferry either. This gives us no option but to kayak back to the mainland the following day, meaning we can spend the rest of today looking around. If there's one thing kayakers love, it's circumnavigating islands.

Now, with more time on our hands, we decide to check out Heligoland from the sea before exploring the land.

Forests of weeds in green, brown and yellow sway in the turquoise blue water, so clear we can see through it for several meters. The shrill call of kittiwakes is deafening as we near the base of Lange Anna, the impressive 47-metre-high red stack on the north-west corner. 'These are Germany's only cliffs,' says Felix, obviously pleased to see them. Birds are lined up on the ledges, the white stains on the rock in high contrast to the deep orange stone. Inquisitive seals pop their heads up all around us and join us as we move on around. It's hard to obey the rule of staying 30 metres away from the seals if they are deliberately following you. In German they are *Seehund* or sea dog, and their friendly canine features, big eyes and good nature make us feel more welcome in these waters. We follow the towering cliffs around the west of the island, spotting gannets swooping and gliding high above us. Tiny jellyfish spin around in the water, their decorated strands and tentacles making them look like fairground carousels or fancy lampshades. It feels like nature is putting on a show for us.

It's sad to think all of this would have been destroyed when on 18th April 1947, the Royal Navy executed 'Operation Big Bang', dropping 6,700 tonnes of explosives on the uninhabited island in an attempt to obliterate it. The explosion, one of the biggest non-nuclear single detonations in history, shook the land and the crater it left changed the shape of the island. It makes me feel lucky to acknowledge that war is an abstract concept for me and my German friends, even if it wasn't so for our grandparents, and isn't so for many around the world.

Doris has saved a small bottle of fizzy wine which has 'Dreams' written on it in Spanish. We've been talking about this trip for months, and since people have stopped shouting at us we're feeling rather more pleased with ourselves. Thinking of the islands' wartime past, it also seems fitting that we can come here as an Anglo–German team, and we toast to friendship and peace, as we swig from the warm, salty bottle of Dreams.

Eventually, we land on a small sandy beach. Doris changes into a pretty summer dress, Felix puts on some clean shorts and I try to make myself look presentable. That's the problem with visiting inhabited islands on foot, especially holiday resorts: you can't just look like a sea urchin. Heligoland's *Unterland*, the lower land near the sea, has a holiday vibe with a collection of hotels along the front and shops selling souvenirs, cheap cigarettes and duty-free booze. We snack on a typical *Fischbrötchen*, a fish roll, from a small fisherman's shed before taking the stairs to the *Oberland*, the part of the town perched on the plateau.

It's quieter at the top, the buildings are smaller and residential, and a modernist church has an impressive spire. Following the path around the clifftop we find Germany's only colony of gannets, seemingly unaffected by the presence of humans. They are my favourite birds, their yellow heads and bright white bodies contrasting with the deep black of the wing tips. Graceful and slick in flight, they can dive to incredible depths, shapeshifting their bodies into a super-charged dart. From time to time one lands, crashing into the perfectly poised group, causing mayhem. Back in the *Unterland*, we wait until after dinner when the ferry isn't running and kayak back to Düne.

The journey back from Heligoland is dreamlike, as if the blurred horizon line reflects a kind of blurred reality. The water lolls around gently. We pass the same marker buoys we saw on the way and then fix a bearing towards Sankt Peter-Ording. I keep my ship-to-shore radio turned on and am excited to hear the German coastguard read out the Shipping Forecast for Deutsche Bucht in a monotone voice and rhythm that seems strangely familiar. The beach at Sankt Peter-Ording starts to appear in the distance, and we pick out our landing spot.

Having bagged Heligoland, I feel a bit like my work in German Bight is done. Still, I've also had my eye on the Frisian Islands and don't want to miss the chance to see them. The long archipelago stretches around the entire coast of German Bight, from Denmark to The Netherlands, into the next Shipping Forecast area of Humber. I have eleven days before I'm due to speak at a kayak symposium in the Netherlands, which should give me enough time to weave my way through these holiday islands. It's about an 80-kilometre paddle from where we are now to Wangerooge, the first of the East Frisian Islands, and when Doris and Felix offer to drive me to the Frisian town of Neuharlingersiel on the mainland, I'm not about to refuse.

It's afternoon by the time we arrive. 'We must have some tea before you leave,' says Doris, going against what Frau taught us, that all Germans drink coffee in the afternoon.

'No *Kaffeetrinken*?' I ask with a smile, demonstrating my local knowledge.

'This is Friesland, they drink more tea than the British,' Felix corrects me. I think back to the amount of tea quaffed in my office and think this seems unlikely, but when I check it out online, the German Tea Association informs me that not only is it true, but that the Friesians drink almost double the litres of tea per capita of the British.

It takes little convincing to get me into the appropriately named Störmhus, a traditional Friesian teahouse in the pretty harbour. A picture of a sailing ship swings above the white arch of the entrance, and inside dark wooden furniture is infused with the smell of Assam as groups of people at every table indulge in the sweetness of the afternoon. On the way up the stairs to the terrace, a wooden ship's wheel hangs with 'Greenwich, London' carved into it, a connection to home. The wind blows the paper napkins around as we sit outside eating generous portions of cake. The tea itself is a complicated affair with some strict rules. I'm about to reach for the cream jug to pour it into the delicate blue and white cups but Doris whispers to me to wait. She uses pincers to place one piece of rock sugar in the bottom of each cup, then pours the tea on top. It's hot enough that we hear a soft cracking sound as the sugar starts to dissolve. She shows me how to add the cream using a special spoon to create the cream cloud.

'Ohhh,' I say appreciatively, as I watch the cream shift and change shape like a real cloud.

'No stirring,' she warns me, and I sip the tea as gently as I can.

'Taste the three flavours,' Felix says. 'Strong black tea, cream and the syrupy bottom.'

It does seem to have three phases and might be the most complicated cup of tea I've ever drunk. I'm encouraged into having two more as we talk about our trip. I must be asking lots of questions because at one point Doris says, 'Okay, maybe we can ask you something?'

'Like what's your favourite colour?' I joke, thinking that it's a question I might even be capable of answering in German.

'No,' she says, 'how does it feel to have visited Helgoland?' I give a long-winded but true answer on how exciting it is to go from a mystical name, to knowing where somewhere is, to actually going there. We agree that it's been a great trip, even if we did end up kayaking further than we thought we would.

'Who needs the ferry!' says Felix.

We talk about my plans for the next part of the trip, which are limited to paddling the 6 kilometres across to the island of Spiekeroog and then figuring things out. 'I'll get you some help,' says Doris as she calls a contact from the Saltwater Union, a group of German kayakers who share knowledge and skills. As she carefully notes down the advice from her contact about where to stay in the harbours, Felix explains, 'Many of the tidal flats are protected nature reserves, so you have to be careful.' Armed with an extensive list of exactly where to pitch my tent in the harbour of each island along my route and who I should speak to about it, I'm far better prepared than I would have been, and worry that my planning may have become a bit laissez-faire. I'm aware of the time: Doris and Felix need to get back to Paderborn – a three-and-a-half-hour drive – and I need to launch.

'I think I should maybe go, which is sad,' I say.

'It's not sad, you're going on an adventure,' says Felix.

'You're doing all the things we always wanted to do,' adds Doris, reminding me of the point of all this. In the back of my mind for a moment, I think that's because I don't have as much time as everyone else, but I push the thought aside as I hug them both. I'm sad to say goodbye, but I know we'll be paddling together later in the summer, so it's more of an *Auf Wiedersehen*, 'until next time'.

Moments later, I've wheeled my kayak from the car to the slipway, with my bag thrown in the cockpit, and I see three other kayakers about to launch. 'Hallo!' says one of them with the enthusiasm I would reserve for seeing an old friend. We don't know each other but Claas seems excited to get more people embroiled in his adventure. When he finds out I'm going to Spiekeroog he says, 'Jonny Glut is playing at the Old Laramie, you have to come!' I don't know what either is, but I agree to go with them. The plan seems to be to go to the gig and sleep on the beach.

'See you later!' I say as they launch, and I'm left to laboriously repack my boat. The paddle over is straightforward, with a slight tidal push as I follow the white-tipped marker poles out to the main channel, aim for the church spire on the island until I see the yellow buoys and go in to the beach next to a campsite in the dunes.

'Welcome!' Claas appears in front of me. 'You want some help with your kayak? Then you must drink. It's tradition,' he says, handing me a bottle of rum. Not one to eschew tradition, I gratefully accept. '*Nich' lang schnacken, Kopp in'n Nacken,*' Claas says before swigging some back himself. Apparently the phrase means something along the lines of 'Shut up and drink' in North German dialect. I try to learn it but eventually stick to '*Prost!*' I leave Claas and his friends to their pre-gig drinks while I sort myself out. No sooner have I selected the spot in the campsite closest to the beach than a man comes over from the neighbouring family encampment to offer me their leftover dinner, a delicious potato salad. After the welcome we got in Heligoland, the kindness of strangers here all feels a bit overwhelming, but I accept it gratefully.

A warm breeze drifts over the dunes and carries the sound of music and salty air of the North Sea with it; there's a feeling of inevitability as I follow it towards the pub. An old marker buoy with 'HM Government' stencilled on it marks the entrance.

The Old Laramie is a small building nestled in the sand whose patrons spill out to a makeshift garden. There's a stage set up under a large tree and a decent-sized crowd are swigging beers in the last of the evening light. I spot Claas and his friend, Helge, who have decided that despite us only having met a couple of hours ago, I will be their guest for the evening and should not buy my own beer. It's very generous and I loosely agree. As we raise our glasses, there's a satisfied, lethargic glow in the air. The balmy evening is tinged with the heat of the day and held under a clear, starry sky. It's a floaty feeling of being on the edge, cast off into the North Sea, and I feel a world away from the cars and buildings on the mainland.

I'm not sure how you would describe the music of Jonny Glut. There was a brief discussion on the beach earlier about whether he could sing or not. The jury was left out. He's supported by a band including guitars, double bass, a mandolin and a saxophone. His music is labelled as Country/Folk on iTunes. It's shouty and anthemic. From what I can make out from Claas's translation between jumping up and down and shouting out the lyrics, it covers topics ranging from wayward sailors, social housing estates in Bremen, lost loves and unemployment as well as the classic, 'Sand in den Schuh'n von Spiekeroog' (sand in my shoes from Spiekeroog) which morphs into Iggy Pop's 'Passenger' with added la la, las. It's a niche fan base and Claas is definitely one of the most committed.

I see Claas squeezing through the crowd, heading towards a man with bright white hair who is carrying a large basket over his arm. He returns, grinning, with three small jars and some cocktail sticks. We open the jars, eat the plum inside with the cocktail stick, clink them together and down the rum the fruit is preserved in. We have another when the white-haired man passes by us, and when Claas tells him about my journey so far, he slyly slips me a few more of these so-called Kutterpflaume out of the basket. It's a brilliant, unexpected evening that reminds me of similar fun times with friends and renews my faith in just letting things happen and seeing where they go.

I wake up sweating in the tent; the morning sun has heated it up to become unbearable. I have a dry mouth and very sore head. An overweight oystercatcher sits seemingly paralysed, staring at a plastic tub filled with water, unable to move except for the occasional shuffle. He doesn't look well and I wonder if he's also overdone it on the Kutterpflaume. I find Claas and the others sprawled on the beach, shielding their faces from the sun, and when I ask how his head is, he points off into the distance somewhere and laughs. I pay for the camping and the warden asks when I plan to leave. 'I need the water to come back,' I say in my best German. At low tide most of the sea falls dry, revealing sand and mud flats, so there is no easy way to leave until the water comes back. He looks at his watch, grins and hands me a 'leaving late' sticker for the tent.

I walk towards the town through the dusty streets lined with trees and small houses. Bikes, trailers, trolleys, child barrows, horses and small electric vehicles are dragging supplies and suitcases around the island. Beached boats lie lazily on the sand and wait for the water to return. I say my goodbyes to Claas and Helge, who have managed to put themselves together enough to launch their kayaks, while I wonder if I'll ever be ready. A group of children on the beach come over and are interested in what I'm doing. It is like a test of my German vocab as they point at everything I have in my bags and strapped to the kayak and ask me what it is. Let's just say Frau would not be proud. I'm struggling and feel embarrassed that my language skills can't even match those of a small child, and am sure I've told them that the stove is powered by cheese, I'm wearing a cake, the camera is made of fish and I'm kayaking back to England. They leave me to it, a bit confused, but I give them a wave as I head off from the beach.

I'm still hungover which might explain why I've waited too long for the water to return. When I launch, mid-afternoon, there are a few hours of the flood tide left, hopefully enough time to do the 20 kilometres to Baltrum, two islands down. Everything I've read, and everyone I've ever asked, has warned me to be careful with timings here. One website says, 'it's easy to end up sleeping in your kayak on the sand,' and another says, 'tidal currents can often be faster than you can paddle'. So, I'm feeling a bit silly as I slog against the current, heading west into the sun. After about two hours, I stop for a rest and some Haribo against the tessellated stones of the harbour wall of Langeoog. I consider staying the night there, but the sea looks okay and since my hangover has lifted, I'm feeling optimistic.

The shallow water is amazingly warm, like a bath – a bath that someone appears to have pulled the plug on, as water is disappearing fast. I'm quite a way out from the shore and only have a few centimetres of water beneath the kayak. A line of sticks, or withies, mark the deep-water channel, and I desperately push towards it as the boat crunches along the seabed. Shoving with my hands and scraping along with the paddle, I can tell it is the kind of sandy mud that you can't trust to walk on. Looking towards the rapidly descending sun, I contemplate spending the night on the mud, in the boat. The thought isn't appealing, and I muster all I can to drag, scrape and pull the boat across the almost non-existent water. Eventually, after what feels like a few hours, I reach the dredged channel, round the harbour wall and breathe a sigh of relief to be within sight of a slipway. I've got a dull headache and am exhausted when I tumble into the tent.

The Wadden Sea (all the sea in German Bight) is a UNESCO World Heritage Site and the largest unbroken system of intertidal sand and mud flats in the world. The sandy flats, salt marshes and dunes make this an important place for migrating birds and seals, and there are many areas that are off limits to boats. On most islands, landing is only permitted in the harbours and on the beaches of the north coasts.

The next day, I'm clear-headed and keen not to make any more rookie mistakes, so after a poke around the island, I sit down and do some proper planning. Calculating drying heights by reading the number from the chart, adding the draft of my kayak, and cross-referencing with the tide tables, is something I don't enjoy doing; there's too much maths involved, which has never been my strong point. But I get an idea about what might work and change my approach for the next harbour of Norderney, arriving on a rising tide with a couple of hours to spare.

With a system in place, I'm able to make my way down the chain of islands, stopping on all those I'm allowed to land on and racking up another 200 kilometres. I survive ten hours with ants in my pants as I unwittingly seal them in the boat under my spraydeck; attempt to look competent as I launch in the middle of a German lifeboat demonstration on Juist; and cross from the last German island of Borkum through the busy shipping lanes feeding into the German port of Emden.

The days blur together as I make my way through the Dutch Frisian Islands. First Schiermonnikoog, Ameland then Terschelling where, with no other option, I camp in a car park next to an industrial estate. I'm nervous about staying here but crash out from exhaustion only to find the next day that my paddle has gone. I retrace my steps, angry and frustrated with myself for letting it get stolen. A quick chat with the harbour master confirms that I'm unlikely to see this £550 piece of kit again and should carry on with my spare paddle. I'm keen to leave Terschelling and join the motorway-like cavalcade of yachts heading out of the harbour on the flood tide. The penultimate island, Vlieland, has a military zone marked on the map and I'm unsure if it's a firing range or a test site, but either way I try to avoid it. Pulling away from the land, I can hear the grinding of tanks and trucks in the grassy flats. A helicopter circling overhead adds to the threatening feeling as I kayak purposefully towards the tower of Texel Lighthouse and out of German Bight.

As I drag my kayak up the beach in Texel, the last of the Frisian Islands, I think how the nine days since I left Doris and Felix have flown by. The rhythm of: wait for the tide, kayak to the next island, explore the island, wait for the tide, kayak to the next island, and a strong will to just keep moving has done me well. It's been as long as the journey down the west coast of Denmark but with the entertainment of nature and islands, it's been more interesting. I feel satisfied that I've done German Bight justice. I would have something to talk about in German class, if only I could remember the past tense. I make do with writing it on my blog and appropriately Frau comments, 'When Marcus was on a school trip in Hamburg he spent a day on Langeoog. Think of him when you're "sailing by".' I did think of him. That day and every day.

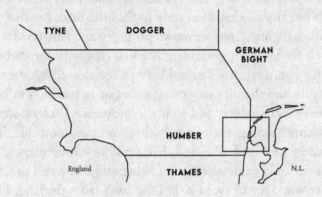

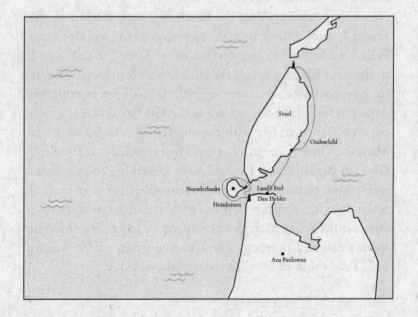

HUMBER: WELCOMED IN THE GATES OF HELL

Nearly a kilometre of sand lies between the beach cafe and the shoreline as I drag my kayak over it on Texel, the last Frisian Island. A couple is taking a sunset stroll. His body is toned and tanned, she has a tight perm and is almost wearing a leotard with high-hipped shorts. She hangs off his arm with light-footed, sparky energy. Together, they look like Jennifer Grey and Patrick Swayze. The sky turns a strong orange colour and the sea gently licks the shore; it's romantic. I feel a bit out of place. To say I've not been very good at romantic relationships would be an understatement, but having never really had one, I don't miss it. Jennifer and Patrick come over and are inquisitive about what I'm doing. 'Where have you come from?' she asks.

'Spiekeroog,' I reply, to which they make impressed noises – once they've checked I'm talking about the penultimate Frisian Island, 210 kilometres away. They're chatty and interested, both Dutch and on holiday here. There is a ferry every half hour from Den Helder on the mainland so it's easy to get here by car. After a chat about sleeping on the beach, they say goodbye and wish me luck, and I watch them walk into the sunset half expecting (and hoping for) them to break into a dance. The sun dips below the horizon and gradually the smooching couples leave the beach so I can pitch my tent and go to bed. Nobody puts Toby in the corner!

I'm nearing the end of this leg of my trip and I still haven't decided what to do over the next few days. I have a fitful night's sleep worrying mostly about the weather. My original plan was to kayak to the Hook of Holland another 140 kilometres down the coast, covering the continental side of Humber and Thames, but my newsfeed is full of reports of big thunderstorms in the UK on their way over here. Being in the middle of the sea with a boat made of carbon fibre (a conductor) and a long, pointy stick made of the same, when there's lightning around, is not a good idea. I've taken some risks so far but none so obviously life-threatening.

A little later, I'm startled by a light shining into my tent and am convinced it's the beach police coming to tell me to leave, but I soon remember I've camped by a large lighthouse which intermittently pans across the deserted beach. I can hear the rumble of thunder in the distance and pick out the flashes of light that are definitely not the lighthouse. It's spectacular to watch as the storms pass across the sea northwards. The skies light up with forks and sheets and there's a cool streak to the humid air. I hardly sleep as I worry about what to do.

I have some fixed deadlines to meet. The first is a talk in two days' time in Den Helder, just across the water from Texel, and the second is a flight to Arctic Greenland from London in ten days' time. My head is full of logistics, plans and 'what if?' scenarios. What if I have to shelter from the storm halfway down the coast to the Hook and miss the ferry? What if I miss my flight and can't lead the expedition? What if I let everyone down? I realise I'm not willing to take these risks, or the more obvious weather-related ones. It's around 5 a.m. when I reach a decision on how to resolve this and the sun is starting to come up. The sky is peachy orange with a heavy purple cloud hanging over it, broken in several places where the rain has dropped in streaks.

My loose plan involves flying back to London, driving to Den Helder via the Eurotunnel and taking the ferry back to Harwich with my kayak on the top of the car. It relies on asking for favours from others and has very little flexibility: two things I try to avoid. A kayak is such a sleek, efficient vessel when on the water but is a difficult travelling companion off it and somehow on-land logistics always get complicated. These changes to my plan mean I won't kayak in the Thames Shipping Forecast area on the Dutch side, but will be able to bag the small bit of Humber that touches the Dutch coast from Texel to Leihoek. On the British side the coastline of Humber is much longer, stretching from just above Filey in North Yorkshire around the bulge of East Anglia to Horsey, just above Great Yarmouth in Norfolk. I'm not going to tackle that for the moment.

I adjust the sandwich boxes I've been using as foot pegs since Norway and as I launch from the north-west corner of Texel, I feel like I've left something behind. The void on my foredeck where my spare paddle usually is stands out as a testament to my carelessness. The wind has picked up and there is light rain. As I'm pushed around the corner without much effort, I look east and say goodbye to the Frisian Islands, the sandy flats, the seals, the birds, and other Northern Europeans enjoying the lightness of a warm summer. I'm taking advantage of a break in the thunderstorms and trusting the forecast to get across to the mainland.

The coastline of Texel is almost entirely manmade, and in fact 'coastline' is a bit of a misrepresentation. The slanting dam walls abruptly meet the sea, with organised areas of marshland for birds to nest, spilling out from the long continuous line. I'm just thinking about the birds in Iceland, when a fulmar glides low over the boat. 'Hello,' I say, 'you're back!' it feels like a friend visiting. Some structures poke up behind the flood defences and I catch a snapshot of some cyclists on the pathway with a windmill behind. I'm excited thinking I've caught the essence of Dutchness and will soon be contacted by the National Geographic. In places, repairs are taking place and diggers perch on mounds of sand. I'm momentarily relieved by the more natural appearance of this and remember the wild mountains of Iceland, before the wall reappears. I pass the harbour of Oudeschild, with several windmills and pretty, old wharf buildings just visible behind the high defences. Shipping traffic picks up and I know that I'm nearing the mainland.

I'm about to cross the Marsdiep, the notorious tide race where the Wadden Sea and the North Sea meet. It's known for being a challenge for kayakers and is made more difficult by a ferry route running through it. There's a fast-flowing tide around a string of yellow buoys forming a barrage alongside a construction site; I'm pushed towards them and glide closely past the final one. I head beyond the ferry route to avoid the tide pushing me into its path. They're big ferries, and by now I am an expert. I can see two of them, one crossing over the channel to Den Helder and another disappearing into the harbour on Texel. In the other direction, I see the tall red lighthouse at Huisduinen marking the point where the coast turns the corner and heads south. If I don't go past this, I should be fine.

It's not pretty, but from this side Den Helder doesn't seem like the Gates of Hell. As the northernmost point of North Holland, it is home to the largest naval base in the Netherlands. Traces of previous fortifications remain in the form of star forts embossed into the lowlands, their distinctive geometry colliding with the shifting coastlines of the charts. The area became known as *Helsdeur*, 'The Door to Hell', although it's not clear why. Some say it's because of the battery of defence structures that would have made it difficult to get to, while others say it was due to the choppy water of the Marsdiep channel.

I pick a marker on the shoreline, a church spire, and head towards it, aware of the westward push. The coast is blocked in by another manmade flood wall, only occasionally interrupted by beach. The tide is relatively high so there are limited options for landing. Axel, one of the organisers of the event I'll be talking at here, has suggested I aim for the beach in front of the Lands End Hotel. I struggle to paddle against the current, and eventually I make it to the small beach, the final point on my journey along the Frisian Islands. I land, so happy and exhausted that I decide to treat myself to a stay at the hotel. The light air-con in my room dries my maps and kit as I retreat to the relative calm of the bar. After nine weeks outside, I enjoy the shelter from the wind it offers.

The next day, I spend some time selecting photos and stories for the talk I'm due to give that evening at the annual Dutch Sea Kayak Instruction Week. I notice how much more confident I feel about doing this than when I spoke to the BBC before I left. It makes me think that Natalie was right to rip up my 'adventurer' card – there is no substitute for going on an adventure. My plan swings into action and Marijn from the Kayak Instruction Week comes to pick me and my kayak up and take us to the campsite 10 kilometres away. We've never met but as his well-used paddling car rounds the corner to the hotel and he tells me not to bother about the sand, I think we're going to get along. Marijn lives in Amsterdam and is one of the few younger members of the cohort of the Dutch Sea Kayak Instruction Week.

'Heeeey! Welcome, welcome, glad you made it!' says Axel, giving me a handshake. I haven't seen Axel since he was my coach on the training course I did with Alina a few years ago in Cornwall. I got back in contact with him earlier in the month to ask for advice on paddling the Dutch coast, and he'd given me some great tips and asked if I'd share my experiences with his group of 50 paddlers. Since this was one of the things I said I would do on the application to the Churchill Fellowship, I couldn't very well refuse. As I arrive there's an abrupt and heavy downpour accompanied by thunder and lightning. It's a bit unclear how much paddling there might be tomorrow, and I feel somewhat justified in having booked a flight.

It's a relaxed event where everyone arrives on the Saturday and things don't start until the evening, which gives me a chance to chat with Axel.

'Den Helder is one of the best sea kayaking areas in Holland,' he smiles. 'Strong currents, sandbanks, and lots of activity. It's great training for Dutch kayakers. From here, most other places are easier.'

'It was harder than I expected,' I admit.

'Come on, you've kayaked in the Faroes now!'

'I still need to get better at drying heights,' I say thinking about how I bodged the calculations a few times around the Frisian Islands. Axel is an internationally renowned coach so I feel a tinge of shame that I still have a lot to learn. He's a kind-hearted man with a gentle persona and tells me of his love of kayaking related not so much to the places he's been to but the people he's paddled with. He just loves being on the water and helping others to enjoy it as well.

Our conversation changes track towards the Shipping Forecast. I soon realise I'm sitting with one of its biggest overseas fans. Axel has spent a lot of time in UK waters over the years, and carries a small, laminated map of the Shipping Forecast areas in his kayak. 'I remember my first trip to Scotland, in the days before 3G, I'd get up at 5 a.m. to listen to the Forecast on the radio,' he says.

'People in the UK are really into the Shipping Forecast', I say. 'There is national uproar when anything changes – and not from people on the sea.'

'I know, I remember when they stopped playing the song before the early broadcast, people were not happy.'

'You mean "Sailing By"? That's still played before the late forecast,' I say, thinking maybe he's got it wrong and taking out my iPad to play it to him. 'They play this at the Last Night of the Prom's. It's very popular.'

'Not that one, that's before the late broadcast, it was a different one.' I note it down to investigate later, and when I do I come across a piece of Shipping Forecast history I'd overlooked. Until 2006, the BBC Radio 4 theme had been played ahead of the early forecast at 5.20 a.m. as a way to signal to mariners that the forecast was about to start. It's a strange bit of patriotic Britishness, including instrumental versions of several popular English, Welsh, Scottish and Irish songs. I can make out parts of 'Early One Morning', 'Londonderry Air', 'Annie Laurie', 'Greensleeves', 'Men of Harlech', 'Scotland the Brave' and, somewhat less explicably, 'What Shall We Do with The Drunken Sailor.' It all ends with a flourish of 'Rule Britannia!' presumably intended to celebrate a proud maritime history. It would have been a morning wake-up call to match the current evening close down sequence of 'Sailing By', followed by the Shipping Forecast, the Radio 4 announcer wishing everyone goodnight before playing the National Anthem and handing over to the World Service.

'Would you mind reading the Forecast for Humber for me? I have it in English,' I ask, thinking of adding it to my collection.

'There's a Humber forecast in Dutch, an official sea forecast,' Axel says, getting his phone out to find it. 'You'll like this,' he looks at me with an excited smile, 'this is in Dutch for Humber and Thames, and there's even a gale warning in it which is always nice!' He reads it in his radio announcer voice and it sounds like our Shipping Forecast. I thank him for making the time to sit with me while also being the organiser of the event.

By the time I get up to give my talk, I've met most people in the audience and feel comfortable. I go through each of the areas I've visited, sharing a couple of stories and explaining what I did. I get a big round of applause which I don't think I deserve, and continue the conversation over a few beers, enjoying the connection with like-minded kayakers.

The next morning I initiate the logistics of getting my kayak back to the UK: leaving my kayak at the instruction week camp, taking a train to Amsterdam, a flight to London, picking up my car, and Eurotunnelling from Folkstone to

Calais, then driving to Den Helder. It takes two full days but it feels nice to be propelled by something other than my arms. As I load the kayak on to the roof of the car in the campsite, I'm pleased to have made it back in time to get in a little bit more paddling in Humber.

I stock up on provisions and drive to Huisduinen. Some of the Dutch kayakers told me about a spot to launch and land for a trip to the Noorderhaaks sandbar – a big yellow blob on my chart. It's a sunny day, the thunderstorms have passed, there's a light wind with a bit of swell on the sea and it looks like I can expect a nice calm paddle. I park the car and am relieved to see the colourful scattering of a group of sea kayaks near the small beach. I get my stuff ready as they pack theirs up. It's late afternoon and I know I'll miss dinner, but I'm keen to see what the sea is like here on the west coast of the Netherlands and to get in one last paddle before going home.

I launch at low tide and plan to arrive as the tide comes in, meaning that whatever happens, I should be washed back to land rather than out to sea. The current has different ideas and doesn't exactly match this. I cross the channel behind some strange-shaped boats leaving Den Helder, and aim towards the sandbank I can see in front of me, negotiating the marker buoys and landing on the shallow flats in the sunshine. Standing on the beach in the middle of the sea, I feel both insignificant and somehow free. The tide is coming in and soon laps against the side of the boat. I get back in and I'm met by an interesting sea, as deep troughs form between steep peaks which curl and roll towards the beach. With most of my stuff in the car, my boat is now light enough to make it more fun than dangerous to play on this water. I push against it to get far enough away to surf back in again.

After a few runs I'm starting to get tired and let myself be gradually washed back eastwards.

I set my sights again on the lighthouse at Huisduinen. The tide is further in and the beach has gone, so swimming is the easiest way to get my kayak and myself ashore. I think of all the ways that I've landed over the last few months and conclude that it's nice to have a new one. I clip a line on to the boat and jump into the water, scrabbling up the sea wall as the waves crash against it. Then I drag, carry, and pull the boat up the breakwater. The Dutch Instruction Week is still running, so I go back to the camp to share my last foray into Dutch waters. 'It's one of the liveliest tide races here,' one guy tells me. 'Glad you got to try it out.' I'm glad too; it makes my messy logistics seem better organised. The next day my kayak, car and I take the ferry to Harwich.

Part 3

THE SEAS BETWEEN

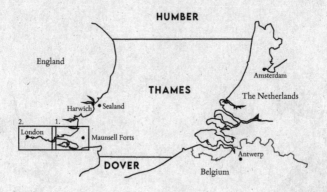

HUMBER

England

THAMES

Harwich • Sealand

2. 1.

London • Maunsell Forts

DOVER

Amsterdam

The Netherlands

Antwerp

Belgium

1.

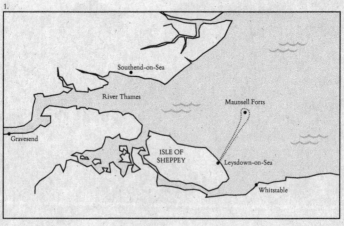

Southend-on-Sea

River Thames

Maunsell Forts

Gravesend

ISLE OF
SHEPPEY

Leysdown-on-Sea

Whitstable

2.

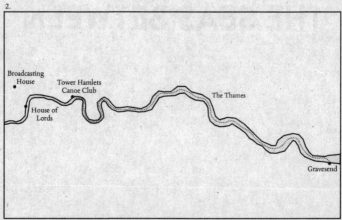

Broadcasting
House

Tower Hamlets
Canoe Club

The Thames

House of
Lords

Gravesend

THAMES: VENUS, THE BBC AND GOURMANDS

If you're an 'adventurer', what happens when you go back to real life? Do you return to your day job, bitter that you can't make a living out of what you want to do? Or can you infuse your life with your adventuring ways? As I sit on the ferry to Harwich, watching the grey of the North Sea pass by, I wonder how to force myself into the second option. Soon I'll unpack my city life and somehow have to squeeze back into it, at least until next summer. My travels since May have taken me to ten Shipping Forecast areas and I've kayaked in eight of them, but I still have another twenty-three to go. Eleven of these touch mainland Britain and my plan becomes to tackle the seas between the UK and the rest of Europe (Thames, Dover, Wight and Portland) at weekends and holidays while continuing my work as an architect in London.

The first opportunity to do this arises before I'm back,

and my Czech friend Michal and I make a tentative plan to go for an evening paddle the next Thursday. A few days before, we sit in the dimly lit, wooden-panelled room of The Prospect of Whitby, surrounded by paintings of ships, battles and stormy seas. Artefacts like ships lights and wheels are hanging from the ceiling. The Prospect claims to be London's oldest riverside pub and is a favourite of mine. Named after a coal barge that used to moor up alongside the quayside in London's old docks, the pub has a noose swaying from a gibbet outside, marking Execution Dock where the fate of lawless pirates would be displayed to those entering the city by river. The Prospect was a regular haunt of Samuel Pepys; Turner and Whistler both sketched the river from the pub's balcony, and it is thought that Charles Dickens also drank here. For me it's also been a home from home, and the inception of this Shipping Forecast project can probably be traced to this pub.

As the nearest decent pub to Tower Hamlets Canoe Club (THCC), it's one of the places I associate with sea kayaking. When I first walked through the doors of their clubhouse in the Shadwell Basin in late January 2012, I was just returning a helmet that one of their members had left in Jersey, and had an idea that I might want to learn to kayak, if the people were nice. The welcome was astounding, and I quickly became a regular at their Tuesday night meets where we'd do an evening paddle down the Thames or training in the basin, usually ending up in the Prospect. There is a very serious side to learning how to kayak safely, understanding techniques and the ways of weather, seas and rivers. As I moved up through the different kayaking and coaching levels, I made lasting friendships. It was a large group of like-minded people from all walks of life, with an age range from mid 20s to 70s.

With no actual sea within a paddle-able distance on a work night, we took everything the inner London Thames had to offer and combined it with other ideas. This led to fun on London's beaches at low tide, unrivalled views of the city, for which I ran a couple of architecture kayak tours, night-time paddles through the Christmas lights ending in singing, appreciated (or not) by Londoners on their way home from work, and the 'Paddling Gourmands Club'.

Natalie and I were the self-selected, non-elected committee and we would propose a theme and insist that everyone bring along home-cooked food (and another random item decided by us) for a shared picnic on one of the beaches. On arrival to the chosen destination, all manner of tasty treats would appear from the hatches of the kayaks. I often contributed a whole steamed salmon, solely because I'd inherited a fish kettle from Mike and as an occupant of the highly valuable space in my tiny kitchen, it needed to be used. We were strict about the rules and shop-bought food rarely got through, although attempts were made: the debate is still open on whether Al's courgette fritters were actually from Sainsbury's.

One Saturday we paddled up to Gravesend Sailing Club, where they were holding their annual sailing tea – an event so popular we weren't invited, but they kindly let us set up our lunch just outside and offered to bring us cakes. Little did they know that this was a Gourmands trip and the theme was Ploughman's Lunch. The impressive spread spilled out over the picnic table including various complicated salads, stuffed tomatoes, and homemade pork pie that Chris had created, having marinated pigs trotters to make the gelatine (we took this very seriously). I had been working for a few weeks on the best recipe for a pavlova that could travel by kayak and nipped back to my boat to retrieve my bowl, whisk and fresh cream. As I whipped the cream, we noticed more people from the sailing club showing an interest in our lunch, some bringing offerings of cake before joining, others enticing us with conversation. There was plenty to go around and I like to think we significantly changed their perception of kayakers.

Our adventures weren't limited to London, and thanks to THCC, I got to discover more of the British Isles than I would ever have expected, long before the idea of kayaking the Shipping Forecast came up. In the beginning it was an easy way to get out into the wild, develop my skills and return to London refreshed by nature. Later I began proposing trips, which involved more work, but also the joy of seeing others do something they otherwise wouldn't have.

'The voyager returns!' says Lindsey, back in the pub, bringing herself and her pint to sit with me and Michal at a dark-wood table in the corner and giving me a hug. I'm quite used to being on my own, but I've really missed these guys. We chat about our summers and make kayaking plans.

Having skipped the Dutch side of the Thames Shipping Forecast area, I'm keen to do the British side 'properly' and we cook up a plan to paddle out to the Maunsell Forts in the middle of the Thames estuary about 9 kilometres from land. It's sometimes easy to forget that the Shipping Forecast area named after the UK's largest river is much more than just the Thames. It reaches from just above Great Yarmouth in the north to Sandwich Bay in the south on the British side. On the mainland Europe side, it runs from 25 kilometres south of Den Helder to just above Ostend. Of all the Shipping

Forecast areas, it's the one my ears prick up for. The one I was trained to listen to from when I was little.

It's early August and it's sunny and hot. I've spent most of the day washing, drying and reassembling kit, waiting for Michal to finish work so we can drive out to the estuary. 'Alright?' he says, arriving, 'Let's go.' Wearing a long-sleeved grey t-shirt, for once he's less colourful than me. It's only when he whips out a bright turquoise-coloured cap that I think he must be okay. We load the kayaks quickly and arrive on the Isle of Sheppey in the late afternoon. There is a scattering of people on the small beach beneath the concrete flood defences on the edge of Leysdown. Motorhomes and cars are parked along the roadside with deckchairs and loungers spilling out across the hot tarmac. People lie around on inflatables tethered back to the breakwater. We can see the Maunsell Forts at Red Sands and Shivering Sands in the distance. Relics of gun defences, they were reportedly one of the toughest places to be stationed during the war. Jointly they shot down 22 enemy aircraft in World War Two, preventing attacks on the capital.

I drop a GPS location marker to have something to aim for on the way back and we leave the beach behind, knowing it will be dark for our return. A couple of hours of paddling later, and we near the splayed legs of the insect-like structures. Birds circle around in the low light, adding to the eerie scene. There is a cluster of seven towers at Red Sands which would have been connected by bridges. One bridge remains linking two of the towers. They are part of a scattering of similar offshore fort structures that occupy the sandbanks of the Thames estuary, the Humber, the Solent and in the past, the Mersey. The Thames estuary forts take their name from the engineer Guy Maunsell. There is another cluster, across the shipping lane at Shivering Sands, and perhaps the most well-known is Roughs Fort or Sealand, 13 kilometres from the Essex coast in international waters. The Principality of Sealand is an independent micronation that was created by Roy Bates, a former army major who ran Radio Essex, a pirate radio station, from a similar abandoned fortress, Knock John Fort, further in.

Radio Essex was one of several pirate radio stations on offshore structures or ships which became popular in the 60s as an alternative to the monopoly and strictured programming of the national broadcaster. Located outside of the jurisdiction of UK laws, pirate stations were free to choose what music to play and comments to make. The most famous, Radio Caroline, attracted a third of the amount of listeners as the BBC's light programming at the time, and broadcast from five different ships around the country. Here in Essex two more pirate stations made use of the abandoned structures. At Shivering Sands forts, Screaming Lord Sutch (of Official Monster Raving Loony Party fame) set up Radio Sutch in 1964, which later became Radio City, and Red Sands was home to Radio Invicta.

Back at Sealand, Bates lost a legal battle for his right to occupy the Knock John Fort and on Christmas Eve 1966, moved to an identical construction in international waters: Fort Roughs. His original plans became bigger and after consulting with lawyers he declared the Principality of Sealand, with its own flag, coat of arms, national anthem and ID cards. A little later, possibly at a loss as to what to buy his wife for her birthday, he crowned her Princess Joan, creating a royal family. The Sealand motto, 'E Mar Libertas', meaning 'from the sea, freedom', strikes a chord with me, and refers to the breaking of the shackles from the mainland. In support of this, I'll admit that I did shell out the 40 pounds it costs to become a Lord of this small nation. Some forts were destroyed in the 60s to prevent further Sealand-like incidents, while others now stand rusty and abandoned, with a few campaigners calling to preserve them.

The hollow clanging of the north Red Sands channel marker buoy echoes around in the waves, with a simple striking noise, it will sing to itself for time immemorial. Its similarity to a funeral bell has a haunting resonance. I remember this sound from my childhood (the channel marker clang, not a funeral bell), when we would sail Hullaballoo out of the river Orwell (further up in the Thames Shipping Forecast area). Here, I could claim to have saved the lives of Katie and Marcus. It must have been before Bron was ill, because she and Mike were inside the Butt and Oyster pub, at Pin Mill, a favourite stop of ours, while we three were playing on the muddy beach. We had probably been told not to go on to the mudflats which ooze like slightly melted chocolate the colour of a Weimaraner, with a special smell that's neither repugnant nor enticing. But we were on them anyway, no doubt imagining that we were characters from an Arthur Ransome book.

I would have been six, so I'm not sure what happened, but Katie and Marcus got stuck waist-deep in the mud with the tide coming in. I was lighter so could still run around on it and took the advice from my scared, screaming siblings and ran up to the pub to get our parents. Some pulling and shouting later and Katie and Marcus were out and safe, and were promptly forced to wash the mud off on the slipway in the river before getting in the rubber dinghy back to *Hullaballoo*.

Back at the mouth of the Thames, the tide is going out, there's a gentle swell and a very light breeze. The current pushes our kayaks slowly to the side, creating a panning effect to the view in front of us. The orange setting sun is intermittently covered by the stalky legs of the perching metal creatures and the heat of the day has dissipated. We drift around taking in the strangeness of the place. It's very quiet; the only sound is the wings of the birds circling the forts and their cries. I feel lucky to be here on such a special evening. The sun dips low and the silhouette of a car transporter slogs across the horizon.

It's dark now and we can see Venus clearly in the sky over Whitstable – it's the brightest thing around and light orange in colour. Heading towards land, we can make out the headlights of cars turning on the road and hear the low-level thrum of civilisation. A light fog floats in and we lose sight of each other. This would have worried me before my trip, but we're both carrying radios, phones and lights and are now used to paddling alone so neither is particularly worried about the other. I find it exciting not being able to see where I'm going; I have to rely on instinct and trust myself to tentatively push on. The water is shallow and the boat keeps scraping on the shingly mud. I try to get out as far up the beach as possible to avoid what happened to Katie and Marcus at Pin Mill. Eventually I get out and drag it over the slippery stones. Shapes and silhouettes are visible and the smell of the estuary mud makes me feel at home. I make out Michal staggering up the beach, boat on shoulder. 'Looking good!' I say, admiring his muddy look.

'You too.' We laugh at each other covered in mud as we try not to get too much of it in the car.

'What's your next adventure?' Katie asks after we've updated each other on our summers.

'The return to work,' I tell her half seriously, as I prepare to get my things out of storage and move back into my small flat. I have one day to tidy my beard, wash my clothes and get my head in the right place to do my job. I don't feel like an architect any more and my flat seems a lot smaller. I think of when I was recovering from my bone marrow transplant, of the phone call telling me Mike had died, and of watching cancer devour Marcus, and somehow going back to work doesn't seem such a big deal. In fact, it's nice to catch up with the small team in the studio, to see how some of the projects have moved forward, and sitting back at my desk is much easier than I thought it would be. I get back into the rhythm of small adventures at the weekends on and off the sea and reconnect with friends and family. The late-night Shipping Forecast is a daily reminder that my project isn't yet done, and I come up with a loose plan to do Dover this year and Wight and Portland before the summer.

A couple of months later I have an unusual day in Thames, the kind that you just need to go with and let unfold in front of you. A visit to the House of Lords has been in my diary for a while following an invite from The Churchill Fellowship. Names were drawn through a ballot and I was lucky to be selected. I've never been to Parliament before, so it seems like a good opportunity to have a nose around.

At lunchtime the same day, I receive a call from the newsreader Alan Smith. 'I'm reading the "Ships" today,' he says. 'Would you like to come?' For years I've imagined the announcers reading the Shipping Forecast, but I'd never seen it, so I have to stop myself from saying something over-enthusiastic like 'Hell yeah!' and go for the more British option of 'I'd love to, thanks!' I've been in contact with a few of the BBC broadcasters who read the Shipping Forecast. Zeb Soanes and Corrie Corfield have both been very supportive of my trip. I'd met Alan only a couple of weeks before when I went into Broadcasting House for an interview and unashamedly expressed my desire to sit in for the late-night Shipping Forecast. This is an opportunity too good to miss and a tingle of excitement runs through my spine at the thought of the invitation into the depths of Broadcasting House, late at night for a live reading.

I leave my flat dressed smarter than usual with the silver-edged invitation from the Lords tucked inside my jacket. I have some work to do before attending, and end up tying my tie in the train toilets: perhaps not the most glamorous way to prepare for afternoon tea at the House of Lords. I emerge from the tube at Westminster to flocks of tourists milling around, and walk towards the Black Rod's entrance to Parliament. I queue up with other guests; it's a sunny winter's day with some wispy clouds in the sky. On the way to the reception rooms, a thick-pile red carpet lines the route, which is peppered with display cases of important artefacts and regalia. On the terrace facing the river, tables are set up inside the marquees that I'm more used to seeing from the other side of the balustrade.

From the river, as you pass under Westminster Bridge, leaving the busy section beside the London Eye and South Bank behind, a series of yellow crosses sit on poles offset from the building line, marking a no-go area. These are special marks and river legend has it that should you stray inside the line, you'll be shot by snipers on the roof. I'm not convinced but have also never tried. Perhaps next time I'll arrive by kayak.

I spend some time soaking up the unusual view down the river from here, sipping a glass of fizz and feeling a bit of a fraud while hearing of other Churchill Fellows' journeys researching suicide prevention, engineering methods, and palliative care seem more worthy subjects than mine. It's always hard to explain my project as there can be several different readings of what I'm up to and what it's for. I'm often tempted to throw the cards in the air and just say 'why not?' without going into the lengthy backstory of the why. Through all my travels so far it is the excitement of experiencing a wild or unusual place and then connecting with people that live in it which interests me the most. It's sometimes difficult to translate this into distinct findings, but as I chat with my co-Fellows I'm reminded that I have a report to finish.

A number of three-tiered silver cake stands arrive on the table with sandwiches, fondants and cakes which look so perfectly presented they don't seem real. Several cups of tea and conversations later and it's time for the tour of the historic Palace of Westminster. We visit both Chambers, the lobbies, libraries and halls before exiting via the great Westminster Hall with its hammer-beam trusses, the largest medieval timber roof in the UK. King Henry VIII used it for banquets and gatherings as well as a tennis court. I emerge into the darkness and am wished goodnight by a couple of policemen before leaving through the turnstiles into Parliament Square.

I have quite a while to wait until my last appointment of the day at Broadcasting House, and decide to go for a beer. Not a regular frequenter of West London, I walk to the only pub I know nearby, the Tattershall Castle, a floating pub that I remember going to with Mike. Sitting on the deck, I look out over the Thames and stare at the lights of the city reflected in the gently moving water, the ebb and flow of the tideway bearing witness to so much history. It's a clear night with a new moon which makes the sky darker than normal. I watch the sparkling lights in the water with a light breeze brushing my face. The bar fills up with Friday-night drinkers and I go home to change for my alternative Friday night out at the BBC.

I've agreed to meet Alan at 10.45 p.m., when he has a break and will be able to step away from the studio to meet me in the lobby. There is a blue glow emanating from the lights of Broadcasting House, spilling on to the plaza where the areas from the Shipping Forecast are inscribed into the ground. The building is not unlike a ship with its prow jutting out into Portland Place, the balconies and lines of windows reminiscent of a huge liner. In fact, the statues decorating the building, designed by Eric Gill, are of Ariel and Prospero from Shakespeare's *The Tempest*, which starts out onboard a ship in stormy seas. The building was opened in 1932 with the radio studios occupying space at the heart of the plan.

I walk into the lobby and meet Alan, a friendly man wearing jeans, trainers and a checked shirt. A reassuringly normal outfit compared to the dinner jacket and evening wear insisted upon by Lord Reith in the early days of the Corporation. I should say now that I don't want to shatter any illusions so if you are happy with announcer Neil Sleat's description that the Shipping Forecast is read from an amethyst pulpit or would like to imagine Corrie Corfield aboard a ship on the seas around Britain, you should stop reading now.

It's calm at this time of night. The open-plan atrium of the news floor has a scattering of desks with multiple screens and a handful of people sitting at them. Alan leads me through the space to an editing gallery at the rear – it's not being used but it is exciting to see the wall of screens flickering input from all over the world, accentuated in the dark space. There are clocks in different time zones and mixing decks on the desk. I can see the circular news studio on the other side of the room as we walk across the vast open space and up a glass and metal spiral staircase. Alan points out the change in ceiling height, signalling that we are now leaving 'New Broadcasting House' and entering the original building. We move through several security-controlled doors and arrive in the Radio 4 offices on the outer side of the building.

'First things first,' says Alan, 'let's have a cup of tea.' Several black square boxes sit on the floor marked with the BBC logo but no other identification. I wonder what secrets sit inside, controversial episodes of *The Archers* perhaps. We take our tea and walk down the corridor through several more security doors and we are standing in a small windowless space in the bowels of the building. Studio 40D is still, there is wooden panelling along the walls and a large wooden-framed window to the adjacent studio. A sofa lounges beneath a large wall print with sayings from the Shipping Forecast and continuity announcements: 'intermittent slight drizzle', 'Skagerrak', 'violent storm 11', and so on. A map of the Shipping Forecast and a series of weather symbols is interspersed with the text.

There is a screen on the wall above the sofa with a digital and analogue clock face. Alan tells me that in the past, all the clocks in the building would have been controlled by a nuclear clock in the basement.

We sit down behind a large mixing desk and Alan talks through what everything is and what it does. On one of the other screens is a display of pre-recorded trails and announcements, including emergency breakdown scripts recorded for each of the announcers if for some reason the live broadcast doesn't work or the studio is evacuated. Virtual buttons with 'Breakdown Nunes', 'Breakdown Soanes', lead me to imagine the usually calm announcers having a live breakdown on the radio. I quickly realise this is not what it's for.

Alan runs through cueing up programmes and listening to the last 30 seconds of 'tape' to gauge the tone of it before jumping in with the continuity. Today it's a programme by Jo Brand and the prerecord of 'Today in Parliament'. We have a light-hearted chat and I'm worried that I might put him off. We decide to move my cup of tea away from the mixing desk – I don't want to be responsible for the close-down of the station due to a clumsy slurp. My elbow is also dangerously close to the slider for the pips; one slip and there would be millions of confused listeners.

As 00.48 draws closer, Alan shows me the script for the Shipping Forecast emailed through from the Met Office. He prints it out and marks it up with timings and calculations based on working backwards, subtracting in 60s rather than 100s to adjust for time rather than decimal. He cues up 'Sailing By'. 'For shorter forecasts the whole thing can play out,' he explains, 'for longer busier forecasts we fade it out early so as to fit it all in.' Alan has circled the word Skagerrak in the script and the pencil notes of timings are listed alongside the text. There are warnings of gales in all areas except North Utsire, South Utsire and Trafalgar.

Before I know it, 'Sailing By' is playing and Alan is announcing in a calm, clear voice, 'Good Morning, and now the Shipping Forecast, issued by the Met Office on behalf of the Maritime and Coastguard Agency at 00.15…' It's a long reading with several long pauses. I'm worried that I'll cough or sneeze partway through, and try to stay perfectly still and avoid any shuffling sounds in the background. As Alan reads through area by area, images of the ones I've visited flash through my mind. Once he finishes – 'Goodnight from everyone at Broadcasting House in London' (which is basically me, him and security) – and passes over to the World Service, we are out of there quicker than you can say Machrihanish Automatic.

It's three minutes past one and I'm walking down the street in the cold night air, unsure if what just happened was real. Before parting company, Alan says, 'Come back any time,' and in a flash, all the late nights, storms, rough waters, difficult times and personal challenges of my trip so far are wrapped in a warmth of familiarity and friendliness with a new dimension to it.

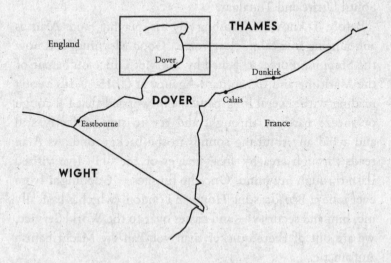

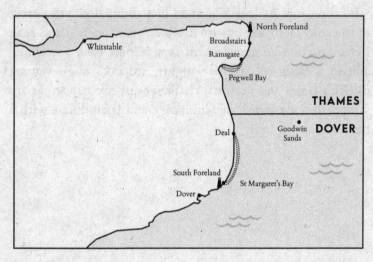

DOVER: THE SHIP
AND VIKING BAY

I don't need a plan! No, I'm a free spirit, a make-it-up-as-you-go-along kind of guy. I'll just go there and see what happens, I thought, before I ended up on the M2 for three and a half hours, crawling along towards Deal and watching the satnav on my phone slowly increase the journey time. I've been watching the weather for a week and dodging a storm over the weekend, shifting a meeting with a new client to coincide with the trip. I've a habit of doing too many things at the same time, and my mind switched into a kind of mental paralysis every time I considered the simple and oft-repeated logistics of picking up my boat, putting it on the roof of the car and driving towards the sea.

I've arranged to meet Charlie Connelly (author of *Attention All Shipping*) in the aptly named pub 'The Ship'. I'm late and ready for a beer. The streets running parallel to the beach are narrow and meandering as the buildings jostle for position, it's dark and the town is deserted (not surprising for a damp Tuesday evening in November), but there is the warm glow of lights reflecting off the wet ground through a light drizzle that's set in. It feels Dickensian, which seems appropriate as I'm just down the coast from Broadstairs, Dickens' favourite retreat and inspiration for some of his novels. I peer in through the steamed windows of the double-fronted brick building. The red ensign of the merchant navy hangs above the door. I'm not surprised it's raining, as Charlie describes in his writing, he is a magnet for precipitation and tells stories of being caught in the most freakish of downpours.

The pub is quiet; there's a small bar on the left with a few local beers and a cluster of wizened folk propped up around it. I recognise Charlie, who's sitting in the corner at a punched copper-topped table beneath a poster commemorating the heroes of the Goodwin Sands, the men and women of the lifeboats sent out to rescue the ships wrecked on the notorious sandbank. He kindly offers me a drink, and the anxiety of the journey starts to ebb away. I feel a bit starstruck – it's been almost a year since I read Charlie's witty best-selling account of his travels around the Shipping Forecast, and I wondered if the real Charlie will come across the same as the hero in the book. I quickly realise that self-deprecating good humour and strong observation are very much part of his real-life character. It's brilliant to share stories; the areas of the Shipping Forecast make for a relatively unlikely set of holiday destinations. A small sign by the bar says 'Cash Only' and I panic as I realise that I've thoughtlessly brought my contactless London ways to this small Kentish town. Despite this embarrassing oversight, conversation flows.

I'm happy to find someone who laughs at my story of the Norwegian exorcist tasked with cleansing the school on Utsira. Charlie applauds my initiative of dragging my kayak 15 kilometres from the dull Danish town of Hanstholm. 'I would have done the same,' he says. We chat about the fascinating story of the undersung father of the forecast, Robert FitzRoy, for whom inventing the world's first storm warning system was just one of his many achievements and who we both hold in high regard. I quiz Charlie about the next stops on my journey once the winter storms have passed. He tells me of the strange beauty and timeless stillness of Finisterre, a rugged headland on the coast of Galicia, marking the end of the world (as the name suggests). As the evening comes to an end, people leaving the pub stand near the door and say goodbye to the others in the room, who bid them goodnight by name in return. Charlie points out the house of a former *Carry On* star as we pass and part company.

I wake thinking about where to start my exploration of the Kent coast. The Dover area reaches from Sandwich Bay around to Beachy Head on the English side, and from just above Ostend to Saint-Valery-Sur-Somme on the Continental side. I've noted 'Viking Bay' on the map and have also spotted the replica Viking ship just outside Ramsgate and this seems like a contender. There are large M.O.D. firing ranges at Hythe and Dungeness and it turns out they're scheduled to be firing all day from 8 in the morning to 11.30 at night over the next three days. While this didn't bother me too much in the Dutch Frisian Islands, I'm not going to take my chances on home turf. I've also lost the aerial to my VHF, and crossing the busy ferry lanes at Dover requires constant contact with the Port Authority. On top of this, although equipped with some charts, I'm missing some maps for the area. I'm familiar with the coast here and have paddled much of it before, but I recently read a story about a sailor who tried to follow the coast to circumnavigate the UK and ended up circling around and around the Isle of Sheppey, so I'm wary.

It's still windy and my head is cloudy so I make it my mission to sort out the omissions to my kit before setting off.

Admittedly a bit more planning wouldn't have gone amiss. I fail on the VHF front; although the HQ and factory of a large UK supplier are nearby in Kent, their stock is mail-order only. I am successful with the maps, always an exciting thing to buy, and I have a look around the harbour in Ramsgate. A series of colonnaded terraces stand on the hill and the red arches below them – home to sailmakers, bike hires, galleries and cafes – get gradually smaller as the road on top of them slopes down to meet the quay. The chandlery that I'm looking for is closed – a large padlock ties together the port and starboard painted doors – a shame as I love a good chandlery. Walking along Military Road I get to the Sailor's Church, a three-storey red brick building with arched windows, its back wall forming the retaining structure to the cliff behind, holding up the terrace that now carries the road. On an adjoining building, tiled letters above the windows read 'The Ramsgate Home for Smack Boys', 'smack' obviously having a different meaning then to its more recent urban appropriation. The building provided shelter for young men working on the fishing smacks and later provided a home for those rescued from wrecks on the notorious Goodwin Sands.

A small door at the side leads into the church, set up in 1878 as a harbour mission and occupying the ground floor. It's a simple room with a high ceiling, painted white and with wooden pews in rows. It's also full of small model boats and paintings on the walls of ships, some in glass cases and some in full sail. There's a stormy painting of the light ship *Kentish Knock* being thrown around in rough waters. Models of the local lifeboats show changes in design over time but a steady sense of pride of the bravery of their crews. A newspaper clipping recalls 'The Tide of Timber' spilt by a Russian ship sailing from Sweden to Egypt in 2009, its cargo strewn along this coast.

Outside, the harbour is full, with a mix of fishing and sailing boats; wisps of clouds whip across the otherwise blue sky and there's a chill in the wind. A busker in the high street wears sunglasses while strumming the blues on an electric guitar; it's a slow morning. This was the point from which, as a young child aboard *Hullaballoo* with Mike at the helm, our family would start our crossings to France and the Netherlands I had little idea at the time that hundreds of similar small ships had made that same journey in very different circumstances as part of Operation Dynamo. In 1940, more than 338,000 Allied troops were stranded in Dunkirk. Churchill called it 'a colossal military disaster' and called on boat owners for help. Over 800 'little ships' including Thames barges, Dutch coasters, RNLI lifeboats and pleasure boats sailed from Ramsgate to evacuate the troops.

The sand on the beach at Broadstairs has formed an embankment rising above the rows of beach huts behind, which hunker down in front of the steep cliffs. Boats are stacked up against the wall, tucked away from the water's edge and sheltered from the wind, and there's a sense of calm preparedness, the place bracing itself for a battering from the winter storms. The old lifeboat station on the beach displays a map with the littering of shipwrecks on the Goodwin Sands. A carved figurehead of a Scotsman, rescued from one of the wrecks, stands tall above a jaunty corner. The building itself has relaxed on its old timber frame and the magnolia weatherboarded sides bulge and lean towards the few cars parked along the short arm of the harbour. A couple sit in the car next to me, staring intently out to sea in apparent silence; I wonder what they're thinking. The tide is coming in. Waves intermittently crash against the small slipway leading to what's left of the beach and sending spray up into the air.

There is an almost painterly quality to the light; the wind has dropped slightly and the faint golden glow of the sun is appearing intermittently behind the grey clouds. A man wheels up on a bright orange, low-rider pedal bike with huge, gleaming chrome handlebars that splay and curl upwards like a pair of shiny horns. He cruises around the car park showing it off, a Confederate flag sticker signalling, I hope, not much more than that he sees himself as a bit of a rebel. 'It's not really the weather for that is it?' he calls in my direction, looking at the kayak, at me and then out to sea. 'It's a bit rough,' he adds, turning the handlebars to stop in front of me. It's a fine ride he has, even if it would be more at home on Venice Beach than North Foreland.

'Nice bike,' I say, looking at it properly.

'I made it myself, I'm not sure about the colour.' He looks at the shiny paintwork, it seems like a test ride.

'Impressive,' I add. He eyes up my boat and wishes me luck before cruising off with a

'Rather you than me'. I'm hungry and walk up the hill, under the stone arch of York Gate on Harbour Street into the small town. A sign advertising the best chip shop in Kent, as voted for by the Potato Council, reels me in to buy a chip butty and momentarily plants the image of a gathering of Mr and Mrs Potato Heads assessing the other entries. After this athlete's nutrition stop, I buy a bottle of water from the supermarket and I'm finally ready to go.

The tide is rising and has devoured the slipway and beach. Tied by the inconvenience of the car, I plan a short trip along the coast to Pegwell Bay, going against the tide as it washes into the channel and then getting carried back along the low chalky cliffs with it. There's a light swell on the water and the low afternoon sun gives it a golden sheen. Occasional houses teeter on the edges of the otherwise uninterrupted line of tufty grass atop the white, wrinkled surface of the chalk. The straight, horizontal lines of flints in the chalk cliff face are perfectly aligned, giving way to clumps of grass, holes and hidden caves. I kayak past Dumpton Gap, where concrete defences are set into the cliff. Many a cold winter trip has been spent with our club in these waters, huddling under a group shelter on the beach, trying to warm up.

Towards Ramsgate, there's a series of small white cliffs with concrete structures securing the soft chalk. The view from the water reveals a sense of geological time and the fragility of human interventions, rusting, broken and falling into the sea. Efforts to retain the land against the force of the sea seem futile and defence structures pockmark the landscape in a pattern that makes much more sense from this perspective than it does on land. The rhythm of intermittent beach shelters inset into the base of the cliffs starts to break up and makes way for larger buildings and high-arched concrete walls holding the chalk behind. I pass through some patches of more lively, bouncy water closer to Ramsgate. The long harbour arms are outstretched like a big hug for seafarers returning to the safety of land. Although how warm that welcome is depends on what passport you have, if you have one.

As I turn the corner into Pegwell Bay, the low afternoon sun hits the sea and shines through the green sloppy water as it peaks and then drops into a trough. I stop on the water to take a couple of photos in the sun and am washed back towards the harbour entrance. A small, high-sided fishing boat turning in for the day chugs in behind me and I realise I should be paying more attention. Heading back, the sky becomes a perfect light show of emerging colours and shapes, the wispy clouds taking the hues of the setting sun, punctured by the bright white speck of the moon. A pink haze grows above the water and brings out the turquoise green of the briny foreground. It's a beautiful experience and grows in intensity until the surface of the water takes on a fiery orange-red set, the silhouettes of houses poking up over the cliffs. I drift in it for a while bobbing around, immersed in the spectacle. In failing light, I land the boat between crashing waves on to a slipway and haul it up over some metal railings and onto the car. Ravenous, I go in search of a curry at the local tandoori before staying the night at the cheapest hotel in town.

I wake early the next day and drive around the coast to catch the sun rising over the abandoned hover port at Pegwell Bay. The buildings have all gone but a pedestrian bridge remains, offering a path over the brambles and shrubs that populate the once busy roadway. The apron of tarmac is still marked with arrows and lines which are being gradually claimed back by nature. It's a clear morning and the sun grows quickly from a tiny line to a shimmering orb. The odd dog walker appears from the bushes and wading birds peep and pip around. There's a sharp metallic smell in the air, the tide is out, exposing a mixture of mud and seaweed. I try to imagine the noise and scale of the operation when it was in full swing, the giant SR.N4 hovercrafts making the thirty-minute crossing to France, killed mainly by changes to the law on duty-free. I find some footage online later and they truly were mad contraptions, hailed as the future of passenger transport and invented by a man with a hairdryer and a tin can.

Above the now silent flats, with the backdrop of suburban semi-detached homes and bus stops, sits a replica of a Viking ship, *Hugin*. Gifted by the Danish government to commemorate the 1,500th anniversary of the Anglo-Saxon invasion of these islands, it is silhouetted perfectly against the rising sun which brings out the gold decoration on the prominent lion's head carving to the bow. A combination of good timing and luck align to let me photograph the sun perfectly surrounded by the swirling spiral of the tail on the carving to the stern. It's an impressive sight. The long oars and shields lined up along the flanks give it an energy which is at odds with the mundane metal fence that now surrounds it.

Hugin landed at Viking Bay, Broadstairs, in 1949, crewed by 53 Danes navigating with just a sextant. The voyage was a project of the Danish Tourist Board who had the replica longship crafted in a shipyard in Frederikssund near Copenhagen. Through an advert in the national newspaper, a call went out via the Danish rowers' union to all the rowing clubs in Denmark and after over 250 applications, the motley crew of insurance brokers, prison wardens, booksellers, a police officer, fishermen, dentists and an ambulance driver, among others, was formed. One stipulation was that all must be over 180 cm tall, be willing to grow a beard and not cut their hair, for the true Viking look.

The ship was sailed and rowed through the Limfjord via Thyborøn to the North Sea before setting off for the main voyage from Esbjerg to Broadstairs to the sound of the Danish and British national anthems. The selected Viking crew ranged in age from 19 to 61 and had costumes on loan from the Danish Royal Opera which they proudly donned on reaching ports along the way. An account of the ten-day voyage sounds like it was by no means plain sailing or even rowing, with the boat facing big seas off Terschelling on the Dutch Frisian coast but carefully watched by a safety vessel. The weather seemingly calmed and warmed up for the crossing itself, and press planes overhead snapped the sunburnt Vikings naked, leading to the questioning in the morning papers of what happened to their pants. The ship and crew were met with huge celebrations on the beach and for several days following, including a trip up the Thames, escorted by kayakers from the special boats service, and a banquet at the Guild Hall with the Major of London.

For me there is a strange pull as I gaze out to sea and the sun reflects off the light swell in the Channel. As an early morning sea swimmer, Charlie had told me the previous night that from the steeply shelving shingle beach it's sometimes possible to see the sun glinting off the French cliffs. Being here reminds me how close this lower lip and chin of Kent and the hungry mouth of the Thames estuary are to mainland Europe. For millennia, this stretch of water has been crossed, fought over and contested, providing a vital connection to mainland Europe. Over the following few days around Dover, I see these reminders everywhere.

Exploring the area on land, I ramble around the Western Heights, towering over the town and littered with military structures, sunken forts and impressive defences. The most interesting of these is the Grand Shaft staircase designed to take troops quickly from the clifftop to the street level. Three overlaid spiral staircases corkscrew into the rock around a central light well with arched openings on to the shaft, giving it the quality of an impossible Escher drawing. I'm lucky to be there on one of the monthly open days and enjoy seeing dogs losing their owners as they run up and down the intertwined steps. Rambling on the chalk downland above, I also pass the remains of a Knights Templar church, built on the arrival of missionaries from Jerusalem in the 11th century. The foundations are all that remain of the walls, which form a small circular area with a protruding rectangular part at the front, making it like a keyhole in plan.

From here you can see Dover Castle occupying the promontory on the other side of the valley – a grand castle with the keep and outer walls intact. Below it is the White Horse pub, a favourite of cross-Channel swimmers. A dignified building with a well-proportioned frontage, the walls and ceilings inside are covered in the signatures of teams and individuals who have completed the challenge. So much so that the barmaid tells me they've stopped adding to it and now swimmers use the walls of the less elegant Fleur de Lys near the police station, which has an altogether different vibe. I walk around as the sunlight streams in through the windows and marvel at the scrawls from as far away as India, Australia and Russia.

A mural by the street artist Banksy adorns the end wall of a terrace in the town: a large EU flag with a workman chipping away at one of the stars, which makes me feel sad. A few weeks ago, I was at an anti-Brexit march in London, flying the European flag and hoping there's some way to stop this awful decision. I still find it hard to believe that the peaceful collaborative European project that has brought us so far from the fortifications and bomb-destruction I've seen on both sides of this sea, is being torn down by lies and cheap political tricks. It makes me angry for future generations that their opportunities have been curtailed.

Back in Deal, the beach is steep shingle, falling in steps towards the sea. By the time I drag the kayak down to the water's edge, the town and seafront has disappeared from view, giving a sense of isolation. The yellow stones almost glow in the morning light set against the contrast of a rich, deep blue sky. The wind has dropped and there's gentle movement on the water. Passing Walmer and Kingsdown, the chalk reappears as the cliffs pick up again. A series of detached villas are scattered around on the flat tops. Their turrets, pointy witch-hat towers and verandas give them a spooky, haunted-house feeling and a definite French air. These more distinct buildings give way to suburban homes.

Later, the cliffs pick up again before stepping down into the small collection of houses dotted around on the wooded hillside leading to the gravel beach at St Margaret's Bay. Three Art Deco villas sit under the cliff; their crisp white lines and mint-coloured window frames contrast with the rough face of the chalk. The sight of ferries on the horizon signals my arrival in Dover. The tower of South Foreland Lighthouse perches on the top with several other watchtowers, aerials and previous signalling structures.

I recall a story Charlie was telling me of a torchlit procession to the now disused tower on Remembrance Sunday a few years ago. Rounding the corner, the harbour swings into view and I sit and watch the constant movement of ships in and out. There is a cleft in the white cliff where a zigzagging path has been cut into the rock face. It stops around 30 metres above the beach and leads to a series of decaying walkways that have fallen into the sea. Holes look like raised caves in the rock with a rusty ladder leading up to one of them from the shore. At first glance it looks like an inviting welcome for anyone landing on this guarded part of the coast. On closer inspection it would make for a treacherous climb. Not, perhaps as treacherous as the route from France made by tens of thousands of asylum seekers to these beaches. The crossing from here is just over 40 kilometres, but cheap inflatable boats and desperation to cross, whatever the weather, leads to great loss of life. I think about how the sea can be a living hell or playmate depending on where you are born. Two figures in black stand beneath a watchtower on the clifftop observing my landing closely, perhaps wondering if I've emigrated in a kayak. I'm in a bright orange drysuit so if I was trying to be covert, this wouldn't be the way to do it. I look up and give them a wave. They don't wave back, but they leave me alone.

I clamber up the first ladder which is pretty much intact. It leads to a flat level and what I can now see are bunkers cut into the chalk. A small stone bench has been made outside one of them, looking out to sea. I wonder about the hours spent here gazing at the horizon in search of enemy craft. Emerging from the cave-like tunnels, the bunkers have cast concrete curved fronts to them and thin slit windows. A pockmarked rusted metal screen to the front creates a shield to the winter sun. There are three bunkers built from concrete and brick, linked together by tunnels cut into the cliff, running parallel to the coast.

It's a good lunch spot. Poking around on the beach, I find the low tide has exposed the rusted metal carcass of a ship, the wet chalk and seaweed making walking turn more to stumbling. Leaving the beach, a misty, low cloud rolls in and the sky turns white. The combination of white sky, white cliffs and underlying chalk turns the sea a milky turquoise green and picks out the impurities in the sheer rock face. The sun burns through the cloud as the afternoon progresses. In parallel the sea picks up slightly and turns a shiny, steely grey. It looks spectacular as the diffused rays of sunlight pick up the surface which stretches out as far as the eye can see. Once I have landed, it's mid-afternoon back in Deal, and Charlie and I go for a celebratory pint. We chat sea stories and classic radio announcers and he kindly agrees to my request to record him reading the day's forecast for Dover on the beach. 'Dover, south backing south-east later four or five, mainly fair, moderate or good, occasionally poor.'

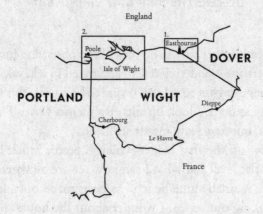

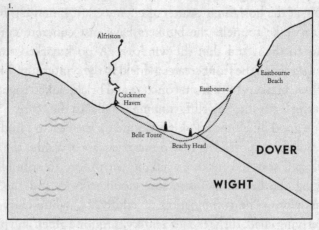

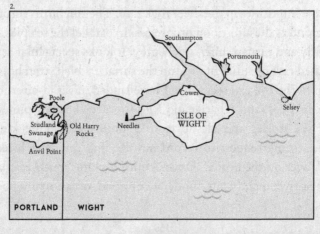

WIGHT: VISITING OLD FRIENDS

It's mid-January 2019 when I next get a chance to propel myself around the Shipping Forecast. I've spent Christmas in Spain and New Year in Iceland and the break has given me the chance to think seriously about what my priorities are. Work is hectic and while the projects are interesting, I'm starting to feel like ten years is a long time in one place and I'm itching to get back on the sea for more than a few days. Wight is next on my list and with a free Sunday morning I go to visit Old Harry.

Located right on the edge of the western side of the Wight Shipping Forecast area, just below Poole, the Old Harry Rocks are three chalk formations including a stack and a stump, off Handfast Point on the Jurassic Coast. A thick slice of Wensleydale cheese nibbled by a mischief of mice, this triangular piece of coast wiggles in and out like the drawing of an overzealous cartographer. It's a favourite of Natalie's, who has recently posted that 'he looks handsome at low tide and high and is probably the best place to kayak in mainland

Britain.' (She and Michal should know this since they circumnavigated Britain in 2012.)

Leaving early from the beach in Studland, I can see the sunrise over the silhouette of Handfast Point, the sky and sea awash with deep yellow, pink, orange and grey. Launching, I head out towards Old Harry – the large stack – in the biting cold. As I approach one of the first arches in the cliff face, I catch the rising sun through it as a flock of birds flies past. The timing is so perfect it feels staged. I round Old Harry, which from this side look like a slice of cake, with a buttress annexed to the back, as if someone has been creative with their spoon. To the right I see the stump, which is sometimes referred to as his wife. She's really his second wife, as his first fell into the sea in 1898. Ironically, the same erosion that took her slowly created a second stack next to him. Further round there are needles like giant crocodile teeth and mountains drawn by a child. The sky is dramatic, Baroque, an artwork designed to inspire awe and obedience, light bursting through the clouds in rays.

The Shannon-class lifeboat from Swanage comes alongside, and I chat with the crew, who are satisfied with my safety precautions but worried I might get cold hands. I tell them I've paddled in much colder waters and they wish me a pleasant journey – as I think maybe I should have worn thicker gloves. I cross the Swanage Bay and round Peveril Point past the RNLI base, the rocks changing from chalky white to the light brown of a chocolate crumble mix.

Old Harry and the surrounding cliffs form part of a chalk ridge created 65 million years ago from the calcium deposits of sea creatures, which runs across the south coast, joining up with the Needles on the Isle of Wight. I make out the top of Durlston Castle on my route south-south-west, and in the distance see Anvil Point Lighthouse sitting like a candle on a lopsided birthday cake. A bit further around, the rock becomes limestone and centuries of pressure have given it stripes.

It's not yet 10 a.m., but I decide to turn back; the tide should be good for the trip back. As I approach the tide race off Swanage Bay, it seems the services of the RNLI might be needed after all as another kayaker is not enjoying her boat surging up and down in the big waves. A fast-moving tide that passes through a constriction, a tide race has bigger swell, eddies and currents, which once you reach a certain level are fun to kayak as long as you're careful. It takes me back to my run ins with the surf in Denmark, and I try to help her but manage to drop my own paddle in the sea. I'm lucky to retrieve it and the other kayaker seems to have got things back under control, so I paddle back past Old Harry with the tide, landing in time to meet my oldest friend Romilly, who I've known since we were born, and her partner Zyggy for lunch.

I'm not satisfied that my morning paddle is enough to tick off Wight so I keep it on my lengthy to-do list. Back in London, I run around doing site visits, giving some presentations about my trip, and I write up the report on the first leg for the Churchill Fellowship. I'm pleased with the result, printed on recycled paper with high-quality images, but it's clear that I still have a long way to go. From here, I state, 'I will break the trip down into chunks.' The first being the southern section (Biscay, FitzRoy, Trafalgar) and the next section around Scotland and Ireland. If I don't leave work, it will take me years.

Let's just say that I'm not exactly able to jack in my job and lead a life of adventure. There are no millions in my bank account or valuable family pile in Hampshire, and the free or reduced kit I've been given by Finisterre and Kōkatat and Werner, though extremely helpful, won't make my trip happen on its own. Nevertheless, by mid-March I've decided to leave work and I have the third meeting on the topic with my boss, Sarah, who already knows this is on the cards. 'I'm really sorry but,' I begin uncertainly, 'I've decided that I think I need to leave in the summer to finish my trip.' As the words come out, it seems so final and I'm engulfed by a feeling of relief, but also fear. Sarah is kind and understanding, no doubt pleased to have some clarity at last.

A few days later, I attend another huge anti-Brexit march with Dafydd, Marcus's best friend since university. Walking through the wide malls awash with the blue and gold of the European flag, we agree that Marcus would have been here. I'm not sure what he would have thought about my leaving work, but he also lived knowing he had limited time. That night I watch the cycle bridge I've designed with a team at work being installed in Kingston. Of all the projects I've done, I'm most proud of this one. João, who worked on it with me, says, 'I think we've designed something London can enjoy,' which captures the essence.

For the next few months, I feel like I'm closing things. At Easter, Katie, Josep, Llorenç and I finally scatter Mike's ashes by the river in the village we grew up in, sloshing them in with some red wine. They've been down the side of my sofa for the eight and a half years since our dad died, and I feel bad about leaving them in the flat while I rent it out. It's sad to be back in the village without Marcus and Mike, but Llorenç is two-and-a-half and distracts us from our sadness as he has since he was born eleven weeks before Marcus died.

Wight hangs over me as a Shipping Forecast area I need to complete before the summer. Stretching from Swanage to just past Eastbourne along the south coast, there are lots of great places to kayak, including the Isle of Wight. To complement my visit to Old Harry, I decide to visit another old friend, the Beachy Head Lighthouse. Along with Dover, Wight was probably the first Shipping Forecast area I ever visited, because my grandparents Betty and Frank lived in Eastbourne and we were in Rutland, about as far from the sea as you can get in the UK.

Keen to get some quality time with their grandchildren, or gluttons for punishment, they would look after the three of us for a week each summer. I'd be woken to the sound of woodpigeons cooing and the wind shushing through the trees at the back of the house (or by being jumped on by Katie or Marcus), and go downstairs to the comforting smell of toast and fried eggs. Grandpa Frank would be reading *The Telegraph* (the cause of much scorn from Mike) and Grandma would be making breakfast in a sunflower apron. It was a happy place, away from the weight of Fanconi anaemia or having a mentally ill mum, and above all it was next to the sea.

We'd scramble up the steep garden, which dripped with bright pink fuchsias and other colourful flowers, to get our beach things off the line. One of us would go to the slim shed by the side of the house, braving the darkness and its potent smell of creosote, to retrieve the buckets and spades. We'd squeeze into Grandma's Fiat Cinquecento (or her 'toy car' as she called it), and we were off to the beach, where we would spend the whole morning. Within the breakwaters of the chosen section, we were free to roam, low tide revealing sand and rock pools, high tide making it easy to swim off the steep incline of rounded pebbles. Grandma would sit against the breakwater, transported to ancient Egypt, reading the latest Wilbur Smith book, occasionally looking up to check on us. I felt so free. We'd leave around midday, back to the house for an al fresco lunch: baguette and taramasalata, olives and sometimes even prawns. In the afternoon we'd go back to the beach or play on the Downs behind the house, climbing over the fence into the dark woods which felt like being comforted under a blanket. Other times we'd drive up to Beachy Head, to be blown around by the wind before hanging over the fence to get a better view of the stripy lighthouse.

Despite bad weather forecasts, I've managed to drum up interest from seven other members of the canoe club who have all escaped London after work this Friday in late April and are on their way down. Al, a small Australian with enough character and talk to fill a room, is sharing a car with me. 'So, at best it's a paddle down Cuckmere River to the sea tomorrow,' she says as we cross the Dartford Bridge.

'Yep, but Beachy Head and Eastbourne on Sunday still look okay,' I confirm. As with most of the trips organised with the club, there is a mixture of kayaking levels.

Matt and Jo are relatively new to it, and I've spent some time this week in the Prospect going through the different options and what we'd need to bring depending on the weather. Working with various scenarios has become second nature to me and I'm happy to share what I've learnt with them.

Al's booked us all into a campsite in Alfriston, a place I heavily associate with Grandpa Frank, who, seizing the opportunity to sit in the sun with a pint and the paper, would often volunteer to drive over and pick up the rest of the family who had walked over the South Downs to the Star Inn. Alfriston itself is a beautiful village in the valley of the Cuckmere River. Many of the buildings are timber-framed with a knobbly flint lower half, with a black and white Tudor-style upper floor overhanging the bottom and making it possible to shelter from the rain.

Al and I are late; I always underestimate how long it takes to get out of London. Some of the others have arrived and Matt has sent us the GPS coordinates, excited to get out the new kit he's bought for this trip. We career towards the dot on the screen, keen to get settled in as soon as possible. We're close, keeping our eyes open for tents. 'Stop, stop, stop!' screams Al dramatically. I brake suddenly and quickly realise what the fuss was about. 'It's Matt,' she points at the caterpillar-like form lying on the ground.

'Phew!' I'm relieved we've avoided running him over in his new bivvy bag where he sent the location from – it would not have been a good way to start the weekend. Tragedy averted, we get our tents up and they rock in the wind. Jo, Zoe, Cai, Patrick and Adrian are already there and none of us are sure if we'll make it down the river the next day, so we book a place for brunch to make sure we will be well-fed before making any decisions.

Storm Hannah is brewing up and the Met Office has issued a yellow warning for winds of up to 70 mph. It's not an ideal weekend for kayaking. 'It's blowing a hooley!' Mike would have said. Brunch was a good idea, and after a few rounds of flat whites and a variety of things on sourdough toast we make a start. It's a long carry from the car park down a lane and over a narrow bridge, where we unintentionally block dog walkers and Saturday brunchers, as we drop the boats into a thin trickle of a river. It's a clear day and the intermittent sun gleams off the dark green water of the river. We make slow progress and I'm struck by how different it is to kayak on a river, guided on both sides by lush green grasses submerged in the water and no horizon in sight. At one point rushes tower over me to the left like spiky ginger hair, and then the river starts to widen below the Litlington White Horse carved into the hill.

This and the Long Man of Wilmington down the road were favourites of ours as kids, when we'd often walk the river from Exceat to Cuckmere Haven for an evening picnic and swim or be driven around on some other mini-adventure through East Sussex. I'm shocked by two things I discover about these landmarks afterwards. Firstly, that the White Horse isn't some neolithic self-expression, but the result of three blokes (Ade, Bovis and Hobbis) going up to carve a horse in the hillside in 1924 under the cover of darkness. I've had some pretty cool ideas late at night after a few beers, but I've never carved an animal the size of a swimming pool into a hillside. Still, it seems, the hill had form for having white horses carved into it, although no one knows when the first one appeared exactly. Luckily it now has the National Trust to look after it.

The Long Man is a different story: although it is also not as old as everyone thought it was, it is estimated to date from the Early Modern period, the 16th or 17th century. The shocking and, if I'm honest, slightly disappointing fact I found about this old friend is that it's now made of lime-painted breeze blocks and not chalk. It seems this is one of the least controversial things the Long Man has been involved in of late. In 2007, he became a she when 100 women dressed in white boiler suits added breasts and pigtails to the carving. While not controversial in itself, the Neo-Pagans and the Council of Druids who regard it as a sacred site were not happy. On the night of the 17th June 2010, in possible deference to the work of misers Ade, Bovis and Hobbis, almost a century before, a massive phallus appeared on the Long Man painted in football-field paint. He has even made his opinion known with regards to fracking approved in the area, with 'Frack off!' written in white tarpaulin sheets next to him. I quite agree.

Having paddled three quarters of the journey, we stop for a pint and a packet of crisps at the Cuckmere Inn, strategically positioned right next to the river. From there it's a straight line to the mouth of the river which is now a deep marine blue. To the left we get our first glimpse of the white cliffs of the Seven Sisters falling away from the dusty green headland. We hear the crashing of the sea before we see it and until we can, it feels like we might be about to paddle over a waterfall in cartoon style. We carefully manoeuvre to the side of the river, drag the boats out over the shingle and amble towards the sea.

Cumulus clouds have been caught, brought down to earth and scattered across the sea and beach as white foam covers everything. Excitement, like opening your bedroom curtains to find a covering of snow, turns us all into children. It's too rough to launch the kayaks, but we are all wearing drysuits so we launch ourselves into this natural foam party. It's like a bubble bath in the sea and inspired by bathing with siblings years ago, we start hurling white missiles at each other, revelling in something unexpected and fun. A few of our group stand on the shore, sensibly suggesting that it might be a chemical effluent emanating from Dungeness just around the corner. It does look a lot like shaving foam, but I also know that lumps of bobbly foam stretching out over the sea surface can tell the tale of a calming storm and, knowing Storm Hannah has just whipped up the Atlantic, I choose to believe this story.

This is not the first time Wight has provided us with a bit of fun. Further around the coast is Selsey Bill on the southernmost point of the Manhood Peninsula below Chichester. Knowing about Selsey as a kayaker who enjoys a bit of a surfy challenge is like remembering which of your local swimming pools has the best slide as a kid (it was Corby for me in case you wondered). Just off Selsey is one of the most reliable tide races for playing in a kayak within a day's reach of London. Michal, Natalie and I often feel the urge to ride some surfy waves, especially as it's good practice for expedition kayaking when you sometimes get caught out by tide races, so we've done quite a few trips to Selsey. Last year we did a photoshoot there, Michal using a massive telephoto lens to capture me riding the waves. The impressive photos were later used on the website of the company who made my kayak, Tiderace. It felt like a recognition of my progress as a kayaker but really was more about Michal's photography skills.

With our tents nestled in a bend of the river, Jo volunteers to make dinner for everyone, while we reduce some of the weight in the boats by drinking the various bottles of wine we've brought. There are several reasons why people usually cook for themselves on these trips: camp stoves are tricky, and preferences and allergies are not easily catered to. But Jo is a novice and who are we to stand in the way of what's possible. After quite an effort she pulls off a gluten free veggie feast which we wolf down, talking and laughing together as the sun sets. I put her on the preferred participant list.

We wake up to the smell of fresh dew on the grass, and the sound of the water babbling as it snakes its way to the sea. It's a somewhat different view than the one from my flat in East London. Back at the beach, the Seven Sisters cliffs stand posing coquettishly to the left, their chalky faces like creases in a wedding banquet tablecloth, falling gracefully to the floor. Everything seems to be desaturated. The colour difference between sea and sky is hardly noticeable and the horizon almost disappears. The forecast is for Force 4, calming to 3 later, so we wait a while, observing the conditions, then launch into rolling waves on the beach.

We paddle east towards Eastbourne, past all seven of the sisters as their teeth bite into the aquamarine-coloured sea. It's great conditions to do this paddle, if a little cold; dramatic stormy clouds in slate grey show off above us but leave us alone. On the furthest headland, we can see Belle Tout Lighthouse, which was decommissioned in 1902 when the

Beachy Head took over. A look at this stumpy lighthouse was a favourite stop on a circular walk we would often do on the headland, and I remember the excitement of seeing it on TV, when engineers moved it 17 meters back from the cliff edge in 1999 to avoid it falling into the sea.

The sea is a bit lumpier as we move further around and get our first look at the Beachy Head Lighthouse. It starts as a dark needle pointing out of the sea, but as we approach, its distinctive red and white stripy paint becomes clear. In 2011, Trinity House – the organisation that looks after the lighthouses in Britain – announced that it no longer had the budget to keep the red and white stripes painted. Thankfully a sponsored campaign raised the money and got the job done. This is the lighthouse of my childhood that was always exciting to come and visit. I haven't been this close to it for a few years and as kids we were restricted to peering down on it over the fence on the headland.

Built between 1900 and 1902 out of Cornish granite, the lighthouse is 165 meters seawards of the chalky headland. As we pass, we can still see the cuts in the cliff made by the temporary cable car used to transport stone and workers to the site. On top of the headland is The Beachy Head Hotel where my parents had their wedding reception in 1971, the cinefilm showing a fashionable young couple, full of hope for the future.

We carry on into the Dover area towards Eastbourne, passing the pier, where we hardly went as kids, making it infinitely fascinating. Arriving at the shingle beach we pull up the kayaks and get ready to go back to London. Standing on Eastbourne beach over twenty-five years since I did as a child, it still feels comforting and familiar and I'm happy to have lots of fun new memories to add to my old ones, this little piece of Wight retaining its mythical 'happy place' status in my head.

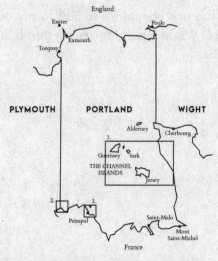

England
Exeter
Exmouth
Poole
Torquay

PLYMOUTH **PORTLAND** **WIGHT**

Alderney
Cherbourg
Guernsey Sark
THE CHANNEL ISLANDS
Jersey

2. 3.
Paimpol
Saint-Malo
Mont Saint-Michel
France

1.
France
St Peter Port
GUERNSEY
SARK
Les Autelets
Brecqhou
Dixcart Bay
LITTLE SARK
Paternosters
Les Écréhous
Greve de Lecq
JERSEY
Le Pinacle
Rozel
L'Étacq
L'Etacquerel Fort
Les Ormes Resort
St Ouens Bay
Corbière
St Helier
St Brelade's

2.
Île Rouzic
Île de Malban
Île Bono
PLYMOUTH **PORTLAND**
Phare de Men Ruz
Trégastel
France

3.
La Croix
Île de Bréhat
Phare de L'Ost-Pic
Paimpol
France
Bréhec beach
Bonaparte Bay
Gwin Zégal

PORTLAND: ISLANDS IN THE MIDDLE

By mid-May, I've got three weeks before I start the second European leg of my journey and I want to get in Portland before I leave. This long, thin Shipping Forecast area, running from Swanage to Berry Head on the British side, includes the Channel Islands. Jersey is home to my aunt and uncle, Nicky and Kevin, who have lived there since before I was born. Teachers by vocation and adventurers by volition, Nicky and Kevin have always known the curative power of the outdoors and have spent most of their lives in nature (often in kayaks) beckoning others to come out and enjoy it with them.

Mike was a supporter of this, so after my bone marrow transplant, at 15, when I'd spent months in isolation in a room that looked like it had been prepared by a serial killer, I was eventually let out and allowed to go on my own to Jersey. Until this jaunt, my knowledge of the Channel Islands was largely derived from the *Joey* books, a series of children's books where a yellow plane repeatedly saves the day, the shapes of the islands etched into my mind by the illustrator.

A week of adventures in Jersey and Sark felt like something worth surviving for: beaches, rocks and endless sea.

For many years I didn't come back, focused as I was on school, university and being an architect. But, at a loss at what to do for Christmas in 2011, after Mike's death, Katie and I decided to spend it in Jersey, knowing from previous experience on the mainland that there would be no moping around or watching Christmas telly. Pretty much fitted for wetsuits as we arrived, we spent the whole time in and out of the sea, jumping off rocks, joining the Jersey Canoe Club Christmas morning swim (no wetsuits allowed) and kayaking on sit-on-tops on Boxing Day (Kev maintains this was the only time he's been on one). It was as if the trip woke something up in both of us: a long-forgotten love of being in, on, or next to the sea.

'Just take this helmet back to Tower Hamlets Canoe Club in Shadwell will you? One of their members left it,' Kevin said to me, as I was packing. I agreed and this nudge was all I needed to start my kayaking adventure and by February I was a member of the Canoe Club in London. Jersey and Tower Hamlets Canoe Clubs already had a connection and regularly met up, swapping the unpredictable murky waters of Central London for Jersey's challenging seas and vice versa. I've lost track of how many visits to Jersey I've made by the time I'm in Poole waiting for the ferry to leave, on my way to the 16th Jersey Sea Kayak Symposium, where I'll be talking about my journey so far and getting a few days of kayaking in. I'm treating this as the official trip for my project.

At around midday the ferry passes close to Sark and makes me think about how far I've come. I'd been kayaking for a few years when Nicky suggested a trip out to Sark from Jersey, a 20-kilometre journey, that most people make by ferry. I'd never done anything like this before and I wasn't very confident with my forward stroke, but I knew I'd be in good hands. We'd launched at L'Etacq at the north end of the beautiful St Ouens Bay in Jersey, which curves in like a tentative bite out of the entire west side of the island. It's funny to think about my first paddle out to an island, with the experience of Utsira and Heligoland under my belt. Back then, I remember it taking ages, Sark sitting on the horizon and the GPS telling us we weren't even halfway. I felt like we were making good progress as we passed the Pierres de Lecq reef off to the east with waves breaking on spiky black rocks. In the 16th century, a boat carrying Jerseymen and their families – granted land in colonisation of Sark – ran aground here and all passengers drowned. Since then, superstitious sailors recite the Lord's Prayer as they pass which has given the rocks their nickname 'The Paternosters'.

Nicky tried to get us in to the rhythm I now know is so important for sanity on these long paddles. Like any project the middle bit seemed to last forever. Eventually we glided into the bay at Dixcart on Sark, with thirty minutes to spare before the tide changed. After a short break, we'd launched again to circumnavigate the island.

I can see the ancient rocks contoured like squashed liquorice allsorts as the ferry passes the length of Sark and docks briefly in St Peter Port on Guernsey. I smile as images of that night on Sark flood into my mind. We'd heard rumours about the Sark Disco, run for over forty years at the Mermaid and DJed by the Silver Fox, so we had come prepared with pirate costumes stuffed in dry bags in our hatches – mine even had a plastic parrot. On hearing of our plans, my cousin Lisa, always ready for a bit of fun, had taken the ferry from Jersey to join us.

A mix of cheap booze, tired bodies, 90s tunes and a feeling of jubilation at having made it over, ensured we were swiftly kicked out at closing time and still dancing outside when the door opened and the parrot flew out, much to our amusement. Unsurprisingly, the kayak back the next day is a bit of a blur and the only thing I'm sure of is that we gorged on Pizza Express in St Brelades Bay before the flight back to London.

Back on the ferry, it takes another hour to reach Jersey's capital, St Helier. It's been five years since my first Jersey Sea Kayak Symposium and I've become one of the regulars. The event draws kayakers from clubs around Europe for a week of sea- and land-based activities on the island. The proportion of each depends entirely on the changeable weather whipping across the Atlantic from Newfoundland. This time, I've forgone the stay at Les Ormes resort (the poshest venue we've had yet) to sleep on Nicky and Kevin's floor, which in many ways is more comfortable.

The first day is a visit to Les Écréhous. I've kayaked out a few times to this group of rocky islands 10 kilometres off Jersey to the north-east, staying the night under the stars. It's a regular haunt of Nicky and Kevin's. Over 40 of us make the smooth paddle over, organised in smaller groups for safety. Clustered houses are entrenched in the rocks as if huddling together; a few cast-off cottages enjoy their own singular outcrops. We break for lunch and sit on the beach looking at the colourful line of kayaks and the deep turquoise of the sea, then have a rather bumpier ride back.

The next day is a busy one starting with sea caves and cliff-jumping in the morning, followed by an afternoon bike ride around the south-west of the island led by Kevin, stopping at the pub at La Pulente, then back to Les Ormes. I'm nervous as I stand up to give my keynote lecture, and Al, sitting in the front row, gives me a reassuring thumbs up. 'Good evening, everyone,' I start, 'for anyone who doesn't know me, I'm Toby Carr and I've been trying to kayak the Shipping Forecast.' It sounds like admitting to an addiction, I think to myself, realising that that is exactly what it feels like sometimes. I've done a few of these since I've been back, and my performance is better than in Den Helder for sure. At the end, a man asks, 'So, what exactly is your next leg?'

'Well, in two weeks Michal and I will take the ferry to Calais and drive to Brittany, where we will spend three and a half weeks exploring the French sides of Portland, Plymouth and Biscay.' I hear myself say this and everything sounds a lot more certain than I feel it is. We do have a plan, just not the detail. 'From there I'll take the ferry to Santander in Spain and somehow get to Porto,' I say, cutting myself short when I realise how ridiculous it sounds to say that I will kayak to Porto – it's 700 kilometres! People are encouraging, though, and by the time I've finished, I'm feeling more confident and a little bit pleased with myself.

A dark-haired man with a beard and a big smile comes over. 'Hi I'm Marc,' he says with a light French accent. 'I'm from Brittany – if you need anything while you're there, let me know.' I've been trying to reach out to kayakers in Brittany and it's a very welcome contact. We talk for a bit and exchange emails.

The next day, I'm coaching a session on rescues and rolling, something essential even for experienced kayakers, as I well know. I lead the group of eight through various techniques, coaxing them all out of their boats and into the cold sea. The evening is a party at the Corbiere Phare restaurant on the south-west corner of the island. I walk down the old railway line and stop to look at the lighthouse. Operational by 1874, it was the first in the British Isles to be made of reinforced concrete. It is impressive; the smooth white lines of the tower and caged light look as if they belong more to the sky than the rugged granite rocks below. On the headland, facing the tidal island the lighthouse stands on, is a stone monument, not to lives lost (and there have been many around these rocks) but to the 307 lives saved when a French passenger catamaran sank in 1995. Inside the pub, there's live music, a banquet of food, a raffle and some dancing. I don't want to destroy anyone's illusions of me being a lonely explorer type, but I do enjoy a bit of a party and have been known to encourage others on to the dance floor.

The next day marks a year since I started my trip in Iceland, and Jenny Mullin at BBC Radio Jersey interviews me. 'You're partway through the trip, have you been getting out of it what you hoped?' she asks.

I muddle together an answer: 'Yeah, I think lots of things have come out of it. One of the most amazing things is the people you meet along the way. Language and national borders go out of the window because of this shared love of something.'

'I know positivity is important for you. Would you say you're inspiring other people?'

I stumble again. 'We all have challenges in our lives, but what's important is how we deal with these challenges,' I state, starting to feel more confident. 'Seeing the positive rather than the negative… I hope that I can inspire other people to spend time out of doors in nature, to rebalance their lives. Probably not everyone will kayak the Shipping

Forecast, but maybe I can inspire others to focus on what they can do rather than what they can't.'

After the interview, I'm introduced to John Searson, the Principal Met Officer on Jersey, and he invites me to go with him to have a look around the Jersey Met Office. I've been trying to visit the Met Office in Exeter since I started the trip, but haven't managed to wrangle an invitation, so I'm excited to visit Jersey Met. Entering the small office, it's comforting to see an isobar chart and a pair of dividers on the desk and weather charts on the walls in front of all the technology. John joined Jersey Met in 1982 and still retains a scientist's fascination with the weather. 'Jersey Met was created in 1952,' he tells me, 'because of the need for a more detailed forecast than the one for the whole area of Portland.'

'I bet the way you put the forecast together has changed a bit,' I say, looking at the mixture of digital and analogue tools around the office.

'Yes, every advance helps us to increase accuracy, and there's no substitute for knowing what the weather is actually doing. We have computers that do the readings now, but weather station measurements are still an important part of how we put the forecast together.'

'When I was in the Faroe Islands,' I say, 'they told me the best way to know what the weather was doing was to look out of the window.'

'It's so changeable there, worse than here, it must be terrible to forecast for.'

'I've read that Jersey was one of the original fifteen weather stations that Admiral FitzRoy set up,' I tell him, thinking about the history of the start of the Shipping Forecast. After two voyages as captain of the HMS *Beagle* and a stint as the governor of New Zealand, Captain Robert FitzRoy was elected to the Royal Society. In 1854 he was appointed as the head of a new department focused on the collection of weather data at sea. He and his team of three developed weather charts and a deeper understanding of how storms work. The loss of 450 lives on the *Royal Charter* off Anglesey in 1859 weighed heavily on him and led to the introduction of the British Storm Warning System for Shipping in February 1861. Fifteen land stations around the British Isles were established, one of which was on Jersey.

'Yes, that's right, we still use his signal system at Fort Regent.'

'Really?' I try to hide my excitement at finding another connection to the Shipping Forecast.

'Yes, from this office we put together the most likely weather scenario for the Channel Islands,' he explains, 'and then we send them out to the BBC, the coastguard and the signal station. It's one of the oldest functioning stations in the British Isles.' John's colleague Adriana is working on the Shipping Forecast for Jersey as we speak, readying it to be communicated to ensure that those going out to sea have the most accurate information possible.

From my sneak preview of the forecast, I can see that visibility and sea state will get worse through the morning. 'Patchy rain and fog' is on the cards and the wind will increase to a Force 6 in the afternoon. The next day, I'm signed up for a morning paddle exploring the caves near Greve de Lecq and the forecast is pretty accurate, although thankfully with less rain. I spend the afternoon in the Maritime Museum in St Helier. I visit Kevin's picture on the redbrick Jersey Wall of Fame. He's well known as a sea kayaker and for his role as a teacher in getting kids to spend more time outdoors, and has been an inspiration to me.

In the harbour near the museum, my eye is caught by the FitzRoy Barometer, a long wood-and-glass instrument set into the wall. These barometers were developed by FitzRoy to save lives at sea before he came up with the Shipping Forecast, and were installed in harbours around the UK to give mariners an idea of the weather before they went out.

As I leave the museum I look up and see the Fort Regent signal station. The large mast was first erected in 1708 on high ground to warn islanders of the threat of invasion. During the Napoleonic Wars, ten such stations were placed around the island and manned by the navy who were well-trained in the use of nautical flags. Semaphore was introduced to Jersey in 1810 and was used to send messages between the Channel Islands and to ships. At the end of the Napoleonic Wars in 1814 the station took on a commercial role communicating with ships docking in Jersey, then in 1861 it became a weather warning system.

The Post Office had laid the first telegraph cable to Jersey in 1858, making it possible for FitzRoy's storm warnings to be telegraphed to Fort Regent and for Fort Regent to send weather observations back to London. On receiving a forecast with a gale warning (Force 8 or above on the Beaufort Scale), a black cone is hoisted up the mast, pointing upwards for northerly and downwards for southerly winds. This technique is still used today, although the messages are no longer sent via telegraph. As I look up at the mast, I can just make out an inverted cone with a ball underneath, signifying dangerous winds of Force 6 or 7. High winds mean no kayaking for me tomorrow, but despite this I'm pleased to see another invention of FitzRoy's still in operation.

Nicky recommends I talk to Brian Nibbs, a retired Jersey harbour master and he meets me for a coffee on my last morning. As Brian enters the airy Museum Cafe, I recognise him from a leaflet about the tours he runs. Wearing a St Helier Yacht Club polo shirt, there's a glint in his eyes of someone who's had some adventures. 'I'm interested in our shared connection with the Shipping Forecast,' I start, as we sit at a table in the corner, and I mention how Guðni in Iceland remembered sitting with his grandfather listening late at night. 'What are your memories of it?' I ask.

'It was easy to listen and miss your area. I was on this small coaster,' Brian says, referring to the coastal cargo ship he was posted on as a young man. 'We had an A4 clipboard covered in acetate and a chinagraph pencil and you'd listen to the areas each side of where you were and write them down. It made you concentrate. "Portland, Plymouth, my god it's gone!"'

'Yeah, and you couldn't just listen again,' I say remembering writing down the Thames, Dover and Wight forecasts on *Hullaballoo* and thinking of Marcus who was annoyingly good at drawing out the weather systems on the photocopied map of the Shipping Forecast we worked with. 'You must have seen some wild seas.'

'Oh yes, when I was deep sea off the coast of Australia, I remember seeing thirty-foot waves right ahead of us.'

I imagine these waves were big enough to engulf a cargo ship. 'Wow, that sounds a bit scary.'

'As a young man it's all part of the adventure.'

'What did you enjoy most?' I ask.

'I used to love stellar navigation. It was accurate; with the stars you can get a proper fix.' Ever since I vaguely learnt to identify constellations and use a sextant with Mike on

Hullaballoo, the stars and particularly navigation by them has captured my imagination too. We talk a bit more about it and as Brian's depth of knowledge becomes clear, I'm glad it's not a skill I need to perfect.

'What do you think makes Jersey special?' I ask Brian, realising I should probably let him get on with his day soon.

'The total difference between low and high tide,' he says, recounting some adventures with the *States of Jersey* tug which drew 3.5 metres and was a challenge in all but high tide. I can imagine this, and am always impressed by the way that the beaches here go from massive amounts of flat sand to the water lapping the sea walls. I thank Brian for the new perspective he's given me on the sea.

I've got a few hours before my ferry and go to St Ouens bay, making a beeline for a fish barbecue restaurant housed in an old German bunker at L'Etacq at the north end of the bay. Run by Faulkner Fisheries, the restaurant serves delicious seafood which you eat on the picnic benches outside. Smooth waves lap the shore in a clear line of turquoise blue into the bay. The sun glitters on the surface and I feel hot waiting for my lunch with the soft sound of French in the background. The weather has improved drastically.

Nicky and I stroll along the flat sandy bay, the light wind in our faces, looking down towards the Corbière Lighthouse on the southern corner of 7 kilometres of sweeping bay. 'Probably the most beautiful lighthouse in the world,' she says, not for the first time, smiling. When she retired as a geography teacher, Nicky recently trained as a Blue Badge Guide (the UK's prestigious tourist guide accreditation) and is most interested in what you can't immediately see. 'Anything newer than the Iron Age, I'm not that interested in,' she tells me, 'but I love taking people around to find out about Jersey's deep history.'

She's keen to show me the submerged forest. 'Here it is.' She pokes something dark submerged in the sand. I touch it with my hand, expecting it to be cold like rock but it's warm and slightly squashy. 'These are peat beds showing that in five thousand bc the island was covered in forest. Isn't that amazing!' she smiles.

'I can't really get my head around that amount of time,' I admit.

'Well, the Palaeolithic artefacts found at La Cotte de St Brelade suggest that people were living there as long as two-hundred-and-fifty thousand years ago.' It's such a lovely place, I can see why. My walk with Nicky brings an end to this trip to Jersey, and as I give her and Kevin a goodbye hug I know I won't see them until I've done the next leg of my journey. Waiting for the ferry, it's obvious something kayak-y has been going on – practically all the cars have a couple of boats on them and some scruffy, windswept owners nearby.

Two weeks later I'm back in Portland, in France, and it's a relief to have started the trip. It's been a rush to pack up and rent out my flat, finish work and get myself organised. This time, I'm in a different boat, a Tiderace Xceed, which I've been testing out since September. I'm still worried about the foot pegs so have a spare pair to avoid using sandwich boxes again. Otherwise, my kit is similar to last time. My newest toy is a solar charger for my phone, a well-thought-out leaving gift from my work colleagues.

Michal and I meet Agnes on the water off Trégastel Plage, among mooring buoys and boats. She paddles over in a green top, wide-brimmed hat and purple glasses, comes alongside and kisses us on both cheeks. 'Bonjour!' she says in a very French kayak greeting. Agnes is a kayak coach and guide based in North Brittany, and today she'll be taking us around the Sept-Îles, an archipelago of 5 islands and two reefs. On Agnes's suggestion we start by paddling out to Île Rouzic, the furthest island about 7.5 kilometres from the coast. We see the island through the mist, and closer in, craggy green humps make me feel like an ancient explorer coming upon uninhabited land.

The island is full of birds. Shags stand on the rocks drying their wings, guillemots perch on ledges and, above, gannets circle and wheel, silhouetted against the light grey sky, like aeroplanes in an air show. We paddle clockwise around the island and the 22,000-strong gannet colony becomes visible; the sound of the birds is incredible, and I've never seen so many at once. This is not a human place, it's an island owned by the birds, claimed by nature. It feels amazing to be back in the middle of it, a visitor to the wild. Even here it's sad to see how much plastic and nylon rope is in the birds' nests. I feel like I could stay here all day watching the amazing spectacle. Puffins bob on the water on the way back, then we see huge seals with long dark horse-like snouts. We drift with them, following their big nostrils.

We visit two more islands, Malban and Bono, accompanied by some storm petrels, then head towards the lighthouse on Île aux Moines, the only island accessible to the public.

Landing on the beach next to a collapsed walkway, it is cold, overcast and damp. The red granite contrasts with the turquoise of the water and the lighthouse looks like it grew out of the rock. The only other people on the island arrive in a rib and unload material to fix the lighthouse, as a man on the lantern cleans the windows, like the main character from the children's book *The Lighthouse Keeper's Lunch*. It's a fast paddle back with seals following us, as the tide pushes between the rocks, land whooshing past.

Coming into the beach the water is so clear that even far out we can see right down to the bottom. Huge pink granite boulders seem piled up to the sides or submerged like hippopotami in the sand, giving the Pink Granite Coast its name. We decide we're not done with the Portland area yet, and spend the evening planning a trip out to Bréhat, a tidal archipelago next to the most northerly point in Brittany.

Happy to see a bit of blue sky behind the clouds, we launch off a small, reinforced iron slipway with views out past huge cardinal markers whose cones in different positions signal where the danger is, towards La Croix Lighthouse. We first see it from the back, a double tower of dull concrete with red tops, but as we pass, we notice that from the front it gives an altogether different impression, painted white with a clear name badge. It reminds me of how I felt dressed up for the House of Lords – although I'm pretty sure my backside was covered.

We feel the tidal push towards the island passing clusters of rocks. These waters have one of the biggest tidal differences in the world, which can be up to 13 meters (even more than Jersey). When we arrive, it's a little disappointing: a posh tourist island. It feels like Salcombe: money, fake castle turrets and very much human land. 'That one would be mine,'

Michal says to me, pointing out a brick mansion set back from the water with what looks like a stone space rocket stuck on the side.

'Well that one's mine,' I say, pointing at a more-or-less tasteful one nestled next to a big lump of granite.

'Too normal.' Michal obliges me to pick a more castle-like one. It's not long before we find parts that are a bit more exposed and uninhabited, and begin to understand why French kayakers like it here so much. Birds surround us once again, as the ancient pink fingers below the headland point to the light-blue sky. As the tide goes out, we see more interesting rock features. The water starts to swirl and bubble, breaking up the glassy surface and becoming choppy, and a tide race invites us to paddle it on our way back.

Marc and I have exchanged a few emails since we met at the Jersey symposium, and he invites Michal and me to his home town of Lanloup. 'It's a good base camp,' he says. 'You can put your tents up in the garden.' He makes us feel very welcome and we sit down with some maps, a few local Coreff beers and squeeze him for information about kayaking in Brittany. For someone who learnt to kayak in the dark Icelandic winter five years ago, he's already got a lot of experience in Brittany. 'For tomorrow,' he says, 'you should go to the "Grotte du Sorcier" – the witches' cave. There is an arch you can go through at high tide, it's very nice.'

'Great,' I smile. 'We've done rocks, islands and a tide race, so it's time for cliffs and caves.'

The next day Michal and I are on Bréhec beach in our big coats, tucking into salami and cheese baguettes, wondering when summer will begin. It's mid-June now but the morning is cold. But we set off south-east and are instantly too hot. It feels good to get into the shade of the coast with its many caves and rocks. We paddle through some of them, foam and bubbles forming on the water as we manoeuvre backwards through the granite caves. We spot Marc's kayak heading across the water and wave to him, pleased he could leave work to join us. He points out Gwin Zégal, one of only two Nordic harbours in France, before we land, have a quick lunch of baguettes, and continue down to Bonaparte Bay.

'This was an important place for the Resistance,' Marc tells us. 'Agents used Morse Code with lights (long, short short short) to tell British ships it was safe to collect people.' From January to August 1944 'Operation Bonaparte' evacuated 136 evaders to England, most of whom were airmen, but there were also French agents and civilians. 'It was Breton farmers who brought people through the tunnels in the rock.'

It's a fascinating piece of history that is easy to imagine as we pass the impressive rock structures. At one point, we spot oysters covering the rocks. 'This is what freedom looks like for an oyster,' Marc says before explaining that a nearby oyster farm recently got smashed up in a storm. We spend the afternoon chatting about kayaking and squeezing through gaps in the rocks before heading back up to the other side of the bay to check out the Phare de L'Ost-Pic, a stunted, castle-like lighthouse, with no obvious difference between the structure and the light. Past the lighthouse we paddle to the Bréhat islands from the other side. The archipelago is very pretty, and bright green seaweed adds texture to turquoise water like expensive wallpaper. A barbecue and cold beers are waiting for us that evening, and Marc and his wife Sandrine's hospitality is a lovely end to our time in Portland.

Part 4

ENDS OF THE EARTH

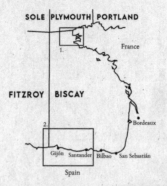

SOLE PLYMOUTH PORTLAND

France

FITZROY BISCAY

Bordeaux

Gijón Santander Bilbao San Sebastián

Spain

1.

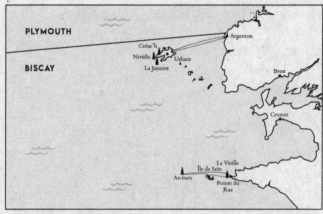

PLYMOUTH

BISCAY

Créac'h Argenton
Nividic
Ushant
La Jument

Brest

Crozon

La Vieille
Île de Sein
Ar-men Pointe du
Raz

2.

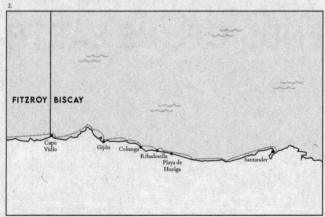

FITZROY BISCAY

Cape
Vidío Gijón Colunga
Ribadesella
Playa de Santander
Huelga

BISCAY: WILD SEAS AND GREEN SPAIN

Michal and I have been building up to Biscay, whose wave heights and tough seas are infamous among paddlers, sailors and commercial ships alike. The Shipping Forecast area traces the edge of the wide inverse 'C' shape created by the coasts of Western France and Northern Spain on the east and an imaginary line from 160 kilometres below the Scilly Isles to just past Avilés in Spain on the west. It has no land in the British Isles and is one of the larger areas whose sea state is often 'rough' or 'very rough'.

We've spent time on YouTube watching expert kayakers paddling enormous waves off Pointe du Raz on the tip of French Finisterre, and as we pass the brown tourist signs, a nervous excitement builds. If Biscay in general is a bit worrying, Pointe du Raz is properly scary. 'Just be careful,' Marc made us promise before leaving, 'and don't forget your helmet, it's like white water on the sea.' We follow a path through purple heather and yellow gorse on the long headland, rocky shards pointing up beneath us. A serious-looking watchtower, converted from the original Pointe du Raz lighthouse, looms over us, and in front of it is a statute of Our Lady of the Shipwrecked. I hope we don't need her help. As we get to the end of the peninsula a sign reads, 'Beyond this point, you proceed at your own risk, over uneven land where your progress will prove extremely difficult.'

'Sometimes that's life,' Michal offers as we step on to the uneven rocks to get a look at the infamous Raz de Sein tide race below. The water is moving fast and breaking below the headland. It's strange to be somewhere that I've built up so much in my mind.

'It's less crazy than other stuff we've done,' I say as we eat bread, *saucisson* and cider.

'Yeah, I think we can do it,' Michal shrugs, and we scramble back to the car. Our confidence subsides somewhat as we head to the intimidatingly named *Baie des Trépassés*, 'Bay of the Dead' to find our campsite.

The waves look much bigger standing on the beach early the next morning, but we launch anyway. It's fast but manageable, and takes us an hour and a half to round the end of the world past the Phare de la Vieille. The waves feel big but not scary, so we play in them for a while, surfing from one to another – all good practice for if we want to be really daring and cross to the Île de Sein or Ar-men, the lighthouse we can just about make out 20 kilometres away.

I had contacted a man called Nico over the internet, having seen amazing pictures of him kayaking the rough, tidal waters of Brittany. In broken, internet-translated French, I said I wanted to kayak wild seas. Let's just say that you have to be careful what you wish for. Nico is a thoughtful, gentle man with a wry smile, he exudes calm, and has short, greying hair and a distinctive laugh. 'Tomorrow we should go to Ouesant,' he suggests. 'There are only small waves in the Raz de Sein so it'll be more interesting next week.' Ushant ('Ouessant' in French) is, at 12 nautical miles off the coast of Finisterre, notoriously inaccessible. Steeped in rich maritime history, myth and folklore, it is a well-known feature for any seafarer crossing or entering the English Channel. Often cloaked in mist, surrounded by strong, fast-moving tides, with submerged rocks, it's exposed to anything the Atlantic throws at it. Ever since reading about it, I've been intrigued by this place, which due to the difficulty of getting there, doesn't have a section in the otherwise comprehensive Brittany sea-kayaking guidebook. Advice from other paddlers has ranged from 'don't go there' to 'only when it's perfectly calm and not spring tides'. We meet in the afternoon to look at charts, tides and bearings while Nico searches for a more agreeable weather forecast.

Later, it's a warm, still evening and the sun is high in the sky. Two women in swimsuits skip light-footedly along the path from the beach, barefoot, shaking saltwater from their wet hair. Nico introduces us to Pauline and her friend, who welcomes us to her impromptu housewarming party. Pauline works for a French surf brand. Her house has a flat roof and a large patio, with steps and a steep bank down to a brilliantly overgrown garden. Large glazed, sliding doors lead on to the terrace; the sofa and chairs are outside and a small group of people lounge around the table. A surfboard sits propped against the wall in the simple lounge with some select bits of furniture, white walls and a concrete floor. The place exudes simple, effortless cool and Michal and I begin to wonder what we are doing here. Other guests start to arrive and the party gains momentum. Women offer hands to kiss on being introduced and respond with '*enchantée*,' which I thought was reserved mainly for spoof French films. One man brings a small gas-powered barbecue and the meal gets started.

It's a trendy crowd that wouldn't be out of place in East London. We watch the sunset over the beach, the grassy humps of the dune landscape silhouetted against the pink-orange sky. At one point I'm quizzed on my level of Englishness as someone has spotted a ginger tinge in my beard, and I explain that my mum's family are Welsh and I have some Celtic heritage, which seems to go down well. Nico's girlfriend Margot asks how we know each other. 'We don't,' is the simplest answer. 'We just arranged to meet on Facebook.'

'I see, kayak Tinder,' says Margot with a knowing smile.

The night drifts on and darkness rolls in with a cooling breeze. Music from the lounge wafts through the air, a mixture of chill-out, remixed piano jazz and soft vocals drifting in and out, mixed with French hip hop and dubstep. We briefly look at the conditions and plan again as Nico crushes ice and mint for mojitos in the kitchen. At this point of the evening, the prospect of paddling seems like an abstract idea, let alone in rough conditions, but there's a chink of wild energy and excitement in the air between the three of us.

I wake up dishevelled, groggy and confused, having fallen asleep on the grass under some tarp strung between cars. 'Up, up, up!' Nico shouts with an otherworldly amount of energy and enthusiasm. I realise it's daytime and crawl out, mumbling something and shying away from the bright light of day like a nocturnal animal. I sort myself out, imbibe a large cup of coffee and sit with the others around the table to check the tides, forecasts and distances once more. We're undeterred by the weather warnings on the radio, of 5-metre waves and a rising Force 7 wind from the north-east. 'That's not right, waves from the north are never that big. Fetch is too small,' says Nico, referring to how far the wind has blown to create the wave. I assume he means it's only had the 200 kilometres from Cornwall to build up.

It's raining and cold (not quite what I expected for the end of June) as we approach Port d'Argenton where we will launch. Looking out over the bay, I can just see the lighthouse at du Four, but the visibility isn't great. We have time to spare so get a coffee at the *tabac* facing the harbour and watch as the cloud lifts, revealing a blue sky. A series of postcards are on display of huge waves in winter storms crashing over the tops of an assortment of lighthouses on the Brittany coast. It includes the iconic image of La Jument, caught as the keeper opened the door to investigate the helicopter noise, then closed it again before a monstrous wave reared up and enveloped the whole structure. In contrast, a group of people on a painting class stand with easels against the harbour wall painting the summer scene emerging in front of us. It's very French. One person may have even been wearing a beret.

Under blue skies, we pack and carry our boats, get changed and check our safety kit. Launching around

2 p.m., we're quickly outside the shelter of the bay, and on our way to Ushant. Nico has a small orange sail on the back of his kayak, which flaps and billows in the wind. There's some movement on the water and it's possible to surf the waves that are intermittently surging forwards. It's exciting and lively. 'Super-fun conditions!' shouts Nico at one point, giving a thumbs up and grinning. The waves steepen and build into a rolling sea, peaking and breaking in places. It's possible to surf some of them but not all. I am bracing hard as they slap and spray the kayak. The visibility drops and we can no longer see land; the lighthouse is far behind us, submerged in the mist. The sea turns a silvery steely grey. We're faithfully paddling on a bearing of 300 degrees into nothingness. The wind increases and, for almost three hours, there's no break from the white noise of it battering my ears. The sea stretches out into big peaks and troughs like a roller coaster. I see a sailing boat briefly on the horizon moving quickly and crashing on to the big grey waves. They become steeper in places and it's hard to turn the boat in the wind or to keep it tracking forwards; some are easier to catch and surge forwards with speed. I keep my eyes focused ahead, looking at the others and the flapping orange sail on Nico's boat. It feels wild and exposed.

We change our bearing slightly; the period between the waves has increased and we briefly lose sight of each other between one trough and the next. Small ridges rippling like tiny scales appear on the water, while the wind occasionally whips the paddle, trying to take it away. Nico takes in the sail as the sky becomes ominous. I sometimes think I can see land but realise it's just the rising waves ahead: from the bottom of the trough, they seem tall and imposing, then they wash under the kayak which rises and falls in rhythm. We shout over to each other. Nico looks at the GPS and starts to count down the kilometres to land; the others say they can see lights, but I can't. Eventually, peering through the mist, a faint shadowy outline emerges, giving a scale to the waves. Michal sees a small white cross on a distant headline. Paddling in these conditions requires clear focus – we can't communicate properly, we just need to keep paddling to get through it.

The height of the waves picks up as we get closer, and they start to occasionally break in the open sea. Rearing up, peaking and crashing, they're too steep to surf with our loaded boats, so judgement and timing are critical. A tower in the distance signals the end of an offshore reef; the waves crash up and over its yellow and black stripes as we aim for a gap between the tower and the land. We head for the shelter of the south-east corner, behind a string of rocks stretching out into the sea. I sit, teetering on the top of a wave, paddling back to avoid catching it. I feel it rising then washing under the kayak and breaking in front of me, the smooth back trailing and washing forwards, our small boats at the mercy of the angry sea. I knew setting off that we were launching into challenging conditions, but I hadn't imagined the intense focus required to push away any doubts that we would actually make it.

Gradually the waves get smaller, the sea calms and there is a break in the constant noise; we're in flatter waters with gentle surf, gliding between small rocks with the dark cliffs looming above. The sense of relief and sharp contrast is overwhelming and surreal. I feel an intense sensation of achievement on reaching the safety and shelter of the land. A beautiful bay opens up with a small, deserted harbour, white sandy beach and turquoise water like some sort of paradise. We land with wild excitement, high-fiving on the beach and jumping on the ground, not quite sure what has just happened but with a deep sense of being alive.

It's nearly 6 p.m. by the time we've carried the boats up the beach, still shaking and gabbling with excitement. We go in search of a celebratory drink to check that this paradise beach isn't just a figment of our imaginations. The narrow road meanders past small, white houses with azure-blue-painted frames. I can still hear the roar of the sea rolling around my ears and the gentle rising and falling motion of the waves which pummel the shoreline in the distance. Multicoloured hydrangeas and the towering stems of tree echiums lurch and bend over walls and fences as we reach the small town. The pub is a triangular room, wood-panelled with photos of lighthouses and stormy seas covering the walls. As we raise our glasses and toast our survival, the slow, anthemic chorus of 'We Are the Champions' rolls out through the pub, and church bells ring in the background. It feels poignant and in our wired state of mind, we're still not sure if it's real.

After a few more rounds, we amble back in the dark; the wind is still howling. The tiny single-storey cottages have red lights on the top to warn low-flying planes – various lights flash and pan around, picking out this elusive lump of rock to the night watch.

'Tired, eh?' says Nico, seeing me yawn as I take my tent out of its bag.

'Yeah, you need so much focus when the sea's like that,' I reply 'It's tiring.'

'It helps me relax,' says Nico, carefully unravelling his tent.

'Really? I'm not sure I'd call it relaxing.'

'I mean in my head. You can only focus in the moment. It's like you are connected with nature.' He says, 'it's not possible to think of anything else.'

'That's true,' says Michal, throwing his things into his tent.

'It's like a cure for whatever's going on in your life,' I say, getting my tent up.

'Exactly,' says Nico. He has had some time off work for stress.

Nico produces a small chopping board, knife and a *saucisson* from one of the hatches in his boat. 'We should rename Biscay "saucisson",' I joke, as he shares it out, and they both agree. Exhausted, content and relieved, we lie down in the tents, listening to the sea breaking on the beach as sleep washes in.

The next day it's still windy and the sea is riled and angry. There are smaller waves lapping at the sheltered beach, and the carpet of yellow lichen on the granite slipway just catches the sun pushing through the mist and low cloud. The light reflects off the shimmering water, turning the view to a silvery monochrome slide. It's still poor visibility and the headlands hang in between the mist. My eyes are bleary and my ankles and neck are sore. Leaning on the parapet at the top of a wall and staring out to sea, I listen to the sounds of the morning. No other people, no boats, no connection to what's beyond the thick enveloping cloak. It feels like the end of the end of the earth and I soak in the sense of glorious isolation.

Leaving the small town, we see the prominent black and white striped tower of the Créac'h Lighthouse. With a range of 69.5 kilometres, it is the brightest lighthouse in Europe. From the middle of the English Channel on a clear night, legend has it that you can see both the light of the Créac'h and the beam from the lighthouse at Lizard Point. It sits on the rocky, north-west coast of the island on a stretch of land that reaches out into the Atlantic like a crab claw on the map. The lighthouse is now home to a museum about these guardians of the coastline and has one of the world's biggest collections of Fresnel lenses. In 1825, French physicist Augustin-Jean Fresnel developed a new kind of lighthouse lens, using prisms that captured all the light from a source, magnified it and steered it in one direction. When he died aged 39, his brother Léonor drove the implementation of his design. Eventually Fresnel lenses were installed in thousands of lighthouses around the world, increasing the power of their beams and saving millions of lives.

The crumbly coast below the Créac'h is otherworldly. Sharp, claw-like fingers reach out, somewhere between drowning limbs, teeth and jaws gesturing at the pounding sea. The gnawed remnants of concrete buildings and structures grow out of this strange landscape: a ruined foghorn, a look-out platform, bridges and steps. Twisted and mangled ironwork, evidence as if it were needed of the futility of our efforts to tame such a wild beast. The tower of Nividic Lighthouse is visible around the corner with a string of tall concrete posts leading out to it like the outstretched necks of giraffes. Now automated, it marks the western extent of the island. The concrete posts would have held a cable used to supply the lighthouse, totally inaccessible in anything but the calmest of seas and even then a risky approach due to the number of sharp rocks just beneath the surface.

It's late afternoon and we seek shade under the awning of a small bar which overlooks a paved square between several small lanes. Inside, while I wait to be served, I notice a pigeon strutting around in the corner, beneath a stand with a keyboard on it, a gold-stranded foil shimmer curtain and handwritten fluorescent signs advertising a karaoke night. It's an odd scene and I'm not sure whether the pigeon is rehearsing. No one seems particularly bothered. Eventually I take the drinks outside. It transpires that the pigeon is a bit of a local celebrity. 'Bob' the carrier pigeon came to the island against the odds, and is only the second pigeon to land there in living memory. He struts along, appearing in the doorway and hopping down a step and on to the street; he's one of the regulars in the bar.

A small car trundles down the hill, momentarily disrupting the lazy afternoon. As we sip our cold lager there's a loud pop, like someone bursting open a bag of crisps. We look round to see a clutch of grey feathers under the wheel of the car. The warm air hangs in the square, which is filled with silence. Onlookers freeze with their gaze fixed on the car in disbelief. The pause seems to last forever. Then, in an instant, the woman behind the wheel drives off, leaving the flapping, twitching cluster of feathers stuck to the cobbles. Before anyone has any time to act, another driver in quick pursuit looks at the casualty and without a second thought drives over what's left of Bob, sealing his fate. The shocked crowd looks on, slowly processing what has just happened: the sudden demise of the most recent local celebrity. Life is harsh here. Nico gets up and prods the flattened body to move it aside from the middle of the square and save any further destruction. It seems Bob has lived out the old Breton proverb that 'He who sees Ushant, sees his own blood.'

Before heading back to the boats to pitch tents, we walk out along the southern pincer of the claw enclosing the harbour, following reports that a dead Fin whale has been washed up. Its huge, deflated carcass is strewn across the rocks in a small bay, decomposing. A strand of red and white warning tape flaps around on the hillside above the beach. The smell, like rotten eggs, is overpowering and we're careful not to stand downwind of it. I've been lucky to see whales close up when kayaking in Greenland and it's sad to see such a majestic creature laid out like an old balloon. It acts as a reminder of the remoteness of this outpost on the edge of the vast Atlantic Ocean.

We launch the following day in poor visibility, but on much calmer seas. A rolling swell and fast current pick up as we cross the Fromveur Passage. We can hear the buzz of boat engines in the distance; it's hard to judge how close they are in the whiteout that surrounds us. Nico radios the coastguard and speaks with the ferry captain, who's well away from where we are. The energy of the sea is decreasing and feels relaxed as I pass a sunfish basking in the water, floating on its side. A counterpoint to the energy of the outward leg, time moves slowly as we drift through the white haze. Eventually, we hear birds and the distant rumble of traffic, signalling that we're near. Distant outlines shape themselves into more certain forms as we hit the coast a little further south than we started. Before we know it, we're having a coffee overlooking the small harbour again, no need for the postcard images of waves smashing on the lighthouses any more as we each have our own, etched in our memory.

'Tuesday should be good for big waves on Raz de Sein,' says Nico as I wonder what 'big waves' look like compared to the ones we've already seen. Michal and I spend four sedate days exploring the colourful caves around Crozon. The sea is like an over-excited family pet, bouncing and bounding. I like to be with it, in its company, part of it. Standing back on the beach at the Bay of the Dead looking out over the swell of the Raz de Sein as it peaks and falls, I'm feeling apprehensive about the 'big waves'. Nico is pushing, careering and rocketing forward. 'Hey Toby!' he shouts as he pirouettes the boat, making it do tricks. I wait like a scared child on the side of a swimming pool, until the wave height drops so I can launch and catch a few. 'I'll do better tomorrow,' I tell them and myself. I hate being a wuss, but I'm not sure I'm good enough for these waves.

'It's only water,' Nico says the next day by way of reassurance. He's right, and I've certainly been in more dangerous, life-threatening situations, so I paddle out. The flow in the first channel is faster but flatter than the day before. We make our way across and explore between the rocks further out. I lean forwards and paddle hard. It's calm beyond the reef but then the waves build in mounds rather than lines, peaking up like globs of cream meringue.

Nico surfs them with rapid ease as Michal tries to keep up. I take a deep breath, think 'it's only water' and get into the tide race. The first pass is bouncy, fast and fun. I can feel my confidence building. On my second pass, Nico is taking pictures. 'Do it for the BBC!' he shouts as I push myself harder. The boat is on the peak of a wave, and I can hear crashing behind me. I feel it tipping and set up for a roll but don't make it and end up swimming in the warm sea. Nobody minds. Refreshed by the dip, I relax and enjoy surfing more waves. I'm pleased I've pushed myself harder and paddled some big scary waves. Nico, however, is disappointed as we paddle back to the beach: 'I thought the waves would be bigger.'

We spend five days in south Brittany with another local paddler, Jerome, while also waiting for a weather window to paddle out to the remote Ar-men lighthouse. When lighthouses were manned, the French keepers categorised them into heaven, purgatory or hell, depending on whether they were on the mainland, on an island or offshore. At 20 kilometres from the mainland, Ar-men is so exposed to the Atlantic it was known as 'Hell of Hells'. Leaving before 5 a.m., Michal and I paddle out on the smooth flat water, watching the sun rise slowly on the horizon. A pod of playful dolphins joins us jumping and turning in a wheel, so close that we can hear them breathing. It's a moment of beauty that makes me feel joy and sadness at the same time.

Crossing the Raz de Sein, we've calculated the tides right and can't believe that something we thought would be a huge challenge is turning out to be easy. As we approach the battered grey and white structure of Ar-men (literally meaning 'the rock'), a man in a white t-shirt and baggy blue trousers calls out to us, 'Bonjour, bonjour,' as surprised as us to meet other people this far out into the sea. A combination of my bad French and his bits of English gets us invited to tie our boats to the ladder and climb on to the base. A few more smiles and gestures and the man, who introduces himself as Antoine, asks 'Would you like to come inside?'

'Yes please!' It's an amazing opportunity and I feel so lucky: the group of engineers are only there for four days a year. Ar-men is small inside, due to the diameter of the base and the thickness of the walls, built to withstand huge crashing waves. A winding staircase leads us up to a kitchen not unlike a ship's galley where Marc is preparing chicken and couscous for lunch. 'You are welcome to join,' he says, 'we don't get many visitors.'

'Ah, *non merci,*' I reply, scared that it would be easy to get stuck here but keen to have a nose around. We walk up to the next level: a tiny bedroom with wooden bunks and a table. The floor after that is a work area and above that the lantern room. On the balcony around the light, the views of the sea are endless, and our kayaks look tiny in the shadow of the lighthouse. 'Not a bad view, eh?' Antoine says.

'Amazing!'

I'm nervous – we need to leave if we are to ride the tide back. The team wave us off on water that feels like we are being pulled along on a shiny tablecloth. I carry the lightness of being on the water with me, through the pink and orange sunset and on to the ferry at Roscoff the next day.

Three days later I'm back in Biscay, arriving on the ferry to Santander. Michal and his car have stayed in the UK and I'm on my own from here. Launching on a grey day with a gusting wind, I remember the start of my trip in Iceland, feeling apprehensive about paddling alone, and I'm pleased I feel much more confident as I cross the wide city beaches of Santander towards something wilder and freer. Before long, lush greenery lines the top of layered rocks and headlands jut out.

I don't have a plan other than to keep the land on the left, the sea on the right and paddle west. There's 200 kilometres of the coast of the Biscay Shipping Forecast area to discover before it becomes FitzRoy. I've heard about green Spain but didn't believe it would be so similar to Brittany or Cornwall. I spend long days paddling between sandy beaches flanked with grey rocks, some striped like plywood and topped off with green. The sea tries on many colours each day before becoming petroleum blue for the sunset. Caves are hollowed out of the cliffs, their dark mouths bearing stalagmites, inviting exploration and reminding me of Mike's love of potholing. I think back to his funeral, where I put together the photos from his life to be projected. So many of them were of him outside exploring. A good way to be remembered, I think.

A little further on, Fernando – tall, tanned and energetic – meets me with his matching white Tiderace kayak. We've been messaging since Jerome in Brittany put us in contact, and I'm pleased he's come to show me his rocky playground at Cuevas del Mar. I've been apprehensive going into caves so far because without local knowledge, it's easy to get into trouble. The sun comes out and the sea has a sparkly allure as we pass through the massive arch at Playa de Huelga. It's like the Dorset coast but on steroids. 'See you tomorrow,' shouts Fernando as he paddles in to the beach where his wife is picking him up, and I continue. The wind increases, causing the waves to crash hard against the flat rock, suggesting I should find shelter for what looks like a stormy night.

Thunder rumbles. I see lightning through my closed eyes and the humidity aggravates the eczema I have developed across my chest and shoulders. I lie inside the tent, itchy, uncomfortable and not knowing what to do with myself, until the clanging of Asturian cows tells me it's morning. Their friendly faces, like Jersey cows but darker, cheer me up and help me focus on the beauty of the place. I'm exhausted but I launch, fuelled by the need to keep moving. I weave my way through caves and arches to Ribadesella, then I wheel my kayak into Fernando's garden.

Sitting in the yellow kitchen, with charts laid out over the checked tablecloth, we chat about my journey as Chisato, Fernando's wife, plays flowing piano music. It's a return to civilisation. After Fernando tells me what to expect on the coast of Asturias, including some dinosaur prints, we talk about the determination needed for expedition kayaking. 'When you see a headland in the distance, you think "I can't do it",' Fernando comments, 'but little by little you get there.'

'It makes me think most things are possible, if you keep going,' I agree. 'And if you have enough time.'

We wander around the town, where blue paddles make up fence railings along the promenade, and many of the houses are *Indianas*, the summer homes of Asturians who made their fortunes in the Americas and came back to build small palaces. They are all turrets and towers, complicated windows and bright colours. 'No two windows are the same,' Fernando tells me. If the design brief was to impress, they certainly do. Looking around, it feels like the rest of the world may not exist beyond this bay.

I sleep in a bed and launch the next day, revived and in search of dinosaurs. The clear green sea laps against cliff faces, which are accident-prone hills that have fallen into the sea. Visibility drops and I'm left with the occasional rock sticking out of the water as a marker. I'm inside a Turner painting, soft pastel shades blurring the line between the sky and sea, on another plane where it's easy to imagine the dinosaurs stepping out and leaving their massive prints on the beach. The mist clears and I notice the bark of the sloping pine trees at the back of the beach curling around their trunks, and a series of boulders stretching out into the sea. The prints are impressive, around 80 cm across: they are the largest in the world from the Jurassic era. I find it exciting. Katie's just had her second son, Max, and I imagine sharing it with him and Llorenç. I've known since my bone marrow transplant that I can't have children, but I do love being an uncle and a godfather.

Sea and sky merge a few more times as I approach Gijón. Passing the last headland before the harbour I see the Eduardo Chillida sculpture, 'Eulogy for the Horizon', its poetic name making more sense than its huge curved concrete structure, which caused a stir when it was erected.

As I glide into the industrial city, focused on finding a landing spot, I think about my five weeks in Biscay, pleased that I've kayaked in the French and Spanish sides of it, caught big waves, paddled through caves and kept on exploring.

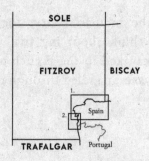

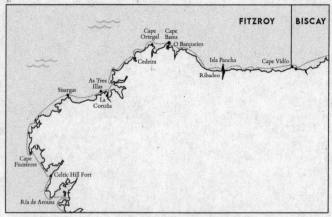

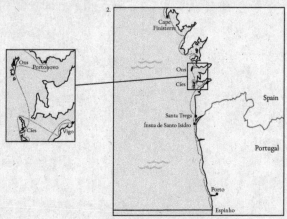

FITZROY: SPANISH FJORDS
AND THE *BEAGLE*

The day I'm due to enter the FitzRoy Shipping Forecast area I wake up and walk to the sea in my pants. The water is a milky turquoise as I hold them in my hands, floating naked. It's liberating, so calm, the temperature – neither warm nor cold – is just there. I think of Grandma Betty making Marcus go in the sea in his pants years ago and Grandpa Frank floating, sculling in the water. The clouds have golden linings and gentle waves caress the shore as I step back on to the tropical-looking beach. 'Free as a Bird' enters my head and I cue it up on Spotify. My parents were big Beatles fans long ago; as kids we knew all the songs.

I wait for the tide and more people arrive. I dry my wet clothes on a makeshift clothesline constructed with my paddles and some rope, until the wind increases, liberating them across the beach. Bigger waves start coming in and I gather up my things. I won't be leaving today after all. There's a movement in the trees like a prelude to something happening in a horror film: pine needles fall, people disappear and the sea rears like an angry monster, further and further up the beach. I'm quickly trapped between it and a rock face as I realise I should have moved to the other side. Thunder explodes across the beach and a wave smashes into my kayak, crashing it into the rocks. A man in peach shorts and a straw hat rushes around the corner to help me. I'm shaken and sheepishly thankful; I know I shouldn't have let down my guard. Later, as the waves beat the shore, I lie at the back of the beach under the intensity of stars, picking out constellations and watching the occasional shooting star. They feel like a connection across time. Nearly 190 years ago, FitzRoy used these same stars to navigate HMS *Beagle* to Patagonia with Charles Darwin aboard.

Over the next few days I slip into a rhythm with nature and the tides, until it finally seems calm enough for me to leave. I choose my moment and paddle fast. Getting over the first few waves, I see steepening faces in front of me which peak and foam into a barrelling mess. I try to paddle back but it's too late, I'm in it, pushed backwards into the foam, surfing for a moment before it whips me around and I'm under. A quick flick and I'm back up, riding a wave sideways trying to get the kayak back under control – it works and I point the boat forwards into the next wave, jumping up and slamming down into the aerated foam. I keep punching through and finally reach the end of the surf zone. Relief washes over me and I take a moment to recompose myself on the open water before nonchalantly rounding Cape Vidío, my GPS beeping to tell me I'm in my penultimate area outside the British Isles: FitzRoy.

Named after the founder of what became the Met Office, FitzRoy is the largest Shipping Forecast area, about the same size as Spain, with around 550 kilometres of coastline in its south-east corner. When I listened to the forecast as a child, this area was called Finisterre, but in 2002, in the most polemic Shipping Forecast decision of recent years, Finisterre was renamed FitzRoy. I feel pleased that the man who invented the concept of 'forecasting' is the only person to have an area named after him.

Ten and a half hours later, I'm celebrating with an Estrella Galicia beer and a packet of crisps in a *chiringuito* beach bar I located on Google Maps. It's been a long day. The constant fight with the boat and the wind has chafed my wrist and the skin is rubbed away and sore. Since there's no place associated with FitzRoy, I've fixed my sights on Cape Finisterre: unfolding the chart, I can see I'm about halfway there, as I wonder whether I'll find a trace of FitzRoy the man in this area. Back on the water, just before I reach Isla Pancha Lighthouse, marking the start of Galicia, the land becomes a crumbly orange, with small islands, lumps of rock and holes. I catch a flash of grey, look around and see several fins, then the sleek, silent curves of five dolphins passing by. It is a joyful thing, so calm and peaceful and a perfect end to my time in beautiful Asturias.

In Ribadeo, Tito – another kayaking friend of Jerome's who I contacted a few days before – invites me to stay at his canoe club, 'Alturuán'. I sleep next to my boat in a clubhouse full of gym equipment and kayaks – it's perfect. The next day, I meet Tito and we paddle over to As Catedrais a few kilometres west. I follow him under the huge rocky arches which tumble out of the headlands, planting their heavy feet in the sea like paddling elephants. Some are easy to get through, others are more challenging. We rock, hop and surf, revelling in the connection we feel with kayaking and the sea. 'You can't always get through all the arches,' Tito says later, with respect, 'it's all about timing.'

'Yeah, I noticed!' I laugh, referring to a failed attempt of mine where I ended up swimming.

'I'm not sure I understand your trip,' says Tito as we sit on the beach.

'I'm trying to kayak in the best places of the British maritime weather forecast areas. Here we're in FitzRoy, which in the Spanish Forecast is still called Finisterre.'

'FitzRoy, the Captain of the *Beagle*?'

'Yes, he also invented our forecast.'

'You should go to Vigo, there's a scale model of the ship in the museum.'

'Really?' I say, excited that I might find a trace of FitzRoy in this rugged corner of Spain. Before I leave, Tito gives me more tips for the next bit of coast and wishes me well.

I spend two days watching the rocks change from jagged grey formations to a sculpture garden for seafarers, spotting golden sandy beaches tucked away in tree-lined bays. On my way to O Barqueiro to meet Raquel, a friend of Katie's, the water is mesmerising, undulating in a blue and silver camouflage pattern. At first I think there are marker buoys in the middle of the estuary, then I make out people frantically waving and shouting. Looking behind me to see what they are waiting for, I realise: it's me. Raquel is a mermaid, knee-deep in the water in a shiny silver bikini with her long curly hair flowing over her shoulders. She's with her sister, Carmela, brother-in-law, Ángel and their two boys, Gael and Roque who are excitedly jumping around. It's a lovely welcome! I find it quite emotional as I paddle in to the beach, the kids running alongside me.

The small town nestled into the hillside seems inviting and open. Three-storey white houses with overhanging balconies are punctuated by a few painted in saturated burgundy, green and blue. I leave my kayak on the stone slipway to go for lunch over the other side. In La Marina restaurant I see why Galicia is famous for food: delicious shellfish of many varieties appears before me. A plate of witches' fingers is served. 'What's that?' I ask Raquel.

'*Percebes* – um, gooseneck barnacles?' she checks the translation on her phone. I've never heard of them. 'It's a local delicacy.'

'You eat like this,' Ángel adds, peeling the outer layer off the long part and holding on to the claw on the other end. I give it a try, the wounds on my hands making it hard for me to open them.

'Mmm, tasty.' I enjoy the sweet fishy flavour, a bit like lobster.

Raquel passes a bowl of cockles, which briefly reminds me of a November day walking round Whitstable with Marcus, Katie and Andy, all knowing it would be our last day out together. I push that thought aside as I enjoy the delicious lunch and the warmth of this family. In the late afternoon, we have an Estrella Galicia at the Fisherman's Association, where nets hang over the balcony, then we all move up to Bares beach.

As the northernmost point in Spain, there's a rumour in Cape Bares that you can see underwear hanging on washing lines in England. It's about 700 kilometres to Cornwall, so few people are gullible enough to believe teasing fishermen. Sitting on the sand in the fading light as the kids play with the kayak, I ask Raquel what she loves about this coast. 'Nature and the weather here are rough, and not for the faint-hearted. We Galicians are like that too,' she jokes, 'especially the women!' We laugh, I give her a hug, despite her comment, and they leave, assuring me that they will catch up with me further along my route.

'Wow, that's an incredible journey!' says a softly spoken German man I meet on the beach the next day. I've just told him I'm paddling to Finisterre. I don't feel incredible right now, I need to be practical: round Cape Bares then Cape Ortegal. It will be a long day. Bares is a long ridge, dipping down at the end; I can see rocks sticking out in a line, grey with green patches. The glass dome of the lighthouse peeks out over gaps in the lichen-covered rock face. On the other side it reminds me of the Faroe Islands or Iceland: burnt rock like charcoal bricks. A smell of smoky iodine hits me as I go inside a cave with gooseneck barnacles on the rocks, where the swell washes over like a waterfall.

Long zigzag paths are they only human marks on the landscape as I approach Cape Ortegal. I know there will be nowhere to land until I reach Cedeira about 40 kilometres away, so I'm torn between spending the afternoon on the beach or paddling the distance in calm conditions. The forecast is for building swell later in the week. My hands are red and sting in the salt water, but aside from that, I feel strong and positive so I decide to push on. The tonal contrast of mountains and sea looks so Nordic that I feel at home. The swell increases and visibility drops, draping the cliffs in cloud and creating a mythical village huddled as if suspended. Cars have their headlights on. Not far now. I round the corner approaching Cedeira; the town should be in front of me, but it's been swallowed by the cloud. Fishing boats are clustered together for shelter. '¡Loco!' a fisherman shouts at me as I go past.

Once I get to Cedeira, it's somehow still summer, and leisure boats play carelessly in its sheltered harbour. I rest, walk around and the next day as I'm preparing to launch, a thin woman wearing a loose red dress approaches excitedly. 'Where have you come from?' she asks.

'From Santander.'

'Wow,' she says, genuinely interested. 'I'm Elsa.'

'Toby.'

'So where are you going?'

'To Porto' I say with a smile, because it still doesn't feel real.

'What?'

I give her an explanation of my trip as she listens intently.

'That's so interesting!' she says. 'I'm preparing a podcast on "dream lives", and how we can live the life we want. It sounds like that's what you're doing.'

'I guess I'm taking control of factors affecting my life and trying to turn them into something positive,' I say, wondering why it doesn't come out like that when the BBC interviews me.

'It sounds like you're facing the sea, connecting with nature and carrying through an idea. That's so inspiring.'

'Thanks,' I smile, feeling happy to be an inspiration to someone.

'Would you like a shower?' Elsa offers kindly. I look a mess and I'd very much like a shower, but I need to leave, so we swap contact details and Elsa promises to feature me on her podcast.

I launch and about an hour in, the fresh sea air changes and there's an oxide smell of rusty metal. I feel the presence of something before seeing the arched spine of an orca, awe-inspiring and graceful. I stay still and watch, breathing the moment in, recording it in my mind for later. I should be scared – they can easily tip over a kayak and have been known to deliberately damage yachts – but this one just swims around brightening my day. On the water, I have time to think about what Elsa said. I feel grateful for the deep experience of nature and human spirit I've had so far. I think if we can explore what we enjoy, we get closer to the idea of a 'dream life', and that is as much a state of mind as anything else, because so much can happen out of your control.

Days later, further down, the hope inspired by a good breakfast quickly descends into joylessness once I get on the water in a strong headwind and rain. I can see A Coruña looming in the distance but there's still a way to go. Visibility drops completely. Alone in the mist, with the deafening noise of wind in my ears, I'm hyper-aware of any bigger boats that won't see me. The fog lifts enough for me to get to Bastiagueiro beach, covered in rotting seaweed, and I decide to stay in a campsite, where I get my first shower since Elsa mentioned it. As the storm rolls in, I sleep under eucalyptus trees, feeling pleased to have paddled the whole of the chart Katie got me for Christmas: Santander to A Coruña. It's taken two-and-a-half weeks of long days on sea, embraced by nature and cheered on by connection with others.

Ángel, Raquel's brother-in-law, is a photographer in the city and has arranged for the regional paper *La Voz de Galicia* to interview me. I spend an hour rambling to the journalist, Mila, about my trip, happy it's not going to be broadcast as is. Afterwards, on the cliff, it's windy and the sea is whipped up and grey. I'm glad I'm not on it. I walk up to the yellow granite Tower of Hercules, the only fully preserved Roman lighthouse still in operation. Renovated in the 18th century, when additional stonework was added to the outside to preserve the original Roman structure, it's a huge lighthouse steeped in maritime history, stories and legends of the sea. A Coruña was an important port for the Romans; trade routes passed up the coast of Europe and this lighthouse marked a point of passage. Later, Sir Francis Drake (or Pirate Drake as the Spanish call him) led a siege here.

When I meet Ángel later at Plaza de María Pita, he hands me a press pass for the Noroeste music festival. I'm delighted, and by the end of an evening spent drinking beer and listening to the wild Celtic rock of Escuchando Elefantes in the wind and the rain, I'm convinced I'm a music journalist. The next day it's still windy so I do some planning, write my blog and go to a Patti Smith concert in the evening with Raquel. It's a brilliant way to sit out a storm, but I think of my card ripped in four by Natalie back in London and go in search of 'proper' adventure, leaving the campsite to sleep on a rocky island.

With the evening sun on my face and the water jumping up, I'm pleased to be moving again towards my destination of Finisterre. As Tres Illas, a rocky outcrop just off A Coruña, looked interesting on the chart and thankfully seems landable now. There is a stone structure with walls on two sides, like a big rock shelter, that will be my tent for the night. My gas runs out so I eat half-cooked pasta as waves crash around and I worry about whether I'll be able to leave. I wait until 2 a.m. in the drizzle to check how far up the water comes, then I go to sleep tired and relieved. Hardly the dream life, I think.

Rain falls on the water's surface creating circular ripple patterns, as I paddle to my next island, Sisarga Grande. The surface becomes a fine mist, making miniature valleys and landscapes on the water: eerie and beautiful. When I reach the island, the gannets circling above me make me feel safe, like they are a connection between places. I have a big view over the sea and despite the dramatic clouds, it is calm, full of possibility. The island has a post-apocalyptic feel, the flowered pattern on the tiles of a derelict cottage, so out of place in this orange lichen-covered territory of the birds.

Two days later a big slab of rock juts out into the sea like a door stop: Cape Finisterre, striking and more noticeable than the other headlands. I've been worried about paddling Death Coast, but now in my tiny boat with the wind behind me, I have a joyful feeling that I'm here and the weather is doing exactly what it was forecast to do. I think of FitzRoy and the idea of the forecast: an invention which has saved so many lives, and made even more adventures possible.

A beam of light silently rotates into the darkening sky, glinting in the diamond-glazed bars and shining on the inside of the glass. A gentle wind blows in the dusk and the soft swish of the swell on the sea wafts in the yellow reflection of the rising moon. The light from the tower picks up a sparkle in the rigging outside the lantern and the last of the pinky orange evening is reflected in the metalwork. I'm sitting watching the sun go down by the lighthouse on Cape Finisterre. It's a cool evening with the trill of crickets and some light jazz music drifting from a bar in the distance. I sit, absorbing the spectacle, until it gets fully dark and I wander back to my hostel with the smell of pine and eucalyptus trees in the breeze. It's a magical thing to see and makes me think of being immersed in a place and how tiny I must look from above, on my own in a small boat that has become my world on the ocean.

The next day my article is out in *La Voz de Galicia*. I buy a copy and sit with a coffee staring at myself on page 30, trying to decipher the Spanish. The map they've included shows me paddling the whole coast of Western Europe and as far as I can make out, the article ends with me saying. 'In times of national divisions, the sea and its shared stories can bring us together.' Not so bad at getting my point across, I think to myself. 'What are you reading that rag for?' the woman behind the counter says. I put the paper away, pretending to take notice of her and make sure she doesn't see my face in it.

In the afternoon, I sit in the hostel garden checking messages. Tom, a friend and ex-colleague of mine, says, 'We've got an associate lecturer job coming up at Falmouth, if you're interested after your trip. It's close to the sea!' I've been trying not to think about what I'll do for work when I'm back in a month or so, but moving to Cornwall is a nice idea, so I open the application form and fill it out on my phone. Walkers with sticks come into the garden, having finished the Camino de Santiago, and I'm pleased to have done my own version of it. I enjoy the idea of secular prayers and everyday rituals and think of Carol Ann Duffy's poem, 'Prayer', which ends: 'Darkness outside. Inside, the radio's prayer – Rockall. Malin. Dogger. Finisterre.'

'Where are you off to?' says the receptionist as I check out of my hippy dippy hostel.

'I'm going to kayak to Porto,' I reply. At a mere 200 kilometres, the journey looks like a hop, skip and a jump, although I doubt it will be.

'Let me take a photo with you. You're the craziest person in here!' I find that very hard to believe given the clientele, but I pose for the picture.

The next morning I'm up and out of the tent early – I want to see the Castro de Baroña Celtic hill fort site before anyone else arrives. On a rocky peninsula rising out of the sea facing north, with beautiful beaches either side of the entrance, I see a series of low terraced walls stepping up the hillside among the rocks, then higher up the structures are almost perfect circles, clustered together tightly. These walls are over 2,500 years old, and a special stillness makes me wonder what they have witnessed. Galicia is often considered to be the seventh Celtic nation alongside Eire (Ireland), Kernow (Cornwall), Mannin (Isle of Mann), Breizh (Brittany), Alba (Scotland) and Cymru (Wales). A Celtic tribe known as the Gallaeci settled north of the Douro River and built these round house or *palloza* settlements which dot the coast. The region still feels very Celtic today.

Making my way back down, I have a friendly brush with a local police lady who tells me off for wild camping. I should have taken the tent down when I saw some people on the beach, who must have dobbed me in. It takes me about four hours to get around the next headland into the Ría de Arousa, infamous for Colombian drug-smuggling in the 1980s, which Raquel told me I could learn all about watching the Netflix series *Fariña*. A few drug cartels still operate here and the name 'Cocaine Coast' has stuck, although not with locals. On my way to the Atlantic Islands of Ons and Cíes, I pass quickly down the coast, sampling the delicious food and Albariño wine as I go. It feels effortless, like I was meant to be here; everything falls into place and I'm happy.

I dodge through the oyster beds floating in the middle of the estuary with huge rocks weighing them down, as I paddle out and aim for the lighthouse on Ons, the most northerly island in the Atlantic Islands of Galicia National Park, about 7 kilometres from the mainland. It's exciting, because with visitor quotas and few places to stay, the islands are notoriously difficult to land on. Luckily, Rodrigo, a local kayaker who saw the article in *La Voz de Galicia*, got in contact and has sorted me out with papers and a place to stay.

He is a friendly, wide-shouldered man interested in lots of things, and introduces me to the group of friends he's brought together on his home island. I find it hard to follow the conversation in Spanish, as it seems to move very quickly between topics, but am made to feel part of the group as they warmly include me in their plans. I let myself go with the flow – it's nice to have a break from constantly worrying about the weather and the tides. The next day I join a kayak tour run by Alberto, an extreme sea kayaker who runs tours for novices and hopes to get more people to do the Camino de Santiago by kayak – a special route he's created where after five days of paddling, the kayaks are left in Padrón at the end of Ría de Arousa and the tourists make the 17-kilometre hike to Santiago de Compostela. He's knowledgeable about the island and attentive to his group. In the afternoon I prepare a presentation for Falmouth University on my experience in architecture, drawing it out by hand because I don't have a computer with me. Work seems an abstract concept from this island in Galicia.

After dinner, Jesús turns up with a heavy telescope. Warm and friendly, he is Rodrigo's cousin and an astronomer who volunteers in the National Park. 'Do you like the stars? Yes?' he says with the excitement of a child at Christmas. 'I'll show you some incredible things.' He fiddles with the telescope for a moment. 'Look, look Saturn with rings.' I skip over light-heartedly to look through the telescope.

'That's amazing!' Stunned, I say, 'I've never seen anything like it.'

'There's more!' he says, before showing me seven of Jupiter's moons; a binary star switching from red to white; an exploding star; and several other galaxies, all explained with overflowing enthusiasm. I'm feeling a bit overwhelmed, then at 1 a.m., like the Cat in the Hat, he goes out and comes back in with another toy: an inflatable planetarium. I have no idea what's going on as the small dome rises from the grass like a bouncy castle at a village fete. Like children, we are quick to scramble inside, where we lie watching films of the night sky projected on the ceiling. Such an unusual and welcome experience!

The next day, refreshed by an afternoon swim, Rodrigo and I climb the hill to meet the last lighthouse keeper in Spain. The light blue sky and fading sun behind the lighthouse cast it into semi-silhouette; from our angle down the hill, it looks huge and impressive. Softly spoken, calm and dressed entirely in white, this second Jesús is exactly the sort of person you imagine to be a lighthouse keeper. The inside of the lighthouse – a scientific instrument – is pristine, with polished brass and beautiful Art Nouveau tiles in greens, blues and yellows. There's been a lighthouse on Ons since 1865, but this one was built in 1926 and must have been state-of-the-art. Jesús explains the various changes in lighthouse technology and takes us up to the light. Looking at the almost normal-sized bulbs, it's hard to imagine that the beam of this lighthouse has a reach of 46 kilometres, one of the furthest in the world. 'That will be thanks to the Fresnel lens,' I think to myself. I'm glad I stayed to see this, but I need to move on. I feel out of control, like I'm losing myself in this group, where I only partially understand and can't express myself, but their warmth and curiosity for nature and life makes it hard to prise myself away.

The next morning, we sit looking out over the sea as the gentle breeze wafts the long grasses on the slope, seagulls glide overhead and waves gently lap. Laughter, coffee and a beautiful view. I know I need to leave today. Three days on land is too long. I'm on the beach saying goodbye to Rodrigo and Alberto and I hear someone calling, 'Carr! Carr!' I see the lighthouse keeper waving from a Ferris tractor, 'Goodbye, goodbye!' Such an emotional farewell makes me feel sad to leave this little island in the Atlantic where I've felt so welcome.

Back on the water, I'm free as I gently paddle to Cíes, another of the Atlantic Islands. The colour of a rusted railway, with soft grass on top that looks like it's been forked, it's home to hundreds of birds that fill the sky and sea, swooping so low I have to duck. Sometimes we need to stop and think about things, I reflect, as I land on the beach overstimulated and in need of some quiet time. I feel guilty; it's been days since I thought about Marcus for longer than a few seconds. It's like I've betrayed the memory of him that I'm so keen to keep alive. I think back to his and Andy's wedding, five years ago, not long after same-sex marriage became legal. It was such a beautiful celebration of love and companionship. Katie and I gave a joint speech in the brick courtyard of their favourite restaurant, as Marcus rolled his eyes at our jokes and the Kylie bingo. Our mum, Bron, brought down to London by her carers, presented the grooms with a drawing of a London bus she'd done, and Marcus, playing host, was in his element. I let my mind wander as I sit on the beach, watching the day go by.

After a day with myself, I'm feeling better and launch the boat for a sunset paddle around the island. I've loved watching sunsets for as long as I can remember. Some of my first photos are of them from *Hullaballoo*, with bits of the boat included because I couldn't hold the camera high enough. I'm calm and content as the colours inject a cocktail of possibility into the last moments of the day, silhouetting different parts of the island as I move.

It's an early start into the final estuary of Galicia and I feel like an outlaw, sitting on a beach just north of Vigo, planning my approach. The sun is coming up and warms the sand, and I might easily be in Devon or Cornwall. After weeks in the fresh air, I can smell the city: humanity and pollution, sweet and dusty. It's FitzRoy's fault I'm in Vigo, and once I've landed and found a campsite I go straight to the Galician Museum of the Sea. Inside it's easy to find the scale replica of HMS *Beagle*, the Admiralty survey ship that FitzRoy captained on two voyages, but is most famous for the second with Charles Darwin. FitzRoy was looking for a 'gentleman naturalist' companion, and had asked his friend and superior, Captain Francis Beaufort (of the Beaufort Scale) to assist him. He in turn asked Professor Peacock at Cambridge University for suggestions, who conferred with Professor Henslow and eventually proposed Charles Darwin as 'a young man of promising ability, extremely fond of geology and indeed all branches of natural history.' FitzRoy accepted and after permissions were granted and negotiations completed, Darwin joined him on the journey. The Beaufort Scale was adopted officially and first used on this voyage of the *Beagle*, before its widespread application in the navy and later the forecasts.

Darwin and FitzRoy were friends after five years on board, but this changed when they arrived in London and Darwin published his discoveries on natural selection. FitzRoy was a devout Christian and creationist and trolled Darwin in the media, which ended in a huge public spat between the two men. Many believe FitzRoy blamed himself for Darwin's theories, endangering his already precarious mental health. The only thing he managed to do successfully after the voyage was promoting safety at sea, developing public barometers and the idea of a forecast. Passionate about the project, he invested his entire personal fortune in it, before he killed himself at 60. A sad end for a remarkable man.

What strikes me most about the beautifully crafted model of the ship is how small the cabins would have been in the full-sized version for such a long journey with 74 people aboard. It's incredible to think about everything the voyage achieved. The *Beagle* is not the only evidence of FitzRoy; the museum also has a FitzRoy barometer. It is like the one in St Helier, but with the full descriptions on it, including the simplified rhyming couplets that FitzRoy invented to help people remember what the barometer was showing them. On the left side for rising pressure it says, 'Long foretold long last, short notice soon past,' meaning that if the pressure has been rising for a long time, the high pressure will be sustained, whereas if there's a sudden increase, it will not last for long. I feel pleased to have found FitzRoy in the area named after him, even if I've been using his forecast all along.

From Vigo, I kayak down the straightest piece of coast I've seen since Asturias, then sit on the last beach in Spain to do a live interview with BBC Radio 4. I manage to condense my answer to their question of 'why?' into: 'A voyage of personal discovery, really... At a point in my life, I wanted to take on a new adventure, and the Shipping Forecast has provided a framework for that.' It's a bit simplistic and I prefer the answer

I gave to Elsa – there are so many reasons. Before launching I raise an Estrella Galicia to an amazing, unexpected journey in Spain, hoping I can come back soon.

I paddle out to Ínsua de Santo Isidro, a fort island just inside Portugal, and watch the sunset. I'm two days away from Porto, so I push down the coast, which is long and sandy like Denmark. As I pass the impressive Farol de Leça, the tallest thinnest lighthouse I've seen for a while, I know I'm nearly there. Entering the River Douro across the bar, a fast-flowing current and waves roll over the sandbank. Brief thoughts of bumping across the River Deben bar in *Hullaballoo* come to mind – it wasn't comfortable then, either! I can see one of Porto's famous bridges as a ferry glides over and eventually I make it to the slipway near the marina in São Pedro da Afurada. Touching the grey stone of the ramp after eight hours on the water, I'm more relieved than anything else but I'm pleased I've made it to Porto.

São Pedro da Afurada is a fishing village now absorbed by the city, whose centre is a bit further up the river. Life here takes place on the street. Fishing nets are strewn around the harbour market, while huts offer barbecued fish, with the polystyrene trays next to hot coals. Washing is blowing in the wind, reminding me of my makeshift line on the beach four weeks ago. In the small mews-like streets, houses are tiled with fishing boat pictures, and the blue flashing light of TVs indicate someone is home. People sit in the street eating at small bars. I can't believe I've made it here from Santander and wander around in a daze.

The next day, it's overcast and rainy as I launch to meet João, the ex-colleague I designed the cycle bridge with, further down the river. Passing forts and embanked walls while dodging the river traffic reminds me of the Thames. I find João standing on the end of a pontoon, smiling and taking pictures. 'Welcome to Porto!' he says, as I think how nice it is to see someone I know after so long. We haul the boat up and slip it on the harbour wall next to another kayak. 'I'll show you my city,' he says, taking me on a comprehensive walking tour around the narrow hilly streets. After dinner in a traditional restaurant where the owner grabs João's face and kisses him on both cheeks like she's his grandma, we stand looking out across the river at the impressive bridges. Then, in the dark, I slip the boat into the flat calm water, my way lit by streetlights, as I pass fishermen with glow-in-the-dark floats shouting at each other. It's a clear night and I can see the stars as the darkness increases towards the river mouth. The river is quiet; I cross under the second bridge looking up at the latticework line in the middle, and land in my neighbourhood, São Pedro da Afurada, probably one of the few in Porto where I can sleep outside near my kayak and not be moved on.

I've been focusing on Porto as my destination in FitzRoy, but Trafalgar starts another 15 kilometres south of the city. It's a grey day and I decide it's worth a final push. Several hours later I emerge from the fog, next to some traditional, coloured fishing boats, pleased to have completed the entire coast of the FitzRoy area. Since leaving Santander six-and-a-half weeks ago I've kayaked 720 kilometres. It's amazing what's possible when you just keep going, I think, as I remember what Fernando said about taking it one headland at a time, edging forwards. I celebrate with a custard tart while I think about what's next.

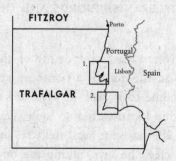

FITZROY
Porto
Portugal
1.
Lisbon
Spain
TRAFALGAR
2.

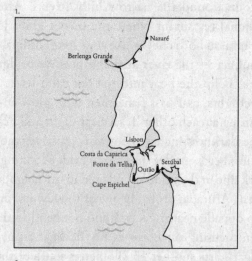

1.

Nazaré
Berlenga Grande
Lisbon
Costa da Caparica
Fonte da Telha
Outão
Setúbal
Cape Espichel

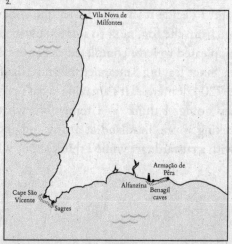

2.

Vila Nova de
Milfontes
Armação de
Pêra
Alfanzina
Cape São
Vicente
Benagil
caves
Sagres

TRAFALGAR:
THE LAST HOT DOG

Four days before I arrive in Trafalgar, Diana Speed gives me a personal Shipping Forecast reading when I'm interviewed on Radio 4. 'Trafalgar North 4 or 5, occasionally 6 later, fog patches and showers. Moderate or good, occasionally poor. And good luck from all of us.' By the time I get to the unwitting border between FitzRoy and Trafalgar, I still feel honoured.

Espinho is a ramshackle town with dusty streets, temporary cables and the feeling that it has seen better times, but my quest to conquer the last Shipping Forecast area in Western Europe starts here. Trafalgar runs from here down the coast of Portugal, around into Spain as far as Cádiz, where it drops south to just off the border between Tangier and Morocco and heads west 800 kilometres into the Atlantic. Having learnt from my surfy experience in Denmark last year, I've hired a car. It's a shift in focus but a necessary one. I have ten days left. I can either do trips like I did in Germany and France where I leave and come back to the same place, or use the trains and buses. I decide on a mixture.

After a night drive south past the lights of Lisbon, I sleep in the back of the car on a dusty unmade road, next to some old campervans. Fifteen kilometres south of Lisbon, Fonte da Telha is as close as I can easily launch to the Arrábida Natural Park, the coast forming an 'L' shape from here, round the corner to Setúbal. I launch into small waves with a lighter kayak, having left most of my stuff in the car, and appreciate how the coast has changed. Yellow cliffs behind white dunes form impressive teeth in a mouth of dark green trees. One minute they are as regular as the pleats in my Grandma Anne's skirts, the next they are giant rough triangular points with horizontal stripes in deep orange, beige and yellow. The long sandy beaches seem endless and much tamer than I expected. Thousands of birds are dotted on the sand and bobbing on the water. The rock starts to prick up into slanted layers, like they've been pushed over, then becomes dark vertical cliff faces. On the corner, Cape Espichel Lighthouse comes into view, sandwiched between the backsides of two rhinos.

There's some swell on the rocks from the north-west and the wind increases a little. Diving boats are anchored near sheltered beaches, and I can get in close to the bubbly, holey rock. There is a warm wind and a pleasant, sweet smell like fruit as I explore small openings and caves. Pleasure boats whizz around, and I wonder if they ever stop to look at the beauty of the sandy rocks and the turquoise sea. The wind pushes the boat from side to side uncomfortably, making me think of a favourite anchorage of Mike's near the Walton Backwaters in Suffolk, where on grey autumn days the wind would rattle the halliards and we'd all struggle to eat our lunch as the boat lurched around.

I still have a long way to go, so I make like the pleasure boats so I can catch the last train. I'm pushing hard and think about the need to give yourself time for challenges, and how hard that is when there is so much to see and do and so little time. One of the things I love about this trip is the longness of time I feel sitting on water or beach, as if the smallest things expand and take on their true importance. I see the red top of Outão Lighthouse on what looks like a white fort and, eventually, make it to a small beach on the edge of Setúbal. I get out quickly, rush to find somewhere to leave the kayak high up the beach near a car park, then march sweating into the town, half of my two-piece paddle in each hand. I know I must look like a state when I arrive, but they let me on the train at least.

I haven't thought this out very well, and two trains and a bumpy bus later, I'm in Costa da Caparica, about 8 kilometres up a long beach from where I left the car. It's a clear night and I can see the stars in the dark sky. A fairground is scattered on the dusty ground. The many beach bars and clubs along dunes are packed and emit different sounds, some pounding house music, some cheesy holiday tunes, some chillout; only the bass pervades as they drown each other out. The sand is hard, making the walk a little easier, as I'm drawn to the orange flashing lights of a tractor moving fast along the beach with people inside a cage trailer behind it. I watch as it speeds off into the distance. The bars peter out, dunes and cliffs fuse and I can see the dusty orange haze of Fonte da Telha in the distance. The music is muffled, and the sea takes over the noise-making. I pick up the car and drive to Setúbal. It takes forty-five minutes, about a quarter of the time it took me to get back by land and a tenth of the time it took me to do it by kayak.

In the beach car park at around 1 a.m., mobs of youths hang around listening to heavy bass music near old cars pimped at low cost. Vehicles line up on the road and race after each other around the car park loop, emitting smoke clouds and loud bangs from their exhausts. I'm tired and want to pick up the kayak and go to sleep, not play the role of unprepared victim in a wild Badlands movie. I get to the kayak and find that someone has been through all the stuff. My buoyancy aid is hanging out and a carabiner has been stolen, but I'm lucky it wasn't a lot more, even the boat itself. I pick it up and carry it on my shoulder. Back in the car park the youths have massed together, more cars are racing and one comes straight at me as I make a beeline for my Jeep. I'm scared and want to get out of there. I quickly get the kayak strapped upside down to the roof of the car, adding a few scratches to both in my haste, and leave to park in a quiet layby with some campervans.

I expected Trafalgar to be dramatic and challenging, but not in the way that my first day here went down. As I make myself a coffee on my camping stove on a steep hillside with ocean views, I try to take it all in. Trafalgar is a special area of the Shipping Forecast: as the furthest from the UK, it's only included in the 00.48 broadcast, preceded by Ronald Binge's 'Sailing By' and followed by the national anthem. The name makes me think of my trips to London as a child, for check-ups at Great Ormond Street and Hammersmith hospitals. These could have been a nasty experience with much jabbing, blood-letting and bad news, but for Mike's instance that we make a day of it. We'd often pass through Trafalgar Square with Nelson high above us on his column, like a lighthouse on a headland, on our way to the National Gallery or Covent Garden. Perhaps that's where my insistence on finding the adventure, no matter the situation, came from.

I drive south some more; I'm keen to get down to the Algarve and see what all the fuss is about. I'm exhausted from yesterday's adventure and my legs are aching. Driving is hot, and trees like cotton-wool balls on flat planes go past as the road winds in between mountains and bridges. The noise of the straps attaching the kayak to the roof grows to a loud hum, and they flap and strum at anything above 80 kph. I should stop to sort it out but I'm still on the run from the Badlands so I turn up the radio and keep going. I've driven all the way to the bottom of Portugal to a beach near Armação de Pêra.

I arrive via a dusty road with horses in a field, who I later see galloping wildly across the beach like an insurance commercial. I sit in the shade of the car and eat some lunch, focusing on my short-term plan: a day trip to Benagil caves, which if the pictures on Google are anything to go by will be spectacular and require relatively little effort. Of course, I make it a bit harder by starting from about 7 kilometres away, although that's because Google Earth shows me it's the closest beach with parking and easy access for the kayak.

I throw everything in a dry bag and I'm off. It's September now, but there's still an air of summer slowness as I kayak past the packed town beaches. Cliffs are whipped-up stone peaks, with holes like sponges but hard. Water slops around lazily as the waves smash in underneath. A temporary construction on the top of one headland and loud piano music suggests a wedding. Remnants of the previous construction are left dangling as the once-luxurious fabric drapes half-way down the cliff. How quick we are to get rid of things when something better comes along.

It's obvious which of the small inlets is accessible from land as they are full of people, where others are deserted. I weave around the rock in and out of caves, bridges, arches, stacks and domes with holes in the roof. It feels like I'm inside a finely crafted clay pot. It's busy; boats of many types are snaking through, plastic kayaks and SUPs with their normally land-based loads. I go as far as the Alfanzina Lighthouse and turn around. The water is calm with an onshore wind; the golden yellow colour of the sun is reflected on the water and rocks.

The beach is almost empty, the bar is shut and the sun sets quickly. I notice a new scratch on the car as I get the kayak on the roof and reach into the dry bag for my phone. Both my hand and the phone come out wet. I breathe in the kind of leaden air that can only be associated with very bad news. The screen doesn't respond. I've seen this many times before, and a hovering sense of loss descends as I shove it in a packet of dry vegetable risotto: a last, futile attempt at resuscitation. The car park is full of large black flies like a Biblical warning. I move the car but seem to be moving the flies with me, accidentally squashing one against the white fabric, leaving a massive bloodstain on the seat. I'm bitten all night and hardly sleep, I'm so anxious about the phone.

The next day, I burn my lips on hot coffee as I watch a piece of melon become enveloped in ants. I'm miserable and feel immensely stupid. I've been so careful for all this time, and now the next bit of the trip will be difficult, if not impossible. I can't believe how careless I've been. No email, no contact, no updates. No weather info, no maps. I think it's probably the end of the trip. I drive to Sagres on the southern tip of Portugal – I've been wanting to paddle around it since I saw a picture of it in a book in the Corbiere Phare restaurant in Jersey. I won't be able to do that now.

I arrive at the headland at lunchtime and wander around as if lumbering under a huge hangover with the same level of self-hatred. I can't take anything in; I photograph things so I can see them later. I hardly register the scorched-earth coloured rocks dropping down to coves where the turquoise sea provides almost the exact complementary colour, long waves dumping into the slightly inclined shore. I drift around the lighthouse, fort and church, forcing myself to take an interest and reading the signs as if trying to convince myself to make the switch from adventure to normal tourism.

At a loss as to what to do, I walk to the next headland, Cape São Vicente, the most south-westerly point in mainland Europe. It is the venue of some exciting happenings over the years, including its own slightly convoluted connection to Trafalgar, or at least the battle of Trafalgar. This was where the soon-to-be-famous Horatio Nelson disobeyed orders and was instrumental in defeating the French and Spanish in 1797. Eight years later he pulled a similar trick at Cape Trafalgar, about 300 kilometres south-east of here, outside the Shipping Forecast.

The first thing I come across is a food truck with a massive smiling sausage on top, marketing itself as the place to buy your last hot dog before America. It's crass and out of place but it reminds me where I am. I did make it all the way here, even if it's not exactly the way I planned. My mood lifts slightly as I wander around the outside of Cape São Vicente lighthouse. It feels good standing next to the solidness of its stone structure, and I'm somehow calmed by this building dedicated to safety at sea with its 60-kilometre reach, the second most powerful in Europe, after the Créac'h lighthouse on Ushant. At the thought of Ushant I miss Michal. I wish I could message him and ask him what to do. I imagine he'd say, 'get the forecast, read the charts, look at the sea and if it looks okay, go.' I decide to get a hot dog and sort myself out.

I can feel my mindset changing. I tell myself it's time to slow down and stop rushing from one thing to the next. A stupid oversight has ruined my phone and maybe my job possibility. I was tired and took my eye off the ball. I don't know how much I've lost but I have my memories. I get in the car and drive two hours up the coast to Vila Nova de Milfontes, which I can see on my chart is at the mouth of the Mira River. I've bitten my fingers worrying about a trip on this coast with its high cliffs and surf beaches and few options if things go wrong: no phone, no tracker and no safety margin. But if I park the car in Milfontes, and go out for a day paddle, even if there is a huge surf I should be able to get down the river and land on the beach. I feel better with a plan.

The next morning, I watch the water flow out of the small estuary. The sky is clear blue and there is a gentle hum of boats in the river, with mountains visible beyond a bridge. I paddle out past the lifeboat station and a group of kids on the beach opposite. Vila Nova de Milfontes is a pretty town with a large fortress built into the hillside, and well-cared for buildings. At the sandbar entrance to the river the waves take on a sweeping motion, beautiful but destructive; a thin line peaks up and gently curves to a full circle, as if I'm watching in slow motion. I try to catch a few, wishing Michal was here to join me in this salty playground. I ride high on a long wave before it sharpens into a sheet and crashes. I'm halfway through shouting, 'yoohoo!' when another one makes the bow dive, and I end up splayed out like a starfish on the back, surfing with totally the wrong equipment. I manage to get back in the boat, which now wobbles around, full of water. I pump it out and get back to touring the coast like a grown-up.

I feel like I'm noticing more again. I breathe in the smell of the sea. Fresh, slightly cold, sharp and pure, I can almost feel it cleaning my lungs. I'm relaxed and happier. As I go closer in to the land on the way back, I see what looks like a piece of purple transparent plastic in the shape of a Cornish pasty, glinting colourfully and floating on the water. I'm about to pick it out of the sea when I realise it's a jellyfish, or correctly speaking a marine hydrozoan. In fact, thanks to a children's book I grew up with, it's probably the only one I can identify without my phone for the slightly worrying reason that it's one of the most poisonous things you can find on a European beach: the Portuguese man o' war. I feel a warning spasm in the pit of my stomach, although I'm sure it's not going to jump out and sting me. What a privilege for one to make an appearance in Portugal.

I put the kayak on the car and walk down the beach to the 07 Ocean Drive Beach Club, with a renewed lightness in my step despite my tiredness. A small single-storey building with blue window frames and coloured triangular fabric sun shades bouncing gently in the breeze, the bar is relaxed and just what I was looking for. I get myself a table and a glass of Super Bock as I watch the lifeguard tie up the floats and seats outside with the care one would take to saddle a horse for battle. The orb of the sun reflects on the water and the sound system sings, 'I don't want to go back home.' Bloody right I don't, I think, knowing I've got one week left in Trafalgar.

The name Trafalgar comes from the old Arabic *Tarif Al Gharb*, meaning either cape of the cave or cape of the west. In the 8th century, Muslims sailed north from Africa and took over most of what is now Spain and Portugal, renaming it Al-Andalus. Initially part of the Umayyad empire, it remained under Muslim rule for five centuries before the 'reconquest' of the lands by Christian rulers. I wonder if Brexiters realise that Britain's most famous square has Arabic origins, like so many aspects of British culture borrowed from others.

From here on, Trafalgar is more like a holiday, albeit one where I sleep in the car and wash in supermarket toilets. I drive back to Sagres, keen to get on the sea in its notorious waters. As small rainbows float above the surface, I half expect sea unicorns to jump through them and I spend most of the day with my mouth open, impressed by the holey, crumbly caves. Fish pass by in huge schools and light shines through the sea in shards, sparkling. It's amazing to be here. Later that evening, I use my Kindle to check the forecast and my email. It's a slow process but worth it because I find out that I've been invited to interview at Falmouth. I feel excited, like things are coming together.

I spend a day visiting more of the Algarve's caves, then head up the coast because Portugal has one island near its coast and I just have time to visit. I'm close to Lisbon as a spectacular sunset plays out its performance of purples, oranges and reds. In this light the electricity pylons sewn across the sky look like beautiful latticework. What is often seen as a mess on the landscape seems lightweight and temporary, touching the ground and stringing out power into the distance. It's almost dark and the exact beach I've been looking for appears before me, and I can see Berlenga Grande island in the distance.

I park, curl up on the back seat to go to sleep. The car has become my home.

There's a cold damp breeze as the fishermen arrive on the pier to load up for the day. I carry the boat down the curved beach, struggling on the slope in the middle before reaching the shore. I pack for the last time in Trafalgar and wonder what the water is like on the unsheltered side of the headland. I can see the lighthouse on Berlenga Grande like a white upside-down T; I focus on it as it appears and disappears behind the waves bouncing and peaking, washing in from the north-west. I'm in a constant up-and-down motion as a man in a rib with two divers shouts across, 'Are you okay?'

'Yes, okay,' I say and signal.

'Radio if you need anything!' he shouts back, making me think about the kind of fraternity you feel with people in other small boats on the sea. Even when our ways of getting around are very different, there's often a connection, a shared concern as humans at the whim of the ocean.

I check my bearing in case the visibility drops and go for it. The islands grow bigger as I close in on them like a lion on its prey, in very slow motion. I can make out colours, forms and headlands. The Berlenga Archipelago consists of Berlenga Grande and two groups of islets, the Estelas and the Farilhões-Forcados. Known to the British Navy as the 'Birling Islands', they are the only islands in the Trafalgar Shipping Forecast area and lie 10 kilometres from the mainland.

Small children play in the water as I arrive. One boy grabs the end of the kayak. It's not helpful but I pretend it is. 'Oh, thanks, *obrigado*, you've got me,' I say, thinking of Llorenç. I realise it's a Saturday and start to walk up to the lighthouse before it gets busier. I'm moving with a steady flow of people as if commuting across London Bridge and get halfway there before I decide I'm better off on the water. The Berlengas are recognised by UNESCO as one of the World Network of Biosphere Reserves, and hundreds of fish are visible below the surface as I loop around the rocks and bays. There's a fine mist over the water and I see what must be the Estelas further out. I explore the peaks rising out of the water, waves smashing into stacks on the outside and a small lighthouse being claimed by the sea.

I later find out this is the edge of the Nazaré canyon, a 4.5-kilometre-deep undersea gorge which allows waves to travel at massive speeds, with virtually no dissipation of energy before they smash into the side of Portugal. I have a quick look and decide not to push it and turn back. The spray hanging beneath Berlenga Grande makes it seem like the island is floating. I paddle back to the mainland, then drive until I see a sign saying, 'Welcome to the biggest waves in the world!' They don't seem that scary looking down on them the next day, but I'm not going to try it. Today I need to transform myself from salty surf dude into someone who might be allowed on a plane. I put a plan in action: wash, swimming pool, Lidl, packing and sorting, visit fort and surf museum, leave and head north.

One of the things I struggled with when planning this trip was how to get my kayak back from Portugal to the UK. After a tentative inquiry, the kind guys at Tiderace and Nelo agreed to ship it with the new kayaks for free. I drive to the Nelo factory, where my kayak was made. Off the car and on a stilt-like kayak-holder it looks a lot more battered than its younger counterparts: I imagine the stories it could tell them on the way home. I feel that same pang of sadness I've felt leaving friends who've looked after me over my trip, and wish it 'bon voyage' before driving off to return my other trusty vehicle: the Jeep. Miraculously there are no extra charges despite the alterations I've unintentionally made and the thick dusty finish it now boasts.

Flying back, I finally get the view I would have had from Google Earth. I see the places I've paddled passing by, waves breaking on the rocks, swell on the beaches. I get a clear view of the island fort of Ínsua de Santo Isidro on the Portuguese border, the river Minho, then Vigo, Cíes and Ons. I think of Jesús in his lighthouse. We go up as far as Ría de Arousa and the plane banks to the north-east, taking me from my adventure and back to London. I've been away for nearly three months. I wash up in arrivals at Gatwick in the same way I landed on the beach after some of my unintentional surfing: disorientated, slightly overwhelmed, but exhilarated and happy to have made it.

Part 5

SOUTH-WEST STORMS

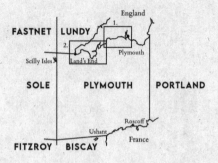

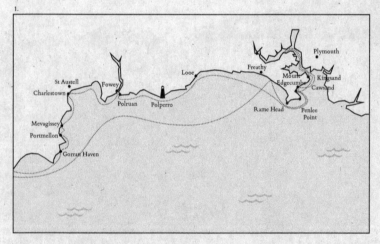

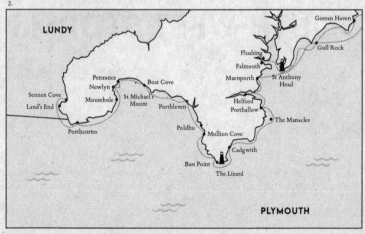

PLYMOUTH: SAFE HARBOURS AND HOME

As the narrow road drops down, I get a spectacular view of the Fal Estuary, with hundreds of boats of all shapes and sizes dotted around the river on moorings. Behind them the white houses of Falmouth stand proudly on the hill. I pass the village church and the Royal Standard pub on the left. I have vague memories of Flushing, and it's incredible to be back with a view to living here. It is ridiculously beautiful, with pastel-coloured, two-storey terraced cottages huddled together and a small harbour. Within two weeks of washing up in Gatwick, I've been offered the job at Falmouth University and take it. I wasn't expecting things to move so quickly, so I keep things simple. I see one house and decide to take it. It's perfect: a cottage with room for visitors, a garden and a log burner I can imagine writing a book next to. Just across the river from Falmouth, it's the ideal base for work and adventures. The village has two excellent pubs, its own FitzRoy barometer and a slipway and a place to store my kayak: I think I'll feel right at home.

The Plymouth Shipping Forecast area stretches from Sharkham Point below Brixham in Devon all the way to Land's End in Cornwall. (And from Trégastel to Kerlaguen in France.) I quickly learn that although the Shipping Forecast unites them, Devon and Cornwall are rivals. My family are firmly on the Cornish side of the debate. My parents moved down to Lostwithiel in the early 70s as dinghy sailors, and soon began sailing larger yachts with Bron's colleague, David. Based on the Fal, they sailed to the Channel Islands, Scilly, Spain and Portugal. Years later, Mike would often talk about Cornwall and it became a mystical place for us all. If it hadn't been for David and his wife Judith, demonstrating how you can still sail with a young family, Marcus, Katie and I wouldn't have spent half our childhood on the muddy beaches of the east coast in *Hullaballoo*.

David and Judith live in the village as far as I know, but I haven't seen them since I was 15 and don't know which house is theirs. At Easter when Katie and I were discussing what to do with Mike's ashes we decided that Cornwall was far too far away; now I live here. I feel pleased to have changed my life and chosen nature, even if I miss my friends in London. My plan is to spend the winter exploring Plymouth and Lundy and bag the remaining Irish and Scottish areas in the summer.

Nevertheless, it turns out that even architecture lecturers are expected to work, and I land in the deep end of my new job running a live build project on the north coast, constructing a temporary cinema for the National Trust to screen a film by a local artist. It's wild and remote and exactly the sort of thing I hoped I'd be doing. I'm well looked after by Tom and his partner Megan. Kind and quick to enjoy life, Tom is now my boss, but takes me sunset surfing and introduces me to interesting people, among them Rachael, a filmmaker with deep curiosity and a dry sense of humour, who quickly becomes my friend.

I make a few dashes up to London to sort out my flat, go to Romilly and Zyggy's wedding in Suffolk (with a stop off at Pin Mill for old times' sake), organise a family party for Bron's 70th in North Wales, give a talk at the Fanconi Hope conference in Grantham, start my part-time PGCE in Higher Education, and before I know it it's Christmas. I need a break, so I go for a four-areas-in-two-weeks mad dash, combining pre-Christmas in St Helens, Merseyside to visit Bron, actual Christmas in Jersey, New Year's in Falmouth and Epiphany in Barcelona. Irish Sea, Portland, Plymouth and (according to the Spanish Shipping Forecast map) Baleares. None of which counts because my kayak is safely in the garage in Flushing.

I start the year committed to being in or on the sea every day in 2020, and I can't believe that my new life includes easy sea swimming, a spot of surfing and a paddle to work in the mornings. At the end of January the UK officially withdraws from the EU. I think of my European friends and the welcome they gave me and I feel shame. Teaching is challenging but in good way; I fly out to Scilly to set up a project, and I've upped my popularity with the students by facilitating the construction of a pizza oven in the department gardens. Soaking in some winter sun in my steep garden, I think about kayaking the entire coast of Galicia and I decide to do the same for Cornwall. I've been reading *The Salt Path*, Raynor Wynn's touching story of how she and her husband completed the South West Coast Path against the odds and feel inspired to do my own shorter aquatic version.

Easter will be perfect to do this, and by early March I'm listening to the forecasts and planning what to do. Then Covid hits and lockdown begins. The Easter break landslides into a rockfall of sudden online teaching, self-isolation and uncertainty. I'm high-risk and receive messages from the NHS telling me not to go out under any circumstances – almost as threatening as the ones the TV Licensing people send about the television I don't own. Rachael, who I only met four months ago, does my shopping for me and is my support bubble; with lots in common and few other people to talk to we quickly become close. A friend of hers, Simon – often serious but quick to laugh – joins us once that's allowed, and we become a cheeky trio of best mates. Performance artist friends of theirs, Katie and another Simon, create an online pub via Zoom, where creativity and laughter unites us all.

The rest of the time I'm isolated but able to walk in nature alone, and I take to listening more avidly to the late-night broadcast of the Shipping Forecast as it leads me through my memories of human connection and the sea. It's clear that this is not the year I complete all 31 areas: Ireland and Scotland are out of the question, and for a long time it hardly seems possible to kayak at all. I try to focus on the bit I've done, the amazing experiences I've already had. At a time when borders are closed, it seems abstract, impossible that I kayaked much of the coast of Western Europe. It's not until mid-June that I get on the water. Despite being an excellent way to socially distance, there is a general feeling that water sports are antisocial: any need for the lifeboat would endanger RNLI volunteers. By July, the rules relax, and I go on Epic Adventures with Rachael and Simon around Cornwall. I buy the cottage I'm in and reconnect with David and Judith.

'Coventry Road?' says Judith, 'what number?' I tell her. 'Well, that's funny, you're living in my old house!'

'Mike would have something to say about that!' says David, as we all laugh.

It's mid-August and I have three weeks before term starts, so I plan to spend a week kayaking the Cornish part of the Plymouth area: Plymouth to Land's End. To avoid parking in Plymouth I'll first paddle the 75 kilometres up from Falmouth. I aim for 12, then 2, and finally I'm on the water at 6, after a torrential downpour as I open the door. Launching from the slipway in front of the Seven Stars pub with a fully packed kayak, it's amazing to just leave from home like this. The clouds have pink edges and a pod of dolphins escorts me out of the estuary. Back in the wild, I breathe out the tension of Covid and can once again just be. I wild camp for the first time in nearly a year, since the night on Ínsua de Santo Isidro. It feels good to be alone under the stars again.

I make quick but uneasy progress up the coast, almost reaching Plymouth quickly, stopping only to sleep. I'm jumping, slamming, bracing, and amid my exhaustion, I see what must be the village of Freathy clinging to the hillside, transporting me to Galicia where the scene was almost identical. I round the headland and land on the first beach I see, in time to watch the sunset reflecting on the water. When the golden-grey sunrise the next morning dilutes to white, I launch for Kingsand, a short paddle away, where a man carries a human-sized inflatable lobster across the beach above his head. The place has a French holiday feel; all the windows and doors of the well-kept houses are open. The forecast looks bad so in the late afternoon I seek shelter in the confluence of the rivers Tamar and Lynher behind Plymouth. The sun reflects on the water and it's hard to imagine that there's a storm coming in, but clouds roll in, muting the sunset to an orange glow in the rain.

A gale warning is issued for Plymouth: 'southerly gale Force 8 imminent,' with sea state 'Moderate or rough, becoming rough or very rough.' There's no kayaking in that. I didn't plan to get stuck in the depths of the Plymouth backwaters, but I spend two days sharing a beach with the birds waiting for the wind to die down. I think about FitzRoy and Darwin on the *Beagle* who in Christmas 1831 also waited out a storm in the Plymouth Sound, a natural deep-water harbour. Having attempted to leave for South America on two occasions, they finally did so on 27th December.

The sun sparkling on the third day entices me to launch, and I follow the sea as the tide goes out, gently surfing past the Tamar Bridge and Torpoint. Then, just as I pass the ferry terminal, I'm suddenly out bashing into the wind. I try to round the corner to Cawsand, realise it's too rough and paddle back to Edgecumbe. With little else to do, I explore Mount Edgecumbe's ordered gardens and listed landscaping. Looking out over the river, past the clumps of tiny purple flowers on the beach, I see white horses galloping across the water and waves crashing up the sides of Drake's Island. I've paddled out to the small island in the middle of the Plymouth Sound before and walked on the bright-green lichen-covered stones above the tideline.

It has a long military history, with the first fortifications built in 1549. Sir Francis Drake was made governor of the island in 1583, having circumnavigated the world from Plymouth three years earlier. Despite the accolades bestowed on him by the crown, Drake was quite the pirate the Spanish know him as, and spent much of his life relieving Spanish galleons and the mainland of their South American riches and bringing them back to England.

Back at the stony beach where I've left my kayak there's a small white-columned folly to the left, partly enveloped by the trees, with a verse from *Paradise Lost* on the wall. When it's late enough, I pitch my tent inside. It's the most obviously non-permitted place I've ever camped, and the grandest. In the morning, I'm up early and out of sight without a trace, launching at high tide into waves dumping on the beach. A strong south-westerly wind means the south coast of Cornwall is fully exposed, and the swell will be high for a few days. I feel the full force of it in my face and nearly lose my cap as I round the point and realise it's not worth putting myself in danger. I land and the water looks wild. Trees taking the brunt of the storm give me an idea of the battering I would have received, their limbs littering the ground. A shimmery silver comes over the water and desaturates as haze and low cloud cover the headlands. I keep checking the forecast.

Later, I head out on a shiny sea that seems to be saying, 'come on then!' in the threatening way someone might entreat you into a scrap at an East London pub. I land outside Plymouth covered in seaweed and ready for some fish and chips and a pint in the sunshine. Standing on Penlee Point, looking out towards Rame and its simple stone chapel, a white highlight at the bottom of the land tells me the swell is still crashing in. I launch anyway, desperate to move on. A roller coaster sea and relentless sound blows all thoughts out of my head. I keep going, accepting the sensation of swooping and gliding on the waves.

Past Looe, things calm down to a beautiful summer evening, and the sun glints off the lighthouse at Polperro on the coast ahead, calling me over. I find a slim harbour with a waiting area and a beach; the pretty white stone houses and narrow winding streets are calm and relaxed. There are small carts left around for transporting luggage, which seems generous, and fishing boats fill the harbour. Polperro's current use seems a far cry from the reputation the town had as a centre for smuggling in the 18th and 19th centuries. After a quick look round, I launch for Fowey, knowing I'll be short of daylight. The sea is metallic; in the big troughs I can see the sun through a thin veil of water, as the green waves jump up. It's beautiful.

I pass point after point, and in the hazy dusk a crescent moon appears through the clouds. I push on; it's getting dark, and I feel invisible. I can hear waves smashing but I can't see the rocks. I'm hyper-alert. I make out the red channel marker but no lights on land. Finally, I see St Austell, but then I start to question where I am. I keep paddling on, then one, two, three small twinkling lights and a green marker. It disappears and I realise I'm heading straight for the rocks. The sea curls and pulls away in front of me. It's properly dark now. Eventually the river mouth opens, showing more lights and a well-lit fort: it must be Polruan. With an immense feeling of relief, I follow the line of moored boats towards a small slipway by a pub. I've reached a safe harbour and I wonder how many others have arrived here with that sentiment. It's 10 p.m. so I get changed and go straight to the pub – I think I've earned it.

Cockerels wake me up at 4.30 a.m., the seagulls are vocal by 5 a.m., and I'm washed and walking around the village by 6 a.m. It's a pretty place and feels comfortable, like Flushing but built on an even steeper hill. Polruan has been a shipbuilding town since the Middle Ages when it was involved in building wine-trade boats. The shipyard is still active today, building and maintaining smaller craft. I walk to the blockhouse, which was originally one of a pair of buildings built in 1380 to keep 'undesirable' vessels out of the harbour, using a chain hung between them. I wonder how successful it was. The sun is coming out through the clouds and it's getting gradually busier: first people with dogs and bacon sarnies, then kayakers and paddle boarders, followed by the ferry. I launch and take a quick look at Fowey from the water. With so many balconies, jetties and steps down, it seems to be all about being on the sea. I paddle around the crumbing rocks and tiny beaches of Gribbin Head, pleased to be making progress at last.

It's a typical Cornish sunny-cloudy day. The wind is gusting, but the sea is significantly calmer, like it's sorting itself out after having been in a mood. A few sailing boats battle the inconsistency of the wind, as I pass Par Sands and land on the beach near Charlestown. It's busy and no one seems to be keeping to the 2-metre social distance rule, so I get nervous and leave – the last thing I need is Covid. Back in my watery isolation, I carry on around a series of rocky headlands with scruffy grass on top and the occasional beach, Cornwall doing a very convincing Brittany impression. In fact, Cornwall, Brittany and Galicia share similar ancient igneous rocks and Celtic-rooted languages.

A pod of dolphins feeds just outside Mevagissey where a self-obsessed jet skier narrowly avoids them. They make a swooshing sound when they swim next to you: first there's an agitation in the water, then you see the fins. It's low tide when I stop at Mevagissey, where the town's substantial trawler fleet lie in the dried-out harbour, their red hulls contrasting with the bright green seaweed under them. The seagulls are possessed, squawking and flocking, unable to understand the idea of Sunday and why the fleet hasn't gone out.

I approach Portmellon, where I opt for the kayak version of what Katie and I called 'National Park Mode' when we crossed the US: driving through somewhere (usually a National Park) with the windows down but not stopping. In the kayak, I go in close to Portmellon and then Gorran Haven, have a look in at their pretty harbours and continue. I'm sure they have more to offer but you can't see everything, no matter how hard you try. Beyond Gorran Haven the rock is dark, shards collapsing into the sea. I can smell farms and the wind picks up, sending ripples across the water. It's a lovely evening so I find a beach in the corner and land. A delicate light casts soft shadows and reminds me this is a special time.

Three people turn up and collect rubbish on the beach in the morning. It's nice to see others caring enough to do it, but sad that it has to be done. On this trip I've made a point of collecting and videoing the plastic rubbish on the beaches. In July, I found an excellent company called Waterhaul, who make sunglasses out of old fishing nets, which make up lots of plastic in the sea. One of their models is called FitzRoy, so I wrote to their founder Harry: 'I don't know how much you know about the Shipping Forecast, but FitzRoy was the inventor,' I'd started, before launching into some Shipping Forecast trivia. Surprisingly, Harry replied and we connected over the challenges of plastic in the sea, before he sent me a pair of FitzRoys.

Visibility is good when I wake up and I can see all the way to Gull Rock, St Anthony Head and Rosemullion about 25 kilometres away. Minutes after launching, clouds gather in the sky, and a castle appears and disappears in the distance. Visibility reduces to total whiteout: I can see the bow of my kayak but not much beyond that. When this happens, I feel I'm kayaking in another world, alone in the whiteness; maybe this is what it's like when you die. Sometimes I imagine Marcus and Mike on another plane, but I think that's just wishful thinking.

I can't see anything until I'm closer to St Anthony Head, the familiar lighthouse at the entrance to the Fal, poking up like a low-key homecoming. Sarah and Owen are staying at my house and I'm meeting them on the beach in Maenporth. I met Sarah at university and her partner Owen later – they are one of those couples you can be friends with individually and collectively. I also got them into kayaking, a habit they have managed to maintain despite having a two-year-old son, Dylan. It's been a long time since Owen and I last paddled together at Lee Valley and I hope he's brought my other boat so we can go out.

We walk around the sandy beach as the tide goes out in the misty bay. Owen and I get in a quick paddle as the foghorn from the lighthouse sounds. 'The forecast's not looking great. You know you could always come home,' Owen jokes.

'Nah!' I say, as I wonder why I haven't considered this option. Mike didn't train us to give up on things; it was more about living the experience and finding a solution. The only time we stopped a sailing trip on *Hullaballoo* was one late August when a severe gale Force 9 stranded us in another place called Flushing in the Netherlands, two days before school started. Mike was cross with the weather and the expense, but we all went back on the overnight ferry from Zeebrugge. Weeks later he picked up the boat with a team of work colleagues and turned the whole thing into another adventure.

It's taken me nine days to do what I thought would take me five, but I am not willing to give up. 'See you tomorrow,' I say to Owen and Sarah as I launch in search of shelter for the night. More strong winds are coming.

The water is clear and silky in the Helford River, with a gravelly shingle on the beaches. I stop at three before settling on one with a rocky ledge. I hear the storm arrive: the wind blasts through the trees and waves race down the river, then comes the rain. Eventually it stops and a sunny morning emerges, the headland casting shadows across the empty beach as clouds speed across the sky on fast-forward. Patches of calm water on the river sparkle in the sun, inviting me in. I swim naked – the immersion feels good, and the gentle morning sun caresses my face afterwards.

On the path to Helford, I walk through hydrangeas, bamboo and ferns to meet Sarah, Owen and Dylan off the ferry. We continue along the coast to a small cove and prop Dylan, who has fallen asleep in his carrier, against a rock. 'Time for a swim?' I suggest, as the wind whips across and the waves crash in. Sarah and Owen change while I strip off, having forgotten my trunks. 'Yooohoo!' we half whisper as we run in, behaving like children jumping and splashing. It feels great to be with good friends.

'Uh oh,' says Sarah dramatically, seeing a brown dog sniffing around Dylan, and we all hobble quickly out to rescue him.

We spend the afternoon outside The New Inn in Manaccan until I eventually walk back to the beach, feeling a bit lightheaded but well looked after. It's so calm, just me and the birds, the sound of the wind in the trees lulls me to sleep.

A quick swim and I'm up, off and in Porthallow too early for anything but a mooch around. Twenty-odd white buildings with slate and thatched roofs provide the backdrop to a shingly beach with fishing boats pulled up. A stone sign marks the halfway point on the South West Coast Path and I realise how much longer it is than mine: Poole to Minehead, a challenge for another time perhaps. The back of the stone displays a poem called 'Fading Voices', a testament to the history of this small fishing and quarrying village, created through workshops with local people. It ends, 'That's How It Was, That's How We're Like We Are.' It's an interesting idea, but I don't entirely buy into the conclusion. I feel like our past shapes us and the lot we are given can limit or enable us, but we can still choose what and who we want to be.

I paddle out to The Manacles, a group of rocks about 1.5 kilometres from the land, responsible for more than a hundred shipwrecks and many lives lost. At high tide they are stacks of black rocks poking out of the sea, with others submerged around. It's easy to see how they could be treacherous if you weren't expecting them. The water is confused and choppy and it takes me a while to realise that the small dome sticking out of the water every now and then is a seal. It comes close to me, and I say, 'Hello, I haven't seen you for a while.'

I'm in a Marine Conservation Zone, and a close look at the rocks reveals a variety of red seaweeds and anemones. I round Lowland Point and see small sandy cliffs near Coverack. The harbour is busy: people are jumping off the wall into the turquoise sea and kayaking and windsurf gear is laid out on the rocky beach. Colourful boats lie in front of thatched cottages, and an old lifeboat station with a ramp lies in the corner. The next bit of coast is wild, cliffs crumbling like the bits left over in the bottom of a cereal packet. There's a small cleft of a bay with people swimming but otherwise it's barren. The greens, yellows, blacks and browns of the coastline look vivid in the afternoon sun. In Cadgwith, fishermen in yellow waders are landing their catch of lobster and crab into big blue boxes on the stony village beach. I have a quick walk around and decide to get out of the way.

Rounding the corner, I see the Lloyds Signal Station and Lizard Lighthouse. As the most southerly point in mainland Britain, The Lizard had an important role to play in signalling the initiations of ships to other harbours around the country. The signal station, a white two-storey castle-like building with 'Lloyds Signal Station' written in large black block letters on the side, is difficult to miss. It was used to communicate through semaphore with seafarers who, in the early 19th century, had no means of communication with the land. Once the information had been received from the ships, messages were sent by post or horse to the nearest telegraph station in Helston, until the telegraph reached the station in 1872. It became vital for maritime trade, and by the late 19th century over a thousand vessels were using it a month.

This no-doubt vast source of income was scuppered by the arrival of radio, the development of part of which can be attributed to the two brown sheds found a bit further round the headland: The Wireless Station, now run by the National Trust. In 1900 the Italian inventor Guglielmo Marconi chose The Lizard for his ground-breaking experiments in radio.

Using two local stations on The Lizard here at Bass Point and further round at Poldhu, Marconi developed the technology to send radio messages over the horizon, something not thought of as possible until 1901 when he sent a radio signal to the Isle of Wight, 290 kilometres away.

I look for somewhere to land but the beaches are too exposed. I continue round the point and camp at the old lifeboat station. Seaweed is piled up – I don't think I've ever seen so much of it; I drag the boat over it and find a place to pitch the tent on a flat plinth. A surprising number of people are watching the sunset on this unpretty beach with the remnants of the old boat ramp crumbling into the sea. The night is clear and a half-moon presides over an expressive sky. Later, the lighthouse beam sweeps over the sea, connecting me to the hundreds of lighthouses I've seen throughout the Shipping Forecast.

I lie listening to the rain drumming on the tent. I can't be bothered to get up. I didn't sleep well and I'm anxious about what to do next. I'm not far from the end of the Plymouth area, so I can either continue along the north coast through Lundy or go out to the Scilly Isles (Sole). Eventually, I get up and get some breakfast. As I launch, a man on the slipway points at the sea and looks at me, shaking his head, and says, 'In there?' I'm not convinced either but I've got an offer to stay in a friend's field tonight and I need to reach Boat Cove – which doesn't appear on any charts – so I get into the churning water.

Further on, I feel the wind behind the swell ramping up, turning the sea into breaking peaks. I'm alert and focused; I tell myself to stay with it. It's so rough that even the horizon is lumpy and there is nowhere to land. It was a silly idea, but

I can't change that now: I'm in the silly idea and I need to get out of it somehow. I push on. It's on the enjoyable side of scary, exhilarating but concerning. Grey water and white sky make it hard to see. I make out what I think is Mullion Island gradually detaching from the headland. Occasionally the sea slops a wave in my face like someone throwing buckets of water at me. It's a good job I was trained for this on summer holidays on *Hullaballoo*. A break in the rocks reveals the walls of a small harbour in the corner and I've found my way out of my silly idea. A hotel dominates the headland, and a cluster of buildings make up Mullion Cove. It's such relief to get into the harbour. I warm up and as the sky clears, I push on.

Passing Poldhu, I think I can see the Marconi Centre on the cliff. It was from here in June 1921 that a message specially prepared by the Met Office for shipping approaching the western coast of the UK was broadcast. Consisting of the forecast and weather observations, this was the first broadcast Shipping Forecast. In October a year later, Marconi and a group of leading wireless manufacturers founded The British Broadcasting Company, as it was originally called, and appointed Lord Reith as its first Director General. In 1924, the Met Office began issuing a Weather Shipping bulletin, which was broadcast twice a day from the powerful air ministry station in London and was capable of being received over 2,500 kilometres away. A year later, this bulletin was broadcast by telephony from the BBC station in Daventry. It wasn't until 1927 that the Company became the British Broadcasting Corporation, founded by Royal Charter.

A modern hotel on the clifftop projects its ugly design across the bay as I approach pretty Porthleven, with its thick stone harbour wall. Old tin mines dot the coast, with towers of rock and buildings growing out of the land near Rinsey. There's a tidal pool here which Rachael, Simon and I discovered on one of our Epic Adventures; I miss their camaraderie and friendship. The wind is against me and it feels like I'm chasing one headland after the other, until finally I see a small stony beach where you could just land a boat, it must be Boat Cove! Kath, a mature student who ran an impressive cafe business before studying architecture, has invited me to camp here, and it's nice to be in a place where I can stay and not worry about being moved on. She leaves wine next to my tent in a special iron holder for the bottle and two glasses. And after a day off the water, giving myself a rest, we drink it in the rain. 'Cheers! To your trip,' she says.

'To the Cornish weather!' I counter. She's kind, and it feels almost too much to let someone care for me. I think how lucky I am to have met such brilliant people down here.

The next day, I watch the rain wash across the bays, headlands wiped out. It's hard for me to leave; I feel comfortable and cared for in Kath's field. I look down at my kayak, lonely on the beach pointing out to sea – it looks like it wants to go. At midday, I head across the bay in choppy water and a strong side wind. Cormorants are diving as I go around St Michael's Mount, the sun glinting off the castle, the impressive harbour and buildings growing out of the rocks. It's wild around the back, and the wind pushes and whips. I fight back, carrying on to Penzance, until the shelter of the harbour brings relief and, eventually, a bacon and egg bap.

Penzance is not a pretty harbour (at least compared with all the others I've seen this week). A large red yacht, *Dynamite*, is on its side propped against the prom and I later find out it broke its anchor outside Newlyn harbour and drifted back to Penzance with its experienced sailor owner aboard. It is a sobering reminder that no matter how much you prepare, you are still at the mercy of the sea.

I launch and paddle on to Newlyn, home of the UK's biggest fishing fleet. There's a strange industrial beauty to this working harbour. The fishing industry is struggling. Cornish fishermen largely supported Brexit as a way to keep European fishing fleets further away from their coast – a promise, like so many, that later wasn't kept. Cornish seafood went for a much higher price in France, but, with no single market, selling it there is now difficult and expensive.

I can see across the bay towards Mousehole, next to an overgrown quarry etched into the hillside. Passing the Penlee Lifeboat house, I notice the flag is at half-mast as it must have been for the 38 years since the Penlee Lifeboat disaster. It was nearly Christmas and blowing a Force 12 when the call came in to assist the MV *Union Star*, a carrier ship whose engines had failed and was drifting to the rocks at Boscawen Cove. An eight-man volunteer crew went out, all from Mousehole, and despite initially rescuing four of the eight people on board, all sixteen lives were lost at sea that night. The impact was huge for the small town and each year the tragedy is commemorated by turning off the mostly homemade Christmas lights for an hour at 8 p.m. on the 19th of December. Another reminder of the power of the sea and the need to be careful.

Past Mousehole, fulmars and oystercatchers hang around on small, stacked rocks. The wind has died, and it's sheltered as I head west, the water a sparkly contrast to the cracked rhino skin rocks. Near Tater Du lighthouse, its white elegance rooted in the green headland, the beaches are full of boulders; hard landings with sharp sand from ground shells. I come in uncomfortably to Porthcurno and get settled as the sun disappears over the headland. A nearly-full moon appears, reflecting its white light on the water; for a moment I can see the stars, then they are gone behind the clouds.

The next day, I walk up to the Museum of Global Communications, where ironically there is no phone signal. Porthcurno was important in trans-oceanic cables, with the last section of the Great Britain–India cable being landed here in 1870. It quickly became the world's largest submarine telegraph station, essential for maintaining the Empire, and more cables from France, Spain, Gibraltar and Newfoundland were landed here afterwards. Even today Porthcurno is the landing site of the FLAG Europe–Asia fibre-optic cable which reaches all the way to Japan. It's fascinating to think of these physical cables still doing the job of keeping us connected.

On my last day in the Plymouth area, I'm joined by a couple of seals, and their friendly faces seem pleased by my company, or perhaps that's how I feel about them. They leave me as I reach Land's End. The rock formations, dark fingers and stacks, just drop into the sea – the black fangs of a smiling beast. Intrepid climbers hang from the sheer faces beneath. I try to see if there's enough water to paddle under, but the sharp rocks lurking in the crystalline water tell me there isn't. I continue to Sennen Cove in Lundy. Sitting on the beach, I feel like I've 'done' Plymouth. I've kayaked the whole of the Cornish part of the coastline in properly stormy weather, testing my endurance – or bloody-mindedness. I feel privileged to call this area my home and to be able to come back to discover more of it when I want.

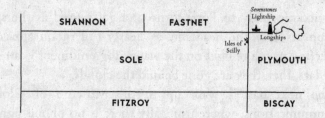

SHANNON	FASTNET	Sevenstones Lightship
SOLE		Isles of Scilly · Longships
		PLYMOUTH
FITZROY		BISCAY

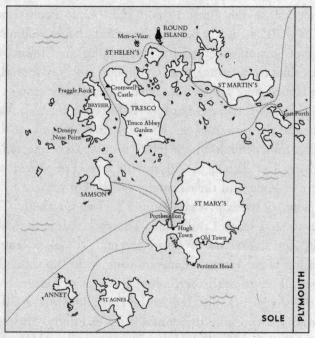

ROUND ISLAND

Men-a-Vaur

ST HELEN'S

Fraggle Rock · Cromwell Castle

BRYHER · TRESCO · ST MARTIN'S

Droopy Nose Point · Tresco Abbey Garden · East Porth

SAMSON

ST MARY'S

Porthmellon

Hugh Town · Old Town

Peninnis Head

ANNET

ST AGNES

SOLE

PLYMOUTH

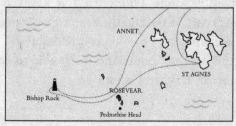

ANNET

ST AGNES

Bishop Rock · ROSEVEAR

Pednathise Head

SOLE (LUNDY, FASTNET, PLYMOUTH): SCILLY STORIES

'Toby?' I hear, sitting on the beach in Sennen, focused on charts of Scilly. I look up and see Simon, Ros, Dan and Sally from Falmouth Canoe Club. I haven't had much of a chance to kayak with them since I moved to Cornwall, but it's nice to see them. 'You going to Scilly then?' Simon asks.

'I think so,' I reply, still a little unsure. 'Have you done it?'

'No, but I'd like to.'

'So it's not a crazy idea then?'

'I know a few people who've done it. It's a long way, but a good challenge.'

The Isles of Scilly lie about 45 kilometres off the coast of Cornwall. I've been four times before but I've never kayaked out to them. The conversation with Simon gives me the confidence I need, the forecast is good and it's closer than Heligoland was to the coast.

Going to Scilly will take me to the top-right-hand corner

of the Sole Shipping Forecast area, which stretches all the way underneath Ireland without touching it and out to the western edge of the Forecast areas on top of FitzRoy. The Isles of Scilly are the only inhabited part of the area and 2,200 people live here, according to the census. For me they bring back memories of Mike, who, having visited the islands with David and Judith on yachts, felt he'd earned the right to make jokes like, 'Look who's gone to Scilly!' at a moment when we found something particularly exciting or fun.

I launch early, leaving Sennen with the fishing boats. It's the last day in August and there's a chill in the air. The sun shines on the Longships Lighthouse off Land's End as the tide pushes south. Flat whirlpools well up in the water and a tide race is just building between the rocks. As I cross each eddy I feel the push of it, altering the up and down movement of the kayak. I feel confident, like I'm doing something I've thought out and planned properly. I leave the land behind but keep looking back to check I'm making progress. Gannets, fulmars and cormorants swoop low under a bright blue sky. I stop for nourishment every hour and check my positioning on the half hour. It creates a rhythm, gives me something to do and keeps me moving forwards. In the middle section, I see fewer birds and less is going on, so I focus on the shipping lanes. I've often thought of Marcus on these long crossings; it's over three years since he died, and I still feel sad about the life he missed out on. He would have seen even more of the world by now, and although he was never boastful about the exotic places he and Andy visited, he could be coaxed into telling me all about them over a few drinks. I know from Mike's death that the sadness never goes away, you just get used to it. About three hours in I see three blocks of land with helicopters flying over.

I hold my course. I've stopped looking behind me now and just focus on what's ahead. Sometimes that's a good piece of advice for life.

The *Scillonian* ferry goes past and land fills my field of vision, making me think I'm a lot closer than I am. Rocks and islands take shape and beaches appear. Seeing the gaps between the islands gives me the energy I need to make a strong push towards the Eastern Isles. As I get closer, pristine sandy white beaches sparkle in the sun like some desert island oasis. It's hard to remember that I'm still in the UK. I land on the beach at East Porth on Great Ganilly, one of the easternmost islands, which is under 1 kilometre long and 250 metres wide and just inside the Sole area. Feeling pleased with myself for making the crossing in about seven and a half hours, I have lunch with the seals. Roman hoards were found near here after a storm and I can see some round stone settlements. The islands have been inhabited since prehistoric times and rumours abound that they might be the real Avalon where King Arthur's sword Excalibur was made. Sitting on the beach of this small island, it feels like an important mythical place.

Back on the water, a small yacht is tacking fast; I try to get out of its way but it seems to follow me. I stop and realise it's Dave who I met when I was over in January for work. Having heard about my challenge on Twitter, he'd written, 'Listening to the Shipping Forecast on the radio was part of my upbringing. Not only did my dad sail but he also ran a flower farm, and we would pick according to the Shipping Forecast to avoid losing the crop to wind damage.' Later when we'd met he described helping pack the flowers, listening to the late-night forecast as the rain pelted down on the tin roof of their barn.

Flower farming in Scilly started in 1879 when an enterprising islander sent a box of narcissi to Covent Garden Flower Market in London. The flower traders in the capital were so impressed that the industry immediately boomed. At its peak in the 1950s, over 90 family flower farms were putting a wide variety of these daffodil-like flowers on the tables of the UK. I'd first come across the Scilly narcissi almost nine years ago when we were struggling to find daffodils in October to top off Mike's tattered ensign on his coffin. An early morning trip to Covent Garden wheedled me a small bunch of not-quite-daffodils from the Isles of Scilly.

Dave had been on the lookout for me all morning, since I let him know I was going to attempt a crossing, but somehow we'd missed each other. 'How long are you here for?' he asks.

'As long as possible,' I reply, knowing that I should be back at work in one week's time. 'The forecast looks good for a crossing back on Friday.'

'Well, if it's not and you need to go back, I can help you get your kayak on the *Scillonian*,' Dave offers helpfully. It's always good to have a plan B. We agree to meet the next day and I paddle across to St Mary's, the largest and most populous island. Landing in Hugh Town, I have a long walk up to my campsite with heavy bags, but it's great to have made it, and finally I feel like I'm on holiday.

My priority the next day is a shower. Washing away layer after layer of salt from my sandpapery skin and matted hair feels so good. The day is sunny with a slight wind – a great day to visit the Bishop. I've been wanting to kayak to Bishop Rock Lighthouse at the south-west corner of the islands since my first visit seven years ago when, as a novice kayaker, it seemed impossible. It's only 10 kilometres from here and 3 from the nearest land so hardly a big challenge for me if I get the tides right. It's interesting how experience changes perspective, making more and more things seem possible. I start late morning, and near Annet, an uninhabited island whose rocks point like fingers, I run into Dave in the *Swift Lady* Royal Mail boat, who stops, turns and comes over. 'You going to Aggie?' he says, referring to St Agnes, an island further on.

'No, to the Bishop! What do you think?' I ask, knowing he has a deep understanding of the tidal flows.

'Should be okay,' he replies. I love the way you just bump into people here. It reminds me of how everyone knew each other in the small village I grew up in.

I can't see the lighthouse until it jumps out from behind some rocks. Wave trains push across the flat water, and small ridges and paths form like those you get in compacted sand. I pass Rosevear, the exposed island where the men constructing the lighthouse lived. The first attempt to build a lighthouse here began in 1847 but it was washed away three years later before its lamp was lit. The second was successfully completed in 1858. South of Rosevear I can see the waves hitting Pednathise Head, the southernmost point of the British Isles. This is very calm weather; I wonder what it is like on a stormy day.

As I get close in to the Bishop, I admire the smooth stonework and a small ornate door; even on this most functional, stripped-back structure a little decoration has been allowed. My alarm goes off, reminding me it's time to paddle back. I've considered a swim landing on the lighthouse with the boat on a rope, but it's not worth the risk so I circle round and leave. As I do I think of something Michal taught me here in Scilly: 'Always leave somewhere with things to do next time,' he'd told me as he paddled off to run the gauntlet through the Men-a-Vaur rocks to the north. Next time, I think to myself.

On the paddle back the wind drops, and it gives the water a mesmerising oily effect – smooth and shiny, it slips around the boat reflecting the sky, pools of blue and green melting into each other. It's easy to get mentally lost in it. Rays fall into the water, making it look like light is coming from the depths. I pass near the site where the SS *Schiller*, a German transatlantic steam liner, sank in 1875, killing 335 people. The lookouts didn't spot the signal from the Bishop and the ship ended up smashed against the rocks. A scramble for the lifeboats ensued, with only 27 people making it into the two seaworthy ones. The women and children were ordered to the deck house, which was almost immediately swept away in front of suffering fathers and husbands.

The disaster was the beginning of a strong relationship between Germany and Scilly because the rescue operation treated the bodies with great respect. It is said that during the war Germany promised not to attack the *Scillonian*. I found it quite emotional when I visited the graveyard at St Mary's church and read the dedications to those who lost their lives. I imagine some of them were just going home to visit relatives and instead ended up in watery graves or the mass burial site in this small churchyard with views of the sea.

I paddle on past sandy white beaches towards the church and marker on St Agnes. The back of the island is rocky and wild, then there are beautiful empty beaches. I stop for my second lunch in Scilly in an equal idyllic spot, the coarse sand warming my bum like an expensive car seat. I'm tired as I round the headland towards St Mary's following the line of the garrison around. I drag my boat up the beach and head back to the campsite for a rest. Parents bicker with their kids as I make the most of my freedom and take an afternoon nap.

Dave suggests an evening paddle over to Samson, the island cursed by William Bolton, the captain of HMS *Colossus*. In 1798 the ship ran aground while attempting to weather a storm in Scilly. The islanders, who at this point were salvage experts, quickly saved his crew and salvaged parts of the shipment, among them the body of another admiral for repatriation which was hidden in a packing case. It was considered bad luck to carry a dead body onboard, and the crew were angry when it was found, blaming Captain Bolton for their misfortune. Bolton, keen to pass the buck, cursed the people of Samson.

In his small rowing boat, Dave sets a good pace and navigates out of the harbour without looking behind him. He uses the names of all the rocks and it's clear just how well he knows the place. In our separate boats we talk about the tides, flow and swell. It's a leisurely crossing to Samson and Dave tells me about his work delivering post to Off Islands: landing on quays in all types of weather. Samson is the largest uninhabited island in Scilly, but it wasn't always that way, as indicated by the derelict houses, their thick granite walls covered in special species of lichen. For many years Scilly derived its income functioning as a motorway service station of the sea: large sailing vessels needed somewhere to stop and take on pilots, food and water before continuing on their journey. However, with the advent of steam in the early 1800s, ships no longer stopped, and the islands slipped into poverty.

In 1834, the philanthropist Augustus Smith stepped in as lord proprietor and solved the issue by depopulating the islands and only allowing larger farms, which would be more productive. A kind of benevolent dictator with a keen interest in education, Smith also introduced schooling for all, eventually making it compulsory. In 1855, Smith depopulated Samson island and made it into a deer park, which didn't go too well as the deer escaped. A walk around the island also reveals neolithic burial chambers and two wells said to be evidence of a prehistoric settlement. 'I wonder what their boats would have been like,' muses Dave, and we try to imagine.

Dave points out some of his ancestors' homes. His grandma was a Woodcock and he is descended from the Samson families: the Woodcocks and Webbers. Dave is a bit older than me and didn't get out of breath rowing, and now he's bounding about through the brambles and bracken, tramping over the low dunes – I'm impressed, and I find it hard to keep up. We talk about the Shipping Forecast. Aside from waiting to pick the flowers, Dave has other memories of it. 'Dad bought his first boat from Southampton when I was twelve and we sailed it down,' he tells me. 'I crewed for him and tried staying awake for the late Shipping Forecast, but I'd always fall asleep before we got to Sole. The fact that we've got more than one sea area here...'

'Yeah, that's what I was looking at. I can bag four areas on one go. Is that out near the Eastern Isles?' I ask, referring to the point where the areas of Sole, Lundy, Fastnet and Plymouth join.

'Yeah, it's not all that far out from St Martin's,' he says, confirming what I thought and cementing my desire to go there. The sun is lower in the sky; grey wispy clouds trail across a patch of red. We watch a big yellow moon rise over Porthmellon and, turning around, see that the Bishop in the distance is set off against a red sky. 'Beautiful!' says Dave, who must have seen the sunset here thousands of times. We sit appreciating the moment, glad that we have learnt to do so.

Wednesday is grey and steeped in thick fog, forcing me off the water. I'd hoped to go to Bryher, the smallest inhabited island, for old times' sake, and then to Tresco, the 'posh' island. Instead, I walk around St Mary's, annoyed that I have to work on Monday and wondering how I can make it back with the current forecast. I walk around Peninnis Head, the faint shadow of the mainland in the distance; from here it's easy to forget that it even exists. In Old Town, the second largest town on the island, I search for something as mundane as a phone charger, then onwards I adventure to find a plug socket. Drizzly rain kicks in and it's overcast and damp, not what I'm here for.

I'm back in Hugh Town just as the *Scillonian* arrives with its daily delivery of slightly lost people, cargo and small boats. The town suddenly becomes busy. I'm told this is nothing compared to this time of year before Covid, when the islands filled up from May to September. Despite many attempts to rely on other sources of income, the economy of Scilly is still dependent on tourism and has been badly hit by the pandemic. It's two months since Scilly opened to tourism and it hasn't yet had any Covid cases. People are especially careful with social distancing and masks, which suits me perfectly.

The topic comes up over dinner and a walk with Kate and Jeremy, who I met in January when I was working on a 'Centre for Life on Scilly', to rehouse the Isles of Scilly Museum and incorporate additional space for cultural and environmental activities. Kate is the curator of the museum, and her partner Jeremy is one of the coordinators of Creative Islands, an initiative to share Scilly's distinct culture and history through the arts. Interested in many things, they are great people to chat with. Initially, I feel a bit sheepish. I'm sceptical about the work we did, but they are enthusiastic and seem pleased to see me again. Our conversation ranges from good ways to die and transient populations to quarantining books and the impact of the pandemic. 'How are you doing with Covid?' I ask.

'There's been a huge loss in revenue,' Jeremy tells me, 'although bookings are up for next year and more people are coming to the islands for the first time.' I'm glad there's hope; it's sad to see everything this virus has taken away from people.

Back at the campsite, I have a fitful night's sleep, annoyed that I might have to go back on the ferry due to bad weather. I can't see across the field in the morning as the thick fog closes everything down. Flights aren't running, but the *Scillonian* arrives dependably. I mooch around, killing time, not sure what to do, but sometimes that's when interesting things happen. The afternoon sun starts to burn through the mist and the islands become visible again. The forecast looks better so I pack the kayak and leave. I'm about to launch when I get a message from Jonathan, a contact of Dave's with a farm on St Martin's, who invites me over to 'pick myself some grapes' the next day. A plan forms in my head, and I might even make it to the mythical meeting point of the four areas.

I tour old splashing grounds as I make my way to St Martin's, through the Tresco Channel between Bryher and Tresco. The last time I kayaked in Scilly was three and a half years ago, with a group from Tower Hamlets Canoe Club including Sarah and Owen. Marcus was dying of cancer and I wasn't sure whether to come. With Andy by his side, he (like the rest of us) was still coming to terms with his life ending. In March,

Katie and Josep had brought Llorenç from Spain at just three weeks old to meet us all and left knowing they might not see Marcus again. The thought had entered my head as I left for Scilly, but everyone including Marcus encouraged me to do it. While I was here, Andy called to say Marcus was moving into the hospice – not good news.

As I paddle to St Martin's, I pass Bryher island to my left. The base for most of our Scilly exploits, Bryher is the smallest of the inhabited islands. I don't have time to go today, but previous paddles around the back of the island have taken me to wild places such as Hell Bay, Stinking Porth and Droopy Nose Point. I do, however, pass in front of Fraggle Rock Bar and Cafe. Nothing to do with the television series, this beautiful pitstop with views of Cromwell's Castle on Tresco has been the site of a pint or two with other kayakers. It's from Bryher that I took out my first group for The Sunset and Moonrise Tour Company – a fictional company Sarah insisted I should start. I'd not long qualified as a kayak leader but was feeling confident enough to take less-experienced members out for an evening paddle. We waited until the sun was about to set and paddled around the islands in the spectacular colours, landing by the light of a full moon. It felt great to be embroiling others in an adventure and took my mind off Marcus.

As the most westerly island pounded by the Atlantic, Bryher has been the scene of many a tragedy, particularly around Hell's Bay where shipwrecks were once common and a good source of income for the islanders. Now its home to the most upmarket hotel in Scilly, after the Star Castle Hotel on St Mary's. I've obviously never stayed in either of them. But, if you're really up for something posh, you go to Tresco – a private island run by Lucy and Robert Dorrien-Smith who also run the Hell's Bay Hotel. On a long lease, it belongs, like most of the land and a third of the residential housing on Scilly, to the Duchy of Cornwall. Tresco is the island to my right as I paddle up the channel. It's the second largest and bills itself as 'the island of luxury and sophistication' and a 'subtropical gem'. Whenever I go there, I can't help feeling a little out of place, as golf buggies bumble around with posh time-share tourists in their deck shoes and white shorts – it's a very different atmosphere to Bryher. Nevertheless, Tresco is well worth a visit.

In 1834, our philanthropic dictator friend, Augustus Smith, chose Tresco as his home and constructed a house and garden near the old abbey ruins. One of the first things he did was create space and conditions for a garden, building strong granite walls and planting seeds to protect the land from the elements. A couple of generations later Arthur Dorrien-Smith (whose father, Augustus's nephew, had inherited the proprietorship of the Isles of Scilly before him) developed the gardens. Arthur had a keen interest in horticulture and brought seeds back from the southern hemisphere, planting them on Tresco. His care – and the Gulf Stream – resulted in impressive gardens with thousands of different species of plants. Dave told me there's a bit of a discussion on the islands, as new species are all very well but there's a need to protect the indigenous ones such as the dwarf pansy, only found in Scilly and even then, only native to two locations. I've been told that Tresco Abbey Garden is lovely and includes Valhalla, a museum of figureheads and other pretty bits of wrecks, but I've never been. Next time, I think, adding it to my list.

The sea is choppy at the top of Tresco, with waves barrelling in, the kayak judders. I pass Round Island, the uninhabited home to another of Scilly's lighthouses, with winding steps and a crooked handrail reaching down into the sea. Passing St Helen's, I can make out the Pest House, where ships put sailors ashore who were ill with diseases from overseas. Good to remember when we complain about Covid lockdowns. On St Martin's, I see the Sir Cloudesley Shovell restaurant, named after the Captain of the HMS *Association* which hit rocks off the Isles of Scilly in 1707 and sank in less than four minutes, drowning all 800 men aboard. Four large ships sank that night with over 2,000 lives lost. It is considered one of the greatest maritime disasters in British History. On this clear night with the moonlight reflected on shiny sands in sparkling fragments, it is hard to imagine. I sleep in the open on the soft sand, only to be woken by the rain pattering down on me, I'm still in England after all. I pull the hood over my head and ignore it.

Jonathan turns up on the beach the next morning. I've never met him before but recognise him from his profile picture. He's tall with blond hair and a beard: we could be related. We walk over the rocks to the organic fruit and veg farm he's been running for seventeen years, and he takes me through small fields separated by tall hedges to protect them from the wind. 'It must be like growing food on the beach – how does that work?' I ask.

'We pick up the seaweed when it's storm-washed in the winter, then spread it on the fields fresh, about 6 inches thick, and it rots down into organic matter which we use in the Spring for the crops. It's a free resource, highly effective and organic,' he says.

'I've heard of something like this in Jersey.'

'Yes, farmers around the Atlantic coast have been doing it for centuries in sandy soils.' As he wanders into the glass house I'm not sure whether to follow him, but I do. A sign on the wall says, 'It's never too late to live happily ever after.' I generally hate those kind of signs, but there's a truth in it that we often forget. He hands over a box of fruit and veg he's picked out for me. 'To give you energy for the crossing,' he says, passing me grapes, cherry tomatoes, carrots, cucumber and sweetcorn.

'Wow, thanks!' It's such a kind thought from a near stranger and takes me by surprise.

We talk a bit about life in Scilly in good weather and bad. He seems to enjoy the challenge of battening everything down during a Force 10, and nipping between the islands on his double kayak with his wife and daughter in calmer weather. He waits on the beach as I laboriously repack my kayak, so I can easily access my healthy sustenance for the route. As I'm close to leaving he says, 'the power of the sea never ceases to amaze me!'

'Me neither,' I agree, mentally preparing myself for the long trip back to the mainland. Leaving St Martin's, I'm reminded of another food-related trip to the island where we inadvertently stumbled upon 'English Wine Week', which may sound like unnecessary punishment to some, but for us meant a chance to match the perfect crisp white to the lobster and crab we'd ordered from local fishermen. The resulting feast was the first Paddling Gourmands meal.

Joined by some porpoises setting off, I'm on a mission to find the point where the four Shipping Forecast areas meet: 50°00' N 06°15' W. I put the coordinates in the GPS. When I'm close, I loop around on the sea until it beeps, indicating that I've bagged Fastnet and Lundy as well as Sole and Plymouth, which are now well and truly ticked off. There is nothing but sea and I float around a bit before leaving.

I see a flash of red in the distance and the tiny speck of *Sevenstones* Lightship appears and disappears through the lurching swell. Lightships are floating lighthouses that are permanently moored near dangerous hazards to warn seafarers. For the next two hours I keep focused on it, sometimes questioning that it's the lightship at all. The waves are massive like rolling hills, fields dipping and rising in the distance. I keep riding them, stopping every now and then to eat my organic veg, taking selfies so I can prove to Jonathan that it did give me energy for my journey back. By the time I get to the lightship, it is bobbing and rocking on its mooring like a small boat thrown around by the big sea, but next to me it is massive, bright red and made of steel, with *Sevenstones* written in huge letters on its side. The first lightship I remember seeing was the bar in Levington marina where we kept *Hullaballoo* for a few years. Occasionally we would arrive early enough from our weekend of getting slapped around by the sea that Mike would get us all a drink and a packet of crisps before the two-hour drive home.

There is something apocalyptic about the *Sevenstones* Lightship; unmanned and self-sufficient with its ominous clanging sound, it will outlive all of us. Marking the Seven Stones reef, which is responsible for over two hundred shipwrecks, there has been a lightship moored here since 1841 and since 1987 it's been automated. I pass behind its stern, reading 'Trinity House London' and I'm in the shipping lanes. Tankers and cargo ships move around and I try to figure out where they are going. I stop paddling and wait; it's hard to tell the direction. A cargo ship approaches, and I see its bearing will bring it close but not directly at me. I know it can't see me and I have an exhilarating feeling of literally passing under the radar.

Everything is grey and murky and the promise of sun never really happens; at around 6 p.m. the water turns choppier, slowing and jamming the paddle, waves breaking over the bow of the kayak. At times the boat is totally submerged and the white of the hull merges with the water, at others I manage to catch some nice surf. It's fast and energising but doesn't feel scary. I make out Cape Cornwall. The last bits are often the most drawn out and I know I have at least an hour left. I head down to Sennen. I can see the red door of the lifeboat station but not the harbour arm, then I realise waves are breaking over it. I find the slipway and land, and as I do a bank of cloud moves revealing a strip of clear sky, and rays of sunlight burst through.

I eat the grapes and tomatoes, go to the Old Success Inn and sleep near some grey sheds. In the morning a ragged herring gull with ruffled feathers and squinty eyes stands next to me, neck tucked into his body, hunkering down, staring out at the waves. It feels for a moment like we're kindred spirits – we must look similar.

The chill of late summer hanging in the air with nothing left to give tells me this is a good place to stop, and I remind myself that I'm lucky enough to have a house to go to and a bed to sleep in. I take my valuables out of the kayak, make sure it's safe, and walk to the bus. The open top 'Coaster' drives around the corner; it's a joyous thing, half of the top deck is outside and half inside. From my elevated position I can see over the valleys and hilltop farms to the grey shimmering sea beyond. I enjoy the pleasure of being moved by something else and seeing the landscape unfold from a different perspective. The bus forces cars off the road like a slow version of a duel – notably, a shocking pink VW campervan with a Devon sticker on it. I can't help thinking they deserved it. We pass through Newlyn before dropping down to Penzance, where I get the Paddington train and find myself surprised by how comfortable and clean it is. Given how tired I am, I make an effort not to fall asleep and end up in London, but get off at Truro for the branch line to Penryn. From there, I walk for an hour to Flushing in the hot sun; I arrive hot and sweaty, take a shower and go to pick up the kayak. I'm glad to be back and spend Sunday in the garden with my own small harvest of beans, cucumber and courgettes.

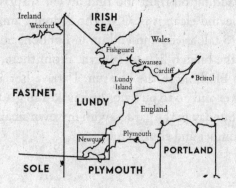
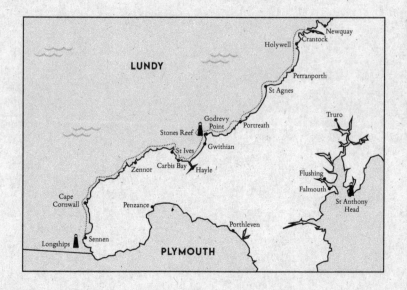

LUNDY: AN UNCOMFORTABLE LANDING

I'm so sure that my journey does not end in Sennen that, after five days of preparing for the arrival of the students at work, I'm back on the beach on Saturday, next to the Lifeboat station ready to launch. I still feel exhausted; I've always found it hard getting used to sleeping in a bed again, without the sounds and smells of the wind and the sea, but I need to do Lundy at least a bit more justice than Sennen Cove.

The Lundy area of the Shipping Forecast runs from near Land's End out west to the point I kayaked to off Scilly, then north up to Morriscastle beach in Ireland and south-east to Traeth Llyfn in West Wales. It encompasses the whole of the Bristol channel, including the island it's named after: Lundy. Right now, I've got a weekend to work with, so I'm hoping to get as far as Crantock, near Newquay.

Things seem to be where they should be: the blue sky, dotted with a few clouds, holds the sun in its place, dune houses sit on the sand and there is a light surf on the water. I can see Cape Cornwall clearly across the bay, accentuated by small breaking waves. A white foam floats on top of the sea, like a bubble bath, taking me back to our fun in Seven Sisters. My paddle scoops up piles of bubbly water, holding the memory of a bygone storm, and leaves trails across the surface. I'm tired, but it feels good to be back on the water and leaving Sennen. Headlands emerge with outlying rocks where the waves are smashing and breaking; spray jumps up over the underwater rocks, churning the water a milky, white turquoise.

I'm supposed to be meeting friends from Tower Hamlets Canoe Club, Wendy and Dave, in Carbis Bay, just past St Ives this evening; it's a jumpy bumpy ride but I'm making good progress. Stunning beaches and bays open up after each headland, cliffs curve and sweep back. The long section from Zennor to St Ives seems to take an age and when I finally round the headland with its World War Two bunkers, I am almost ready to go in. Coming past St Ives I first see the bay and Porthmeor Beach with the Tate behind, then Tregenna Castle further away. The green of the headlands dips down to town, like the saddleback of a well-ridden horse.

I'd visited the Tate and St Ives last year before I moved, when I found myself with a bit of time in Cornwall. Wandering around its pristine galleries, some with views across the bay, I was torn between appreciating the artwork or the natural seascape outside. Turner was one of the first artists to visit St Ives, on what must have been quite an adventure in 1800 – a much more challenging journey down than it was for those arriving at the beginning of the 20th century, when it was possible to pop on the train from London to appreciate the Mediterranean-esque light. As fishing declined in the town, it became known for art, attracting artists such as Bernard Leach and Barbara Hepworth to make it their home. It was the latter who eventually drew the Tate offshoot to St Ives after it took over running her museum in 1980, five years after she died.

I paddle past the undeveloped end of St Ives Head, until tall houses seem to grow out of the rocky base, windows appearing in the rock, following the long harbour wall with a lighthouse on the end as it protects a small cove with a slipway in the corner. Looking out, I'm in a wide bay stretching into the distance, past Hayle, Towans and Gwithian, to where I can see Godrevy Lighthouse, 6 or so kilometres away. I paddle in close to Carbis Beach; the ripples on the surface of the crystal-clear water are reflected off the bottom. It feels calm and safe, slow and drifty. I'm early. As the boat runs aground in the dropping tide, I wonder if I'm ready to pack it in for the day and rest in the harbour until Wendy and Dave arrive.

Nevertheless, I decide a better use of time is to continue across the bay to the lighthouse. If I start now, it should be about an hour and I'll have the tide with me. I'll send them a message later to meet me further up. At Godrevy Point the rock is black in shelves and ledges and, looking out to the white octagonal lighthouse sitting on Stones reef, it's easy to see how this part of the coast has claimed many a vessel. It wasn't until 1854 that the lighthouse was built on public petition following the sinking of the SS *Nile*, which claimed the lives of 40 people. I get a bit closer and enjoy the ordered enclosure of Trinity House planning. The wall around the lawn of the lighthouse is painted perfect white, drawing out the divide between wild and tame lands. The symmetry and simplicity of the buildings contrasts with the natural forms. I send Wendy a message to say I'll meet them in Portreath and start the journey over.

Rounding the headland the rock changes and the sun drops. The deep orange light of early autumn sun floods the cliffs, casting dark shadows. It's a glorious evening. I see settlements tucked in between long stretches of headland: harbours and towns opening up and revealing themselves as I approach. It's been a long extra paddle and I'm looking forward to getting off the water. The light is low as I come into Portreath, the setting sun reflecting on the breaking swell and bringing with it a cooler breeze. I'm going to have to surf in to the beach. A nervous swimmer waves at me as I turn and point the kayak straight at him: it's strange to be the bigger, scarier thing in the water!

The gradient of the sunset fills the sky and reflects off the beach, magical light making a short moment last a long time. Wendy and Dave arrive, having driven from Carbis Bay. 'We were so worried about you,' says Wendy, a retired primary school headmistress. 'We went from bay to bay asking if anyone had seen a lone white kayak.'

'We spoke to the lifeguards at Carbis Bay and St Ives,' Dave adds. It sounds like they've had a bit of an adventure, but I feel sorry I've made them worry.

I drag the kayak up the beach, find a spot to bivvy and we head to the pub. 'I've never seen you look so exhausted,' Wendy says as I come in; I feel it too. I order a pint of squash and a beer, and join them at the table. After the pub, Wendy and Dave go home; like many nights before, I stay up waiting for the tide to reach high, making sure it's not further than I think. It's a clear night, moony, cold but cosy. A cool wind blows over my face as the kayak and I sleep on a comfortable ledge on a retaining wall at the back of the beach. My eyes adjust to the morning, watching the stars go out one by one, invisible but always still there: like good friends and family abroad.

The swell is forecast to build throughout the day, so I'm on the water early. It's cool and autumnal now but I can feel the warmth of the sun trying to break through and taking the edge off. Mist is hanging in a series of noses and beaks sticking out above the dark black rocks: a softness to hard edges. As I sneak out through the light swell, I recognise the land from a walk earlier in the year, although the perspective is different: St Agnes lies clustered and clinging to shelter behind the headland, then the shore curves around to the long dunes and straight beach at Perranporth. Small winding routes cut out of the dunes lead down to breaking surf. I feel relief, counting down as the deep bays stretch in, and wild cliff rocks reappear at Holywell: two more headlands to go.

I'm aiming for the tidal river at Crantock, hoping it will be easier to get into, but when I get there, waves are crashing into the outlying rocks, pushing through the gap and foaming with building swell to smash on to the beach. I feel weak and there is nowhere obvious to land. I paddle across to the other side where waves are breaking close together. This is the kind of situation I've been trying to avoid. As I line up close to the rocks, the surfers in the water move out of the way. I try to judge the timing as a long wave surfs in, followed by another. I bump towards the beach and brace into the wave. Just as I start to rebalance, my paddle comes apart in my hand and I lose the ability to push down into the wave. I go over into it, holding the bits of the paddle in my hands; I pull the deck and grab on to the boat, which is now full of water and heavy. I try to get back in it a couple of times, but end up surfing in on the back like a body board, as I'm tipped and pushed by the waves.

I'm close to the shore now and people are enjoying a Sunday stroll along the beach and cliffs, oblivious to the power of the sea. A rip current is pulling me out but I manage to nudge the waterlogged boat into a small inlet, empty it and pull myself together. Some Sunday walkers on the beach come over. 'Are you okay?' they ask.

'Yes I think so, thanks,' I reply automatically, unsure what they've seen. I'm more annoyed and I hope no one calls the lifeguard. It's a slow, careful ride down the inlet for me, where Dave meets me. My weak legs hardly support me in the sinking sand. It's so different here in this small river; calm waters hold novice paddle boarders as they drift around. It seems surreal. I've been looking forward to a lazy afternoon on the beach, but I end up passing out in Wendy and Dave's beach tent and sleeping all afternoon. I'm so glad to have made it and even gladder to have a lift back to Sennen to get the car.

Thinking about Lundy later, I realise how much more there is than the small part I've completed: puffins and conservation, Bristol, the Severn and the Avon, estuaries. Atlantic coasts, the Celtic Sea and Welsh edges. I make a note to add the last bit of Lundy to next summer's final trip to Ireland and Scotland when I will complete my challenge. But by the next summer, things are very different.

Part 6

ROUGH, BECOMING VERY ROUGH

THE UNFORECASTABLE

I always knew that I was working within a window of good health, an undefined parameter that I would try to stretch out for as long as possible, and it was foreseeable that sooner or later I'd be challenged by another bout of one illness or another. I try to think about them as periods of bad weather, like stopping to sit out the storm in Reykjavík, Galicia or Plymouth. Stop, reflect, replan and continue within what's possible. At first, it's tiredness that overwhelms me. I try to ignore it, put it down to the stress of the pandemic, I feel like the whole world is exhausted, so who am I to complain. I get out locally in my kayak when I can, launching from the slipway or the beach. I sketch the plants in my garden and go on Epic Adventures with Rachael and Simon. Christmas comes and goes and the forecast for 2021 is not looking good. I find it hard to keep my energy levels up and struggle to sleep.

Awake early following a restless night, I miss the deep sleep you get from physical exercise and can't seem to stop different, useless, and disconnected thoughts running through my mind. The shutters on the window make long crosses of the soft morning light which seeps in around the edges. A blurred dawn, sodium lamps in the street outside fizz through the hazy air. It's 4.30 a.m. and I'm wide awake. I give up on the idea of any further sleep and reluctantly get up, get dressed, and leave the house into the emerging morning.

The light blue sky is streaked with wisps of clouds which are soaked in a pinky glow. The sun has not yet risen but its arrival is imminent; there's a stillness in the air of gentle anticipation. A cool breeze tickles the side of my neck as I drop down the hill towards the small beach. It's high tide and I'm surprised to see so little beach left and the old quay so low to the water. It's as if I've caught the sea up to something. The water slowly spills in and pulls back, leaving sparkling trails as it turns and shrugs off the sand. There's a slowness to the slack slop that whispers in and out. It laps the thinly strewn line of the high tide mark for a fleeting moment then it sets about as if it wasn't there. The pink glow grows into a golden orange which lights up the sky tracing the edges of low hanging clouds. This accidental but near perfect alignment of high tide and sunrise feels like the satisfaction of a final jigsaw piece fitting in place.

A low mist hangs over the water and I can hear the distant hum of Falmouth docks. A thrumming engine but nothing to see. A tanker sits on the horizon, suspended in front of the next headland that has been erased by the mist. The grass is wet and the mist hangs silently among the trees. Yellow and grey stones are scattered between the gaps like melted butter on the blackened surface. Occasional clumps of bright pink Parma-ham weeds are strewn about over the ridges with messy abandon. I listen to BBC Radio 4 live on my phone to catch the early morning Shipping Forecast as it's announced: 'Plymouth... fog banks... occasionally poor.' I turn it off.

Here, I feel like I'm floating, suspended and blissfully cut off from everything. I stare into the whiteness and lose myself in it. The breeze catches the sharp smell of the sea, which instantly clears my head; iron, sand, salt. It gurgles and sloshes between the low rocky ridges sounding like an old dog lapping at a bowl of water. I feel totally calm for the first time in a while. I soak in the cool air and feel it in my nostrils. I'm in Iceland, Denmark, Galicia, Portugal, on different beaches on different mornings simultaneously.

Cornish sunsets, sunrises and clear night skies become my tonic to an ache which develops in my shoulder and eventually shifts into a realisation that I'm not very well. Covid restrictions are relaxed and university reopens; I'm expected to go into work. The white blossom in the department garden is a piteousness of doves, perched on dead, leafless branches. A spring that I find hard to enjoy and all I want to do is sleep. My tests reveal stranger than normal blood results, but there's hope I'm getting this sorted out. Palmed off with some antibiotics and the diagnosis of an infection by the GP, I start to think it's something more. A storm is brewing on the horizon and there is little I can do about it but follow protocol and rest. I have the feeling of waiting to be rescued that I've never felt in my kayak.

Hospital admittance, tests, scans, check-ups, consultations, ultrasounds, MRIs, biopsies – I remember this all too well. I refuse to believe these sterile, controlled places are now my natural habitat. In late May, one day shy of the three-year anniversary of my flight to Iceland, I'm summoned to the Royal Cornwall Hospital in Truro to be served with the devastating news that I have uncurable liver cancer. I sit in my car, filled with remains of past adventures, and cry. It takes me half an hour to call Katie; I hate having to share bad news. Rachael comes over and only her presence holds me together.

Three days later, I'm on the night train to Heathrow and on to Barcelona. Everything is complicated by Covid, international travel still seems irresponsible, and I will have to quarantine on my return. Katie can't even leave Spain. She meets me and we hug for the first time in a year and a half – we've never been apart for so long. We go straight to the beach, the warm golden sand filtering through my toes as we walk. Katie is kind and practical, another health challenge of her brother's to be overcome, but I know she's sad and worried. My nephews Llorenç and Max are delighted I've come to visit at last, freed from the prison of the tiny screen on the phone. We talk, rest and paint. In our only tourist visit we go to the Sagrada Família. It's not the first time I've been to the half-finished cathedral, overt in its celebration of nature. Coloured light streams through the stained-glass windows creating a manmade sunset over the elegant tree trunks which open into a forest canopy of stone. We joke that in being slightly complicated and unfinished it's like my project, and I wonder how I will complete it.

Quarantined back in Cornwall, I receive the positive news that immunotherapy might be able to slow the growth of the cancer, and I start treatment soon after. I feel a glimmer of hope that I will navigate my way through this rough patch. At first, I'm concerned that I have no side effects, then I have too many: one set of pills treating the effect of others. The day I receive a letter from the NHS planning my treatment into next year, I feel positive that at least someone thinks I'll be alive by then. Whenever I have a bit more energy, I swim in the sea or take the kayak out; I have a feeling this does me more good than the treatment. No one seems willing to give me any kind of timeline – I guess it's impossible to do. I try to keep it out of my head and plan a trip to Jersey, one to visit Bron and one to Scilly. In Jersey, Nicky and Kevin carefully plan activities I can do in a morning, or an afternoon, then rest. Somehow, they make it feel like a normal Jersey trip and I find it a relief not to think about things for a change. I have fun with the Jersey Canoe Club and I'm glad they can remember me like that.

Visiting Bron in St Helens is always an emotionally empty experience, and this time is compounded by my illness and staying in a hotel that turns out to be a homeless shelter. We drive to Formby beach, and I look out across the expanse of mirror-like sand to the flat grey sea. I have fun memories with Katie and Llorenç here from two years ago, where I had to put myself between my nephew and the sea to stop him running right in – a clear sign he's being brought up on the Mediterranean and not the Irish Sea. It's so much easier to visit Bron with someone else. By the end of the visit, I'm tired, frustrated, and I nearly crash the hire car. It's not the easiest of days, but then it never is. I'm happy when I eventually give the car keys back and fly to Cornwall.

A few days later, I'm feeling so bad I'm admitted to hospital, where an overzealous auxiliary nurse knocks my new phone on the floor, smashing the screen. At least the phone is easy to fix, I think to myself: I, apparently am not. They order another scan and I dread what it might show. Blood clots on my lungs but no growth in the cancer: good news, then! There are many days when I don't think I'll be able to go to Scilly, but on the late August day I have the booking on the *Scillonian*, I'm feeling okay, so I go. Wheeling my packed kayak down the tarmac, up to the side of the grey ferry, I leave it next to one carefully protected in bubble wrap. It's a smooth crossing, sun glinting on the water and amazingly, everything arrives inside the boat.

The water gently laps the gravelly beach, fizzing between the gaps in the stones. I head straight to Bryher. As I sink my toes into the white sand, I notice how weak I am compared to my last visit and I find the familiar colours and calmness of the islands quite emotional. I fall asleep on the beach, thinking of the Frisian Islands and Ons and Cíes. I spend four happy days in Scilly, finally exploring Tresco's manicured jungle, imagining shapes in the rocks round the back of Bryher and pushing up to St Martin's through light movement in the sea to the faint chorus of the seals. Coming back, I'm tired, in pain, and my energy is low; I dip the paddle in the water and just drift for a while, grateful for the calm weather. On the penultimate night, I get myself a proper dinner at the Fraggle Rock Cafe, in anticipation of paddling out to the Bishop the next day.

The craggy faces of the Western Rocks rise out of the flat sea. I can see the Bishop in the distance and feel like I'm paying a visit to an old friend; as always, I try not to think that I might be going to say goodbye. I manoeuvre the boat close to the rusted iron steps descending into the dark sea and step off, holding the boat on a line before tying it up with too many knots. The steps are covered in rust and are hot to touch. I'm careful where I tread, avoiding birds' nests. The view is amazing from the top; I breathe in that special satisfaction of having achieved something difficult that turns out to be worth the effort, then I undo the tangle of ropes, relieved not to have to use my personal locator beacon to inform the coastguard that I'm stuck on a lighthouse.

As I carry on around into a beautiful, sheltered bay, I see a small yacht with a dark hull tacking confidently around and recognise the way the boat is being handled. I paddle over and Dave, his wife Julie and I greet each other as if it's the most normal thing in the world for me to be kayaking these waters. I put a brave face on it, but I'm sure Dave can see how much weight I've lost, and he says he's been worried since I dropped off Twitter. I haven't posted anything because I didn't want people to worry, and I've tried so hard not to make my life about my illness. I make my slow way back to Bryher, allowing myself a stop on a beach for a little shelter, food and pain killers, then it's back to the slow slog in the early evening sun. As I fall asleep under the stars for the last time, I consider myself lucky to have been able to make this trip and it feels like running into Dave and Julie was supposed to happen somehow.

Back in reality, I'm finding it harder and harder to eat. The treatment leaves me with no appetite and some side effects make it more comfortable not to. I've lost a lot of weight and I'm having to learn to accept help from friends. Eventually I decide to post something on social media. I don't want to worry people, but I don't want them to feel I'm hiding anything either. The response is overwhelming, people I hardly know say beautiful things and wish me well; I find it all hard to read, as if they are talking about someone else. I've often wondered how Marcus felt towards the end – now I'm getting an idea.

It's coming up to my 40th birthday, which I'm pretty sure will be my last, and friends and family rally around, understanding the situation and trying to make the best of it. My uni friends, Lizzy, Helen and Sarah, and their partners, rent a beautiful cottage for us all in Cornwall to make it easy for me to go. On Saturday night a lovely dinner is cooked for us with pretty foraged foods and some nice wine. It's the sort of thing I would normally love, but I feel sick, in lots of pain and I end up with a nosebleed so can't enjoy it. I try to hold it together but get upset, then annoyed with myself for ruining such a lovely weekend. Ten years earlier we'd all stayed in the House in the Clouds – a weird but fabulous building in Suffolk – now I feel like I'm burdening them with my problems.

Back at work, two days later, I struggle to walk across campus with my laptop. I remember Marcus giving up his work as a GP when his cancer was diagnosed as terminal and it's not a route I want to go down right now: teaching and tutoring the students is one of the few things that helps me focus on something else and keeps me active.

The actual weekend of my birthday goes slightly better, although mostly because I've spent a week preparing Nicky, Katie and Llorenç, who are flying in, and my friends from Cornwall who are coming over: don't expect much of a celebration. I can't rely on myself to be able to do things any more but go out on a limb and book a drive-it-yourself motorboat that we all have fun with. Intermittent nosebleeds and general exhaustion almost make it impossible, but in the end it is – a small adventure I can manage. In the evening, friends come over, we make pizza at home, share stories and silliness and I feel embraced by the expressed but unmentioned love that surrounds me. I spend most of my 40th birthday in bed, but eventually make it to Gylly Beach to watch the end of the sunset, put my feet in the sea with Llorenç and share a bit of cake.

I try to focus on small adventures – going to the geothermal pool with Katie and Simon, having a feeble walk and a chat with Racheal, Simon and Tom – but I know things aren't going well. My nosebleeds have become so recurrent that after his five-day visit Llorenç draws a picture of me having one; he's now four and for him it's a fact of life. On a call my Fanconi consultant, Stefan says, 'If you were ten years old, I'd say you were being a very brave boy!' It brings a lump to my throat and reminds me of the RNLI saying, 'With courage, nothing is impossible.' I have to keep thinking that way. It annoys me when people speak about 'beating cancer', placing the responsibility of winning or losing on the person who's ill; sometimes no matter how hard you try you can't win.

In mid-October, I get the results of my latest scan: the cancer is not responding to treatment and I'm being referred to palliative care. I call Katie to give her the news. I hope the end won't be too traumatic. It's like a bad dream. I think of my nephews, my goddaughter and other children of my friends, and I'm so sad I won't get to see them grow up. I discourage Katie from getting on the next flight, and Owen comes down from Bristol to be with me. We talk things through, and I don't feel so alone. When he leaves, I stay with Tom and Megan in their beautiful house lovingly decorated by Megan, who offers me home-cooked meals, a hot bath and a hug: I accept all three gratefully.

Julie the Palliative Care nurse comes around. Her direct talk about my demise in near-certain terms is something I'm not ready to accept. Katie arrives the next weekend, alone and seemingly ready to talk things through. I find it nearly impossible, and she coaxes me by talking about scenarios. Scenario A is a full recovery (my top option, although the least likely), Scenario B is at least a few years living with cancer (also not very likely) and Scenario C is months to live (my least favourite option). Somehow it's easier to talk about it this way, making it possible to accept the harsh reality and not give up hope. Friends and family rally around me, never knowing how I will be when they arrive. Katie and Nicky come over when they can, Natalie and Michal happen to be in Cornwall a lot, Lizzy makes the trek from the Lake District and Wendy and Dave have been so often that the staff of the Seven Stars think they are my mum and dad (I joke with Wendy that this could technically be possible, just). I turn a lot of people away, end up with an extensive collection of tea and wonder what I've done to deserve such support.

I try to tell myself that this is not how I die. I was diagnosed with throat cancer at the same time I started kayaking and I got over that. I put some faith in Chinese rainbow mushrooms, having watched *Fantastic Fungi* with Racheal, and I start taking them every day, just in case. I know I need to eat, but I find it so hard; I can't look at myself in the mirror now and I'm constantly cold. Christmas is nearly here and as I watch the lights being turned on in Penryn with Katie, Llorenç, Andy and my group of friends, I wonder if I'll make it until then. My scan says maybe not.

The plan was to go to Jersey for Christmas, but I can hardly leave the house and I know it's not a good idea. I keep thinking maybe I'll feel better, and put off deciding. A few nights in the hospital, and I book Katie and family on the Galicia boat from Santander to Portsmouth, so they can get to Flushing for Christmas Eve. I'm feeling awful by now and spend most of the time in bed; Nicky comes over as I decide to stop treatment and I find myself losing hope. I'm no longer mourning just Marcus and Mike, but my own loss of life. Julie the nurse suggests I take some steroids which promise to give me a boost and make me feel like myself again: they work like magic. I start them and on Nicky's last day I have a bit more energy, which we use wisely to do a recce on the Eden Project to see if it's somewhere I could bring Llorenç and Max: it is. I feel pleased to have a small plan and to have bought some Christmas presents in the shop. I'm so up and down over the next few days that I can't buy the rest, and Natalie and Michal end up wrapping the presents which are a combination of bought things and stuff I already have that I think people will like – among them the two soft toys I've held on to from my childhood, a panda and a lion. 'These have helped me through tough times,' I write to Llorenç and Max, 'please look after them.'

The hordes arrive and my house is full of laughter (and quite a few shouts of 'No!' from Katie aimed at the owners of little hands touching stuff that I'm not worried about). I've watched their progress up the coast of Biscay, in between Ushant and Pointe du Raz, then round into Plymouth and Portland on Vessel Finder. I know from the forecast that it hasn't been the smoothest ride (there was a gale warning), but it's Christmas Eve and the boys are ready for the traditional 'Catalan pooing log', adopted as a family custom long before either of them was born, involving hitting a log with a stick until it poos presents. Dressed as dinosaurs, they are as overexcited and silly as we used to be at Christmas as children.

I feel the effect of the steroids kicking in and on Christmas Day, I'm able to prepare and eat the dinner. On Boxing Day Natalie and Michal come for lunch and we all play games while Llorenç tries his hand at cheating. There are moments when it feels like a normal Christmas. I'm still very tired but, now free of nosebleeds, I plan one mini (or epic as Rachael would say) adventure per day. Lots of these involve food because I finally have an appetite. The Pier Cafe, Pizza Express, the local curry house – all have been off-limits to me for months. Just before New Year's we have an afternoon at the Eden Project. I've spent the whole morning in bed to save energy and Josep pushes me in a wheelchair, racing Max in his pushchair from time to time. I have two things I want to do here (I call them epic challenges): walk across the skywalk and listen to the live big band music.

I'd seen the skywalk, high up over the canopy in the Rainforest dome when I'd visited with Nicky, but I didn't have the energy for it. This time we go straight there, the kids overwhelmed by a totally new atmosphere with huge biodiversity. Ditching the wheelchair and the pushchair at the bottom, it was foreseeable that we might get told off, but at this point, I'm past caring. The bridges are more stable than they look, and as I step on holding carefully to the sides, I can see two-year-old Max's look of 'what the hell is this,' but also a smile. A light spray drifts over my face and I breathe in this smell of different nature, as I gingerly walk across the bridge. On the other side, two officials have our wheels, but one glance at me tells them we need them back and probably weren't messing around. The kids feel at home in the Mediterranean dome, as Katie pushes me through the crowd to a front-row spot for the concert. I haven't heard live music since before the pandemic and it stirs up a lot of emotions. I feel Katie's hand on my shoulder and hold it through my thick mittens as the band sings:

'*Through the years we all will be together, If the fate allows…*'

No we won't, we both think, but say nothing because we're trying hard not to cry.

On New Year's Eve, we make some biscuits and have a nice Vietnamese meal in Falmouth, only marred by a call from my surgery saying my liver indicators are very dodgy; my heart sinks as I think they are going to make me go into hospital, but they don't. We're all in bed by 10. Woken by the ships' horns blasting in the river at midnight, I open the sash window to let the new year in as Mike always did, hoping it will bring something better than the previous one. Katie hears me struggling with the window, shuts it and gives me a hug.

I wake to an ashen overcast sky with low clouds and the remnants of a rain shower: a typical Cornish morning. There's a slight promise in the forecast of the sun making an appearance around lunchtime. The days are short, with a faint glimpse of clearing skies to be cherished and savoured for brighter days ahead. I often go for a paddle on New Year's Day and today, I feel like it could be possible with help. Katie is keen to make it happen although she probably worries whether I'll make it back. I might not. I slowly gather my things and consider each carefully. The drysuit is baggy and clumsy; I struggle to put it on and need help to tighten the zip, the rubber neck seal flops around my thin body rendering the whole thing a bit pointless. With layers underneath it feels warm and dry and strangely comforting. The cold has stopped me considering going out until now, but strengthened with a newfound appetite I've developed energy within. It's also an exceptionally mild day to start the year.

It's been relentlessly windy over the past week, blowing in from the south-west. I'm launching from the slipway by the pub on an incoming tide and onshore gusts. My small safety crew are armed with throw lines and phones in case I get into trouble (although none of us think too much about what use these would be). I'm planning a very short trip along the quayside, to the sailing club and possibly over to Falmouth, depending on how it feels. I often find these small steps the hardest but also the most rewarding and emotional to make. I've been thinking about it for a long time and wondered if I would ever make it into the kayak again.

As I gather my things, each bit of kit starts to feel familiar, the weightless paddle, the fit of the buoyancy aid, comfortable and reassuring, like a protective hug. We start our procession down to the slipway, Katie and Josep carrying the empty boat and Llorenç and Max running alongside. As predicted, the clouds break and patches of blue start to appear. Ever since I started to get ready, I've noticed a sense of being more aware of what is going on around me. The birds, the temperature, the clouds and the wind. It's a reconnection and grows stronger as we negotiate the slippery granite slope down to the beach. The tide has turned and is gradually seeping back in, over the mix of pottery shards, old bricks, seaweed and shingle.

With all the kit and helpers on the beach I make my final adjustments and perform the familiar ritual of launching the kayak into the water. It takes more strength than usual and gently starts to bob in the small waves as if ready to go. I stand astride it and lean on Katie to lower myself into the seat. It immediately feels comfortable. Perhaps it's something to do with the closeness of the water, the movement of the boat or the familiarity of the seating position, but with a quick fiddle of the foot pegs and a shufti around in the seat I feel a sense of being back in the right place. There's a shove from the launch party and a push from the paddle, a gentle glide backwards and – I'm floating.

In this short moment, I can feel my body relax; the boat bobs up and down and I move effortlessly with it. My breathing changes and I'm hyper aware of where I am. The sun breaks through with a golden touch on the water, bringing the quayside into silhouette and picking out the small but pushy waves on the surface. The few boats moored in the river now catch the low winter light and seem to come alive. The faded pinks and oranges of the moorings recapture their former brilliance. The gap in the clouds opens up to reveal a cluster of altocumulus high up in the atmosphere, shimmering in the golden light like a shoal of fish. A small group of gannets whirl around the headland while being propelled by short gusts that push across the water. The smell is fresh and salty; it blasts straight up my nose and washes over my face, I tilt my head back and just feel the sun on my skin.

The paddling seems effortless despite my wasted muscles and skeletal frame. Llorenç runs and waves along the quay while the rest of the party follow and take photos. I paddle up to his favourite boats and give them all a wave before setting off across the other side. I push into the wind and it's great to feel some resistance in my body, with little jumps and splashes as I go. The low cloud eventually gets the better of the blue sky and covers up the shimmery world above. It's a magical time and I don't want it to end, but I start the short crossing back to the beach, carried by the wind and the incoming tide. The welcome party arrive, helping me get out and start back on our short procession through the narrow streets, lunch, a warm shower and a rest after the big expedition. Big for me at least and a brilliant start to what might be a very uncertain year ahead.

The next day, Katie and family are leaving early, they've got a long trip up to Portsmouth, across to St Malo and down through France, and there's still some worry about whether France will let Katie in. I entertain the boys with Christmas crackers while Katie and Josep load the car. As they leave, they give me massive hugs, Max running from a distance and headbutting my liver. I've told myself I won't get emotional, but I can't help it, the idea that we may never see each other again hangs unmentioned in the air as I wave them off from my front door still wearing a paper crown.

Wendy and Dave come over in the afternoon and I'm grateful to have some company. Kath from Penzance brings round the most beautiful pie I've ever seen, and I eat it over the next two days with Rachael and Simon, and Tom and Megan. I feel a little hope returning and come up with new projects: taking the ferry to Santander to show Llorenç the dinosaur prints at Colunga; getting an electric bike; buying a big sculpture for the garden to remind me of our visits to Eden; a trip to Jersey.

Even so, I know now that I won't finish my project and kayak in all areas of the Shipping Forecast. Nicky and Kevin have offered to help me complete it; Katie suggested she would hire a van and drive me around Ireland and Scotland, but I've had to downsize my plans. For a long time, it was still there in my mind as a possibility, but eventually I have to let it go. There are six areas with land that I have never kayaked in: Fair Isle, Cromarty, Forth, Malin, Shannon and Rockall. I spend a morning imagining what these places would have been like, looking at beaches I will never see on Google Earth and wishing things could have been different.

*On 10th January 2022, Toby died in Mount Edgecumbe Hospice
in St Austell, Cornwall, surrounded by friends, having left
his cottage in Flushing for the last time the day before.*

*That morning, the Shipping Forecast issued by the Met
office at 11.30 mentioned 'rough' 21 times. It was.*

*The late Shipping Forecast that day, issued by the Met
Office at 00.15 hours on the 11th January 2022, contained a
reference to Toby, made by broadcaster Andrew Crawford.*

*'Wherever you are tonight, either on ships large
or kayaks small, whatever your voyage, whatever
your destination, take care, Godspeed.'*

FLOTILLA

Katie, June 2022

I'm woken by the sound of the rain falling on the slate roof of Toby's cottage. A grey day wasn't part of the plan, it's Midsummer for God's sake! I've been on edge since yesterday when it became clear that the worst-case weather scenario for this event is about to play out: south-westerly 5 gusting 6 with a big swell on the sea.

Nicky and I came up with the idea of a Kayak Flotilla back in January when going through Toby's notes on his funeral, and we realised that one of his hopes was for everyone to have a nice weekend in Cornwall enjoying the sea. That seemed a little more challenging at the end of January, when we held his funeral, than in June, although 30 of us got in the sea in January for a swim in his honour. We have gathered over 50 of his friends and family who are due to meet in kayaks, boats and other floating devices in the sea just off the St Anthony Head Lighthouse at the entrance to the Fal estuary, to float Toby's ashes and have a picnic on the nearby beach. It's a lovely plan and one that I know Toby would approve of.

It was sitting facing forwards, looking at the darkness of the road in Toby's dirty car, that he and I discussed what he might like to happen to his ashes. 'I don't really believe that they will be me,' he said, 'but just in case, I'd like to be put in the sea. There's a lighthouse with a beach past St Mawes; that would be a good place.' I made a mental note and we never discussed it again.

It was a pretty good plan – I tested it out a month before with Llorenç, in *Moonshot*, David and Judith's yacht. The dark turquoise water was calm, the sky a Magritte painting, the deep green trees above the beach gently swaying; it all seemed perfect. But today it's different, it's colder and greyer than January with a light drizzle that invites you into the nearest pub but not the sea. We need to change plans and make sure everyone knows. It's clear we can't go to the original beach because it's totally unsheltered and the waves will be dumping on it, making it difficult to land a kayak or anything else there. The trip out to leave the ashes off the lighthouse is now a challenge only the most skilled kayakers are willing to take on, and the idea of me going in a double kayak with Nicky needs revising. Somehow a new plan falls into place, involving more people on the headland, both of Toby's kayaks going out, six of us in a rib and four adults and three children on the yacht. As the plan comes together, grey gives way to bursts of proper summer sun, and I wonder if this is some kind of challenge from Toby on the other side.

Once everyone's informed, I take a moment to look around Toby's garden, the little bit of nature he managed to cultivate and enjoy during Covid times. For me, it's been hard looking after a garden from another country for the last six months, but with local help, the flowers that Toby planted are coming into bloom. I pick a small bunch, one of each out that day, their bright colours set off by a small leaf from his favourite Gunnera plant. The flowers will look quite different when they reach their destination but for now, I hold them delicately, worried I'll forget this part of the ritual in the rush.

Toby – or Toby's ashes – has spent a month in the garage sitting in his kayak; it seemed like the most appropriate place for him, surrounded by all his gear, the detritus of his adventures. But the night we arrive, I bring them into the house – it still feels strange us all being there without him. I put them on the green chair he's had for years, and he's subjected to watching *The Octanauts* with Llorenç and Max – it's a cartoon about sea adventures, so he would probably have quite enjoyed it. He leaves the house for the very last time in a yellow dry bag that looks like it's spent more time on the sea than the Octanauts have. I walk through the village the same way as we did on New Year's Day for his last kayak, past the pastel-coloured terraced houses, down the middle of the road to the slipway in front of the pub. I hold back my tears. I don't think the real him is in those ashes either, but I wish this wasn't all that was left of the physical him.

Natalie and Michal have prepared the kayaks on the beach for themselves and for Nicky and Kevin, who are driving last minute from Newquay airport. I slip the dry bag with Toby's ashes into the front hatch of his white kayak, ready for Nicky to paddle them out. The wind is clearing the clouds and Natalie and Michal seem pleased they will get a more interesting paddle than they originally expected. As the most experienced kayakers I have earmarked them and Nicky and

Kevin for the job of taking the ashes out off the lighthouse if no one else can make it.

I go back to the house and dispatch Josep and the boys to the Sailing Club slipway, where they will be picked up in a rubber dinghy by Judith to take them onboard *Moonshot*. Sarah and her son Dylan join the yacht crew, Owen having won the coin toss on who gets to kayak. They are delighted to be going on the sea anyway. Nicky and Kevin arrive, ready as always for adventure, change in less than five minutes and make their way to the slipway, which is now busy with other kayakers who have arrived from London, Bristol and Jersey. Lindsey, Wendy, Dave, Al, Alex and others are preparing themselves for a rather more challenging sea than they expected. The rumour reaches me that the rib is at the quay, and I set off in four layers of clothing with my little posse through the village with my cousin Lisa, who has taken a break from training for the Commonwealth Games to come down. Halfway to the quay we bump into Elsa and her partner Francesc who I've invited to join us on the rib.

In many ways, we're a long way from Elsa meeting Toby on the beach in Galicia. I'm delighted and touched that they made the effort to come from Madrid. Toby spoke at length to me about Elsa, who is a well-known writer and speaker; he was keen for us to connect, and finally we have. My layers of clothing are a stark contrast to Elsa's thin shirt and gilet; I wonder if she will be okay on the water. She's not worried and seems excited about the adventure. Apparently my WhatsApp wasn't very clear and they think they've signed up for some group rowing vessel. They are game anyway, but they are visibly relieved when they see the solid rib with its large motor and skipper, Gary.

I sit in the bow of the boat with Elsa. As soon as we leave the quay we are thrown around by the wild river, waves constantly crashing over the front of the boat, leaving us drenched. It takes me back to the times as a child when I'd sit in the front of our much smaller rubber dinghy, Mike driving, Toby next to me, Marcus and Bron in the middle, all getting a lashing by the sea before even reaching *Hullaballoo*. Sometimes it hits me from nowhere that I'm the only one left. Luckily, the conversation with Elsa is interesting and I'm distracted by other things. She tells me that the day she met Toby, she was feeling particularly uninspired with a deadline for podcast content fast approaching, and decided a walk on the beach might bring her some kind of inspiration – and there it was in the form of Toby. Since then she's featured him on the podcast and mentioned him in a book. I feel exhilarated by the water and the constant movement, the excitement of looking out for the kayaks, and am calmed by the horizon that I spent so many hours as a child looking for answers in.

For the time being the question seems to be, will we be capable of rounding everyone up and floating the ashes. In the distance we can see *Moonshot* proudly displaying Mike's nautical flags spelling out TIBY (due to a last-minute encoding mistake, as I picked the flags in the 30-degree heat of Barcelona before we left). Judith suggested it's just Toby in an Aussie accent so I feel a bit better about it. It makes me think about Toby's kayaking friends Vicky and Janice in New Zealand who are going out in the middle of the night now to be on the water at the same time as us. A large part of *Moonshot*'s newly painted blue keel is visible as she is thrown around and I wonder if my kids are okay.

As the owner of the Arvor Sea Kayaking school on Maenporth beach, Gary is experienced at rounding up kayaks on the water, and quickly slips into the very necessary role of making sure everyone is okay and going towards the right spot. We go back and forth in the rib, playing sheepdog to the barely visible kayaks. As we get closer, we can see a line of about 30 people on the headland near the lighthouse – Toby's supporters from the land. I find myself worrying that they might be bored as we struggle to get everyone together. It becomes clear that we really should have distributed some of the many VHF radios we have, across the different boats. David on *Moonshot* has been calling the rib but we don't hear his call. Eventually Josep calls me on the phone and I respond on the Apple watch like a wet, shabby Inspector Gadget. They are doing okay, but he asks, 'when are the kayaks coming?'

'Maximum twenty minutes,' I shout into my watch, 'if the kids are sick go home.' We come up close to *Moonshot* in the rib and everything is okay, David is trying to give the kayaks a wide birth until it's time to do the ashes.

Eventually Gary manages to round us all up, and Nicky brings Toby's kayak alongside the rib so that I can lean over and take the dry bag with Toby's ashes out. *Moonshot* comes in as close as she can and the kayaks gather around. I reach in and pull out the heavy urn, designed to be floated at sea, made from sand which will dissolve. I've had enough experience with human ashes to know that the idea of romantically scattering them is a myth, so I'm pleased with this solution which is supposed to float for a moment then gently go down into the sea. It might have been the height of the waves or perhaps I dropped it from too far, but the urn doesn't float gracefully at all – it makes the loud plop of a badly skimmed stone into the sea. I think Toby wouldn't have minded; he loved a bit of rock jumping. I throw the now sodden flowers from Toby's garden on top and watch them float on the sea. There's a moment of silence from everyone. My eyes well up. I think 'We've done it, Toby! We've bloody done it,' and half of me expects him to reappear in his kayak. If there was an incantation to bring him back, this would be it.

No one is sure what to do now. I should have thought of that. Someone sings a round of 'For He's a Jolly Good Fella,' but even the singer realises the celebratory song is a little out of place. I revive a verse of the song I sang with Rachael at Toby's funeral: Alfred Lord Tennyson's 'Crossing the Bar':

'Sunset and evening star,
And one clear call for me,
And may there be no moaning of the bar when I put out to sea.'

That seems to do the trick. A moment more of silence and we go our separate ways, each person finding their own way of remembering and honouring Toby. Alex plays some sea shanties he and Toby got into on a speaker strapped to his kayak and Michal and Natalie go out to the big waves to play in the surf as they had so often done with Toby. *Moonshot* sails for her mooring, my children wondering what all that was about. The friends on the headland return to their cars for the long drive around the estuary, and in the rib we turn back up the river. We will reconvene on David and Judith's sheltered beach in an hour or so.

Gary speeds up the rib for some fun; I feel a bit like I'm in a James Bond movie and not for the first time that day, I wish I was wearing my black wetsuit. Elsa is not enjoying the speed, having done amazingly after admitting she didn't really like being on the sea earlier. Gary quickly realises this and reduces the throttle. The slower speed means we can talk, and it turns out that Gary also has a connection to Toby, although he didn't realise it when he offered to take us out in the rib. He tells us that his son Eliot was interviewed by Toby for a place on the architecture course at Falmouth and that Toby spent an hour with him helping him to decide if it was a good fit or not. Gary remembers Eliot talking about how kind and helpful Toby had been. Later he refuses to let us pay him for his help or the rib rental, saying he's repaying Toby's kindness. We wouldn't have managed to make it happen without him so I feel hugely grateful. As we get back towards Flushing, I think, now I'm able to offer Elsa the shower she offered Toby in Galicia, but we drop them off at the hotel quay and I take one at the cottage.

Messages come in on social media. Around the world, Toby's friends have taken a moment to remember him on their adventures: Esther is paddling the Yukon River in Canada, candles are lit for him in the harbour at Skomer. Some, like us, have been challenged by the weather: the New Zealand kayakers had a false start in a Force 6, but honoured Toby with a Karakia, a Māori chant. Jennifer, Toby's literary agent, and her friend Peter in Tilos, Greece, are forced off the water but make an alternative route towards the distant haze of the outlines of a Turkish peninsula. Charlie floats a tiny Toby Playmobile figurine on a Scottish loch and tells me, 'The loch was unusually choppy and the wind was in our faces so "tiny Toby" needed a bit of assistance to be on his way. (Actual Toby would have dealt much better with capsizing.)'

Showered and somewhat less salty, I make my way to David and Judith's house across the village, picking up our picnic contribution of some Estrella Galicias, Albariño wine and a selection of Spanish cheese and meats. I walk down the rickety path, whose safety is slightly improved by a rope rail that Mike put up in the 70s. The tide is up and there's about 4 meters of shingly sand for us to sit on; by the time I get there, it's full of people spread out along the beach, friends from different parts of Toby's life mixed together. David is sitting on a chair quietly enjoying seeing his beach so full of life and Steven – Mike's brother – and his wife Lynn have come down from Yorkshire. It feels good to have some connection to Mike here, although he would never have imagined this event. We chat, we laugh, we share stories of Toby, there's some swimming in the river and Llorenç gets his first rowing lesson from Judith. The atmosphere is light and hopeful; kayakers and non-kayakers alike talk about their next adventures. Toby would have loved it!

THE CHALLENGE

Katie, December 2022

There is no greater responsibility than telling someone else's story, especially when they are no longer around to correct it. This is not something I've taken lightly. When Toby died, he had written the book proposal with a clear outline and three chapters. We had talked about the book at length, but he never asked me to finish it for him; he was pretty sure he'd manage that himself. Leafing through his notebooks the week after he died, it was so clear that he wanted his story to be told that I emailed the editors and asked them not to cancel the publication: I would finish it.

I was under no illusion that it would be easy, mourning the loss of a second brother, the last member of my close family and a supportive friend, organising his affairs, continuing my own work and bringing up two small boys: at times it was too much. I've lost entire days going back through our WhatsApp conversations, getting stuck in memories of him and crying at my desk. Like Toby, I've tried to think of it as one headland at a time, breaking everything down into sections and edging forwards bit by bit. Many days the tide was against me, but I just kept going. I think this is an attitude that we both have from the family history we share.

It's mid-March before I take a good look at everything and decide to dedicate the next nine months to writing it up. I sit in my studio in Barcelona, which Toby encouraged me to rent and helped me to furnish. My desk is clear and I'm ready to start. I grab his weather-worn notebooks which still smell of him, open Google Maps, plug in his phone and settle down to try to understand his trip in detail.

I've chosen FitzRoy as the chapter to start with. I'm not sure I'm ready to listen to his recordings – just feeling his voice coming out of the page at me through his scrawly handwriting is hard, but I start anyway. I try to imagine how happy he would be to see his story in print; finishing it would be the greatest gift I could give him. There are times I burst into tears, wishing I could have hugged my brother on that isolated beach, rewriting a history where I wasn't stuck at home with a newborn but able to be part of Toby's journey. But there's no point in thinking about 'what ifs' Toby would say... better to ask 'why not?' So why not finish this bloody book then?

It takes me a while to get used to how Toby's notes work, jumping from day to day in a way that only makes sense after a bit. I worry constantly about doing his trip justice, about making the book as close to how he would have wanted it as possible. Sometimes this paralyses me, then I remember that the worst I can do is not try, because then no one will read it. I get back to it. I feel like I'm with him on the journey.

At times I'm a detective piecing together Toby's movements, thoughts and feelings using his blog, logbooks, notes, emails,

WhatsApp, recordings and photos. I am grateful to live in a time where some of those have automatic geolocation included, but many do not and I spend hours trying to identify lighthouses from photos via Google. I've never tracked anyone else's movements so closely, and sometimes it's fun.

I feel like I'm climbing a mountain as I flick forward to see how much more I have to go: 'a lot' is the answer. Better not to look, just keep edging forwards. When I'm hungry, I leave the rugged beaches of Galicia, Portugal, Cornwall, Iceland or wherever on my desk and venture out into urban Barcelona. If I didn't have children and responsibilities, I would get in the car and drive to those windswept beaches, but I know I'd leave disappointed, unable to find Toby there. The voice recordings are the hardest. I'm listening to Toby explaining his trip in Spanish Biscay: 'Oh, a shooting star just crossed the sky, amazing!' he marvels, and it feels like he's still on that beach. Later he says, 'I feel like I'm probably rambling a bit now, so I'm going to shut up and try to get some sleep before the tide comes in.'

'Night night Toby,' I say automatically, as tears well up in my eyes.

It gets easier with time, like grief itself, and writing the book becomes more of a therapy and less of a torture. I often find myself stuck in the same places he was, if only on the page. It takes me several weeks to get to Vigo from Finisterre – longer than it took Toby, and I'm putting in around the same number of hours a day as he did paddling. When I finish Trafalgar I feel sad – the adventure is over for a while, even though the next day I pick up the Plymouth notes and continue. I often listen to the music Toby mentions, Spotify confused whether I like Jonny Glut or Escuchando Elefantes. Later when I'm writing drafts, I treat his chapter summaries as a treasure hunt, creating a bingo-style checklist. I feel childish excitement as I set out to discover what Fraggle Rock has to do with Scilly or radio with Cornwall. The day I identify a Shannon-class lifeboat from a silhouette at a weird angle, I feel quite pleased with myself.

Once I have a full picture and feel satisfied that I've listened to the hundreds of recordings, read all the notes, know what he did each day and have checked it with others, I can start with the creative part. A lot of the work I do is related to creativity and storytelling, so I'm excited to get my teeth into sculpting his story out of words. I try hard to balance giving myself creative freedom and going back and checking it fits with what Toby might have written. With no way to know this I settle on making it as good as possible and keeping my own agenda out of it.

By September, I have a full draft and since it now doesn't have to be in until October, I find myself with time to let it rest (or stew as Mike would say). A few weeks and some external opinions later and I take it with me on a two-and-a-half-day trip to Cornwall. I expect to be able to sit at Toby's desk and work on it but instead I feel the pull of the coast he found so much solace in. I drive up to Crantock, the location of Toby's last surfy landing. Wendy and Dave are there, and we meet on the immense windy beach at low tide. Wendy indulges me with an in-situ description of how Toby landed that day, and we walk to the cafe for a coffee which turns into a beer before we've ordered.

The next day, instead of tidying the cottage or editing, I find myself walking along the coastal path in the rain to Lloyds Signal Station and Bass Point. I stop for a moment; the bracken below me is the same colour as my hair and I imagine diving into it. Grief is a slippery creature but I have to keep on track for my boys. After sorting a few things out, I spend some time on the book looking out over Toby's garden and feeling the bear hug of the rain pelting on the skylights as he would have done, had he written it.

By November, it's back from the editors; it still needs substantial work. I bury myself again in recordings, notes and photos. Max gets his first bike while I'm shut away. Our Christmas tree comes out, Toby's decorations evidence of his absence. Eventually the book goes in. 'Toby left me an unfinished book and an unfinished adventure', I tell myself, 'I can tick one of them off.'

This is not the book Toby would have written, but it is as close as I can get to it, a co-creation about his experience where his words are mixed with mine to tell his story as best we can. For me, this book is a way to keep Toby alive, letting him continue to inspire others to find and start their adventures.

ACKNOWLEDGEMENTS

Wading through the many ways Toby recorded his trip was often tough, but gave me a sense that anything is possible – a message I hope this book passes on. So, the first thanks has to go to Toby Carr for creating this story and for continuing to be an amazing brother, even after his death. All your hard work recording your trips was worth it. I'm so sorry you never got to hold this book.

Toby would have thanked all those who offered him kindness, companionship and fun on his trip and in his life. In order of appearance in the book: Andy Carr, Marcus Carr, Mike Carr, Bron Carr, Nicky and Kevin Mansell, Sarah Outen, Owen Rutter, Natalie Maderova, Michal Madera, Aasmah Mir, Dave Cook, Lindsey Harris, Gunði Páll Viktorsson, Arian Ne, Ari Benediktsson, Jan-Egil Kristianssen, Heini Heinesen, Alina Natalia, Ivar Kim Rokke, Morten Vogelius, Thomas Neilsen, Irma Roberts, Felix Drueke, Doris Hoelterhoff, Claas Meier, Axel Shoevers, Alan Smith, Zeb Soanes, Corrie Corfield, Romilly Witts, Zyggy Dreja, Sarah Wigglesworth, Dafydd Bevan, João Sousa, Betty and Frank Stow, Alison Randall, Matt Boston, Joanne Read, Zoe Gillard, Caihua Sim, Patrick Macleod, Adrian Simpson, Lisa Mansell, Marc-Henri Trancart, Jenny Mullin, John Searson, Brian Nibbs, Agnes Penisson, Nicolas Daviau, Jérôme Le Ray, Fernando Rey, Tito Rodríguez, Raquel Calvo, Ángel Manso, Elsa Punset, Francesc Guardans, Tom Ebdon, Rodrigo Arbones, Alberto Rocha, Diana Speed, Anne Carr, David and Judith Eastburn, Megan Beck, Rachael Jones, Simon Andrews, Katie Etheridge, Simon Persighetti, Sarah Hollingworth, Kathleen Hawkins,

Simon Osborne, Daniel Purkis, David Mawer, Kate Hale, Jeremy Brown, Jonathan Smith, Wendy and Dave Heffernan, Lizzy Mackinnon, Helen Lovesmith, Stefan Meyer, Julie Trestrail, Alex Hester, Gary Bullen, Vicky Bostock, Janice Barret, Esther Wheeler and Jennifer Barclay. Many of you have been a huge support to me as well, thank you.

Thanks to the excellent brands who gave Toby free or reduced kit: Finisterre, Kōkatat, Tiderace, Werner and Waterhaul, he did love your stuff!

Thanks to the Churchill Fellowship. Your support of Toby's 'mad idea' gave him a boost more valuable than the grant you awarded him (which he was also very grateful for).

Toby would have given a big shout out to Charlie Connelly who encouraged his voyage around the Shipping Forecast and his foray into writing. Charlie has also been a great support for me through emails about the challenges of writing, a very specific piece of FitzRoy history and of course, the foreword. Thanks!

Thanks to Holly Astle, for the beautiful cover illustration. You immediately captured the essence of the book and were a joy to work with.

This book would never have been written without our literary agent, Jennifer Barclay, who spotted the potential in Toby's story and helped him finesse the proposal. In autumn 2021, while Toby received nothing but bad news about his health, Jen successfully pitched the book to Summersdale, giving him something to look forward to. Thank you, Jen!

The baton was then passed to Debbie Chapman, our managing editor, who has seen the project through to completion. A couple of weeks before he died, Toby was very ill and devastated that he would not be able to write it. Debbie came up with creative solutions and Toby left the call buoyed that his story might be told anyway. When I contacted Debbie a week after Toby died to say I would write the book, she believed me and has given me her full support ever since. Few people combine such kindness, professionalism and creativity. Debbie, I feel honoured to have worked with you. Thanks, too, to the rest of the Summersdale team, especially Hamish Braid, Emma Stuart and Jasmin Burkitt.

The structural edit was done by Ross Dickinson, who pushed me to make this book far better than it would have been. Thanks, Ross, for your careful suggestions, your sensitive but firm approach, and for putting up with getting back an almost entirely rewritten first half. It took me a while to get over the fact that you didn't know much about the Shipping Forecast, but I've forgiven you now that you're an expert on it!

Before the manuscript reached Ross, I sent an earlier version of it to Bill Stow and Wendy Heffernan who battled though it. Thanks for your words of encouragement and ideas for improvement.

Over the many months spent at my desk, two people became my cheerleaders, the slim and expensive Andy Carr and Aine Doris – neither of them strangers to grief. Our text conversations got me through some of the darker times and helped me keep thinking that finishing the book was possible.

Special thanks also go to Nicky and Kevin Mansell for all their support of many kinds, to both Toby and me. For me this included answering my many kayaking questions, lots of WhatsApp messages and getting me in a sea kayak for the first time.

In the family category I'd also like to acknowledge our dad, Mike Carr. It had bothered me for a long time that we didn't say goodbye properly, but recently I realized that what was left unsaid was 'thank you'. So thank you, for everything you did for us in awful circumstances, imperfectly but with good intentions.

Lastly to those who have had to put up with me every day, facing the ups and downs of the research, writing, editing and book promotion process. Listening to my moaning and my excited explanations depending on the day. Thank you Josep Sayeras for the emotional support and for doing more than your fair share of the childcare. Thank you Llorenç and Max Sayeras Carr for taking my mind off the book (with moderate or good behaviour). I'm glad you will be able to read Toby's story once you are old enough.

In memory of Toby Carr, Marcus Carr, Mike Carr and Bron Carr (I hope I did you proud).

ABOUT THE AUTHORS

Toby Carr was an architect and senior lecturer at Falmouth University, who loved being on the sea and out in nature. In 2018 he set off to sea kayak the Shipping Forecast, keeping detailed recordings, notes and photos. He shared his trip on social media under the name 'Moderate Becoming Good Later'. He died aged 40 in January 2022.

Katie Carr is an author, artist, educator and coach who never imagined her first book having anything to do with sea kayaking. After a year tied to her desk writing the book, Katie can now be found outside, learning to kayak and finishing off the Shipping Forecast. She lives in Barcelona with her partner and two young boys. www.katieannicecarr.com

See Toby's original posts and Katie's new ones:
Instagram and Facebook: @moderatebecominggoodlater
Twitter: @KayakForecast

For additional content: www.m-b-g-l.com

ABOUT THE ILLUSTRATOR

Holly Astle is an illustrator based in Falmouth. She is greatly influenced by her local surroundings of the coast and her love of the natural world. She aims to capture an essence of Cornwall in her work.

Katie found Holly's work in the beach café in Maenporth a few days after Toby's Flotilla and contacted Holly via Instagram. After a chat outside the Pier café in Falmouth, Katie was convinced that Holly would create a beautiful illustration for the book cover. And she did.

www.hollyastle.co.uk
Instagram @hollyastle

Four charities made Toby's life better in different ways. If you'd like to know more about their amazing work, or throw some money their way, here's where to find them:

Fanconi Hope: www.fanconihope.org
Macmillan Cancer Support: www.macmillan.org.uk
The RNLI: www.rnli.org
Cornwall Hospice Care: www.cornwallhospicecare.co.uk

Have you enjoyed this book?

If so, why not write a review on your favourite website?

If you're interested in finding out more about our books,
find us on Facebook at **Summersdale Publishers**, on
Twitter at **@Summersdale** and on Instagram and
TikTok at **@summersdalebooks** and get in touch.
We'd love to hear from you!

Thanks very much for buying this Summersdale book.

www.summersdale.com